Storytelling in Radio and Podcasts

Sven Preger

Storytelling in Radio and Podcasts

A Practical Guide

Sven Preger
Bonn, Nordrhein-Westfalen, Germany

ISBN 978-3-030-69631-3   ISBN 978-3-030-73130-4   (eBook)
https://doi.org/10.1007/978-3-030-73130-4

Cover design by eStudioCalamar
Cover image: Malte Mueller/Getty images

This Palgrave Macmillan imprint is published by the registered company Springer Nature Switzerland AG
The registered company address is: Gewerbestrasse 11, 6330 Cham, Switzerland

PREFACE

Neither Anne nor I are normally the silent ones by any stretch of the imagination. But right now, neither of us can think of anything else, no humorous comment to break the silence and dissolve the tension. And it's still too early for professional analysis, what we have just heard is still affecting us too much.

We both, Anne and I, have a kind of, well, tradition might be a bit exaggerated, but it is something we do regularly. And it is a good sign if we both feel like it at the same time because our heads are not full of all those everyday work questions. We are both audio professionals and specialise in complex narrative forms. When we have a long car journey ahead of us, we sometimes listen to podcasts together. It means we are once again looking for inspiration and are eager to hear and learn something new. We both love *Radiolab*, Anne also *99% Invisible*, me *More Perfect* and *Invisibilia*. And, of course, the show we just listened to. Afterwards, we often discuss what we liked and didn't like and what we can and cannot adapt for our own productions. But this time we stay silent, at least almost.

It's June 2020, the first Corona shutdown in Germany is over and people can visit their families again. That is exactly what we are doing. If everything goes well, it's a 75-minute drive, more or less. We are not far from our destination and we are both struggling to find words. We have spent the past hour listening to an episode of *This American Life*. We were at the refugee camp in Mexico with Ira Glass and Aviva DeKornfeld. We heard Molly O'Toole talking to US asylum officers and we heard Emily Green meet a man who is being sent back to Mexico and is afraid of being kidnapped. And is then kidnapped.

It's the episode that won a Pulitzer Prize in May 2020, the first audio production ever to do so, and under the title 'The Out Crowd' it deals with the consequences of Donald Trump''s asylum policy. It is exciting from beginning to end, developing a narrative that is told authentically. *This American Life* proves once again why the programme is often called the 'mother of storytelling podcasts.' It is no coincidence that *Serial* was a spin-off of *This*

American Life. The influence of particularly the first season, also on the European (podcast) market, was immense (and I don't just mean the number of true crime podcasts that ensued).

The storytelling techniques, which are perhaps a bit more American, meet a great feature tradition, especially in Europe (podcasts were also available here, of course, but they didn't attract nearly as much attention as in the US). Right now—and this is a snapshot at the beginning of 2021—the market is still very buoyant (with the first signs of consolidation), the big platforms have created (or conquered) formative structures, production companies are on the rise, publishers are investing in podcasts and audio is experiencing a renaissance hardly anyone could have imagined.

For me, the developments of the past few years are reason enough to finally write this book. From numerous workshops, format developments and story consultations I took away the same impressions time and again. There is a great deal of enthusiasm and inspiration out there, but also a great deal of uncertainty about the narrative craft. Storytelling techniques, in particular, do not only help improve large-scale series or stories, but all narrative forms, short and long, radio and podcast.

This book shows how documentary audio stories can be told in an exciting way, which dramaturgical techniques help to tell a story, what exactly storytelling means, and what effects it has on the work processes of the reporter, editor and director. Storytelling is a craft and can therefore be learned. And if you know and master the rules, then, fortunately, you can be creative in breaking them again.

Bonn, Germany   Sven Preger
February 2021

Acknowledgments

I am always looking for people who inspire me or are crazy enough to work on projects with me. There are so many great ideas out there! Therefore, I would like to say a big thank you to some inspiring people. They share my enthusiasm for storytelling.

Stephan Beuting. When the first season of *Serial* came out in autumn 2014, we accidentally ran into each other in the newsroom we were both working in (we tend to do that!). We were both so impressed by Sarah Koenig and her team and responded with one of those things you say during these short conversations: 'If one of us ever comes across a story like that, we'll do something like *Serial* in Germany. Or at least try.' We definitely weren't the only ones to think like that at that time nor are we today. It's hard to believe that this all somehow came true. A few months later, Stephan and I met for dinner in Bonn and Stephan suddenly started talking about this hitchhiker he met at a petrol station. You can listen to the rest!

Leslie Rosin. Leslie has given *The Hitchhiker* a home. She recognised the potential in the story and made the first WDR serial possible. She fought with us for this form, always keeping the quality of the product in mind. She also opened the door on the European feature world to me. And with her constructive comments on the German manuscript, she also made this book better.

Ralph Erdenberger. His stories always get to me. I hardly know anybody who handles the medium audio as lovingly as Ralph. As author, director and presenter. Together we have spent innumerable hours on ideas, plot designs and in the studio. For *The Unsolved Mysteries of Science*, *Evo-Solution* and of course *Faust Jr*!

Mira Brinkschulte. The former boss of Igel Records, the publishing home of *Faust Jr*, Mira was crazy enough to give Ralph and me our own series and (almost) a free hand. She was always straightforward, affectionate, reliable, humorous, enthusiastic and warm-hearted! The degree of trust Mira placed in us would motivate anybody to get the best out of everything.

Team *Quarks Storys*! In late summer 2019, we started this podcast project which is very close to my heart. Complex and moving science stories with a daring sound design. Together with a team of 15 reporters, editors and directors we were able to develop something unique!

Timo Ackermann. He was the sound engineer for *Faust Jr*, *The Hitchhiker* and numerous *Quarks Storys* (including the pilot!). Need I say more? Anyone who can make three such different, complex productions sound like this is simply one of the best in his field!

Svenja & Uwe Walter. If you love storytelling as much as you two do, you will always inspire others. Just like you did me.

Barbara Emig-Roller, the responsible editor at Springer, immediately recognised that the time was ripe for this book on the German market. Together with the editor of the 'Gelbe Reihe', Professor Dr Gabriele Hooffacker, she has given my pet subject a high-quality environment.

And she put me in contact with their sister publisher Palgrave Macmillan. Without the help and guidance of Emily Wood, Bryony Burns and the responsible editor Mala Sanghera-Warren the English edition would not have seen light of day. Esther Gonstalla designed the great graphics! And finally, Dr Lynda Lich-Knight not only proof-read and polished the manuscript but was a magnificent co-translator!

And Anne, for the biggest adventure stories!

CONTENTS

1   Acoustic Narration: A New Beginning   1

2   A Good Story: Delivering an Experience   23

3   No Story Without Structure: Plot Development   43

4   Character Development: The Actor Drives the Story   91

5   Dynamic Storytelling: How to Build Suspense   115

6   Scenic Narratives   147

7   Who Speaks: Developing and Implementing a Narrative Attitude   175

8   Staging: From Script to Sound   195

9   Ethics and the Limits of Narrations: Is This Still Journalism?   219

10   Work Routine for the Narrative Reporter   229

Index   243

LIST OF FIGURES

Fig. 3.1	Ladder of Abstraction	47
Fig. 3.2	The Hero's Journey	58
Fig. 3.3	Hero's Journey and Act Structure	64
Fig. 3.4	Plot Point Paradigm	67
Fig. 3.5	Hero's Journey, Acts and Plot Points	68
Fig. 3.6	Scenic Narrative	74
Fig. 3.7	Scenic-Reflective Narrative	75
Fig. 3.8	Explanatory Narrative	77
Fig. 3.9	Argumentative Narrative	78
Fig. 3.10	Narrative Anecdote	79
Fig. 4.1	Story Interview	109
Fig. 10.1	Storyboard	234
Fig. 10.2	Workflow for Narration	238

CHAPTER 1

Acoustic Narration: A New Beginning

1.1 WHY WE NEED STORIES

One of my happy places looks like this: I'm sitting in an almost empty train which moves smoothly along the tracks. I look out of the window into a September morning. Outside, life and the landscape pass by, there are fields and small villages. This film, swiping by, forms the blurred background for what is happening inside me. With headphones over my ears, I am immersed in one of those stories that take me into a cosmos that I don't know (yet). These are not invented, fictional stories, but non-fictional, documentary narratives. They explain a piece of the world to me that I have not understood before. I would love to have a sign around my neck: Please do not disturb! It is these moments that feel to me as if the world is a place of possibilities that somehow make sense (especially if the stories are true and not invented). This may all sound a bit cheesy, but maybe I'm not the only one who can indulge in stories like this and react accordingly. "All tales, then, are at some level a journey into the woods to find the missing part of us, to retrieve it and make ourselves whole" (Yorke 2014, 72). These are stories I am looking forward to. Even if I sometimes don't yet know what sort of a journey they will take me on. They are special stories, which—as different as they may be—have certain characteristics in common. And which rarely appear in news programmes, for example.

When was the last time you really looked forward to a news programme? If you are German and like football (unofficial estimates put it at 84.3% of the population), then perhaps it was on 14 July 2014 because you anticipated seeing the best pictures (of the totally exhausted Bastian Schweinsteiger) or hearing the commentaries (like Tom Bartels shouting out to Mario Götze: "Do it, do it – he's doing it....") of the World Cup final the day before

S. Preger, *Storytelling in Radio and Podcasts*, https://doi.org/10.1007/978-3-030-73130-4_1

(after the German team's elimination from the preliminary rounds of the 2018 World Cup, such moments are even more precious in my home country).

Otherwise, we probably watch the news more because we want to keep informed and know what is going on. Enthusiastic anticipation of reports on a political party conference or the last debate in parliament is usually relatively limited. These are stories we see, read or hear because we think it makes sense. And that is a good reason. Dramaturgically speaking, they are stories we want to see, watch or hear to keep updated. We consume them because there is an external reason for doing so. The stories themselves don't capture our imagination. But such stories do exist: They are not stories we want to hear, but need to hear—they give us pleasure, insight or move us on a deeper level. This book is about these stories and how they are told.

When we think of stories that cast a spell over us, we often think of fictional material: films, books and television series. We don't expect to find them so often in media that cover reality—in daily newspapers, television magazine programmes or in radio and podcasts. Yet these stories and the corresponding need for them exist in the audiences and editorial offices. Soft news factors such as conversation value have become much more important in recent years (although this has not always led to a dramatic improvement in programmes, quite the contrary). The actual message behind it is that the creators want to deliver stories that readers, viewers, listeners or users like to consume. However, this effort often leads to rather odd approaches. A practical example shows what I mean by this: Reporters should definitely and always include one emotional moment in their 2:30-minutes piece (e.g. when the shopkeeper enters his shop for the first time after the flood and is shocked by the full extent of the destruction). These moments often seem voyeuristic and artificial, in the worst case even cynical. Because we, as viewers or listeners, have not really got close to this person before (mostly not even as reporters), we don't accord the situation real respect. We suspect the editorial offices and reporters do not really take this person seriously but use him purely as a vehicle. This also results in the same formulations every time, such as "After this dramatic day nothing was the same for Marc Smith ever again…!". Statements like this are often peppered with adjectives, which is a clear indication of a violation of the old storytelling rule "show, don't tell," because the adjectives are supposed to tell me as a recipient what impression I should have of the situation. The story as such obviously does not convey this. The example also shows why narrative attitude is so important. What is the journalist's or storyteller's attitude towards the subject and the people in it? The audience senses that, too.

Another example is radio presenters who try to link good mood programmes with current disasters. In this case, it may be moderated in analogy with the music bed of a pop song: "You have just heard it on the news. In Bavaria, six young people have died from poisoning. Why carbon monoxide is dangerous - right here with us in just a moment… and now (imagine the pop song of your choice!)". In 20 s, you cannot create deep emotions. Like novels, films or TV series, deep stories need space even with real material.

Then, they unfold in a way we like. There are at least five reasons why we as humans love stories, even need them. These reasons partially complement each or overlap.

1. Stories create order in chaos and are therefore meaningful in a complex world. Everyone has probably experienced the feeling of being overwhelmed at one time or another. One's own life (What do I want? What is good for me? How do I find happiness?) is complicated enough. Add to this the great complex crises of this world (climate change, Corona, world peace). It is relatively easy to lose track of all this. Stories work against that. They are told as a logically structured plot and thus provide orientation on cause and effect (how exactly this works will be explained in Chapter 3); they explain problems and clarify contexts. The effects of Donald Trump's asylum policy on a refugee camp on the Mexican border, for example, are shown in *This American Life*. The episode "The Out Crowd" from November 2019 illustrates how stories fulfil one of the main tasks of journalism in a particularly convincing way (we will also discuss the danger of creating contexts of meaning that may not be there later, see Chapter 9).[1]

   So, pleasurable stories explain and sort the world. Because there is often a deeper truth in them, a realisation beneath the events. These stories not only show what happened, but what it means, be it in the form of a moral or beliefs and statements about the world. This is how, for example, the first season of *Serial* always conveys the message: It is worthwhile to pursue the truth and fight for justice. These messages are often not formulated explicitly but are transported in the subtext of the story. When real stories convey this kind of message, they unfold a special power. Then, they can even explain the world much better than short news, articles or forcibly balanced reports (party A says, party B says, party C says, done), which in the end hardly explain anything at all and reproduce similar stereotypes again and again. Somewhat provocatively formulated: Forcibly balanced reports are often a justification for not doing the research.

2. Stories bring the world to us. They take us out of our familiar surroundings and show us what is still going on out there. We don't even have to leave our homes, or we can immerse ourselves in these strange worlds on a train ride. Stories can take us into other areas of life and make them accessible. These stories not only show us other perspectives and are therefore instructive, but they may even be a wake-up call when they point out a problem, for example. This is especially true for journalistic stories. They show us how the Supreme Court works in the US (*More Perfect*), what secrets are waiting for us out there (*The Untold*), how we can get in tune with our bodies (*The Heart*), why a homeless man kills several people (*The Nobody Zone*), what forces and beliefs influence our actions (*Invisibilia*), what stories are behind design (*99% Invisible*) or

what a life can look like that doesn't fit into a small town (*S-Town*). This selection is very small and highly subjective. But all these different products have at least one thing in common: They are narrative podcasts; they tell one or more stories. These stories convey a differentiated perspective and thus provide a deeper understanding of the world and its interrelationships. Podcast stories in particular, with their space for complexity and nuances, are also able to depict contexts in their appropriate form. It is not just a matter of briefly highlighting a news item, but of providing the context, arguments, analysis and possible solutions, and telling a story accordingly. Storytelling and constructive journalism go hand in hand here.

And stories do something else: They can transport us into this other world. In this sense, listening to stories is a highly immersive experience which has two great advantages: It distracts us (e.g. from stress, anger, cold) and it lets us experience the moment. We forget everything around us, go with the flow. We are so fascinated that we don't take a toilet break, even if we have to go urgently. Only when we emerge from this state or wake up (because we fell asleep while listening) do we notice that we are thirsty, hungry or that time has passed. A wonderful state until we realise how urgently we need to go to the toilet!

3. Stories connect. This aspect contains two different arguments. One is the phenomenon of different people hearing, seeing or reading a story and then sharing it. In this sense, they form a community. The other is the idea behind this that stories are able to awaken understanding and empathy for other people. If you listen to the *Radiolab* story 'On the Edge' about Surya Bonaly you get a deep insight into her world, her worries, fears and experiences. Those who deal intensively with the lives of others, also in the form of stories, will find it much harder to condemn these people. On the contrary, we will get to know them, and they will be closer to us than they were before. Stories connect us because they enable us to experience that basic human needs and emotions are common to all of us. We are not alone. Particularly, podcasts with their great closeness and empathy are especially powerful in this respect (*Love & Radio* or *The Heart* are just two examples Spinelli and Dann write about in the second chapter titled 'In Bed with Radiotopians: Podcast Intimacy, Empathy, and Narrative') (2019, 69–97).

4. Stories give hope by showing us what is possible. This has a lot to do with the characters because stories show how people deal with crises and challenges. In doing so, causes, motives and inner conflicts are also made tangible. In particular, crucial decision-making moments play an important role because they show which options can become reality. And it is precisely these moments that serve as role models and are remembered: They show how people try to make the morally appropriate choice even in difficult situations, although the choice itself may be just as difficult. Experiencing such moments in stories generates hope. They also help to

ensure that we do not collapse in a complex world, despite the feeling of being overburdened. "We watch stories not just to awaken our eyes to reality but to make reality bearable as well" (Yorke 2014, 181). Those who can stand reality and find their way in it will always sense the chance to experience their own ability to succeed. Stories are thus the glue of society.

In this sense, stories can even heal or at least make us feel healed. In playback theatre, for example, there is a basic guiding idea: A person in the audience tells a story, which can consist of special moments like the first kiss or a (nightmare) dream. Essential parts of this moment are then performed by the playback group on stage. It is a sign of appreciation. The message is: Your very personal story is so important that we feel it. The storyteller thus has the opportunity to relive their own event, this time as a spectator. For many people, this is a very special experience. This kind of appreciation plays a crucial role in the *StoryCorps* interviews and *The Listening Project* (a collaboration between the BBC and the British Library). In psychodrama, patients are even given the chance to stage their own story with the support of a therapist. The spontaneous play is intended to help them distance themselves from old role patterns. So, stories can actually help us heal.

5. Stories make us happy. I can make this claim not only from experience, but also because neuroscience confirms it. "Brains love control. It's their heaven," Will Storr writes (2019, 193). And stories manage to give us a sense of control through their meaning which makes us feel good. Stories also make us happy for another reason. When they bring us closer to the world and explain it, they trigger a eureka effect in us. We have understood connections that might not have been so clear to us before. Stories are therefore teachers for life in the very best sense. And sometimes they are simply the best entertainment.

So, stories allow us to experience something and feel emotions, they touch us, whereby our feelings do not know the difference between fictional and non-fictional stories. No matter whether we are mourning the demise of Sherlock Holmes with Dr John Watson after he has jumped off the roof of St Bartholomew's Hospital (in the BBC series *Sherlock*) or are shocked at the end of the second episode of *S-Town* (spoiler alert!) when we learn that the hitherto central character John B. McLemore has taken his own life. Emotions always feel real, even when we know that one story is true and the other is not (which helps to sort and change emotions). And they are the key to remembering a story. Memory research shows that we remember better when emotions are associated with an event or story (Shaw 2016). This can be a major dilemma, especially for non-fictional stories. On the one hand, we naturally want our piece to be remembered. On the other, when dealing with emotions in journalistic products, we still experience either great uncertainty and immense reservations (not least about objectivity!) or suspect ourselves of inappropriate sensationalist tendencies. Neither of these is helpful. Stories are about the appropriate depiction and staging of real events and emotions. If you want to tell such stories, you should not be afraid of emotions, but need to handle them confidently.

A good story often creates key moments that seem bigger, truer, more real to us than our own lives. The one scene remains in our memory, the one sentence or sometimes even just the one word (all fans of the TV series *Castle* know how important the little word "always" can be). The third episode of our six-part WDR documentary series *The Hitchhiker*, for example, ends with a scene in which we as reporters want to reveal the family history of the psychiatric victim Heinrich Kurzrock. Heinrich had previously asked us—Stephan Beuting and me—to investigate this background. After months of research, we meet up with Heinrich to report the results, but he doesn't want to hear them. We make several attempts, but Heinrich remains firm. This scene conveys a deeper message beneath the actual plot: Everyone has the right not to know. That is what makes this scene so powerful, plus the tension that arises from the situation: Why does he actually not want to know?

Not every story unfolds its effect continuously and evenly on all levels. An investigative story about the impact of Trump's asylum policy on refugees on the Mexican border will generate empathy and understanding, but probably little hope. How journalistic audio stories can unfold their effect in detail is also the subject of this book.

A few years ago (probably before autumn 2014), you might have read the following paragraph at this point: If you look at media use, there is one medium that is least suited to this kind of pleasurable story: radio. Its trademark: It is fast and thrives on short, concise contributions. Features and documentaries have always had fixed broadcasting slots that were hardly noticed, however, by a large audience.

But radio and podcasts can do so much more. Namely, they can tell stories. Audio formats in particular seem to be the ideal place for those quiet, intimate emotions that unveil themselves cautiously, very cautiously, to unfold their power. All the more so because we carry these stories around with us on our smartphones. We can immerse ourselves in them at any time, on the train or bus. Then, we just have to be careful not to miss our stop. And as is often the case at the beginning of a story, there is a triggering event that sets something in motion. Since it probably marks the biggest single break in audio production to date, I'd like to briefly discuss the first season of *Serial* from a storytelling point of view.

1.2   What Has Happened so Far: *Serial* and the Consequences

This beginning has become a modern classic: just a few notes on the piano and then a voice from a tape says: "This is a Global-Tel link prepaid call from…" This is the opening of the first season of *Serial* which was released in autumn 2014 (one story told week by week, well kind of). At the same time, Apple had integrated an 'easy to use' podcasting app in its iOS8 software, which added to the momentum or perhaps facilitated it in the first place. The American podcast series changed the world of audio stories and especially of podcasts. It was immensely successful, was published, at least in part, during the ongoing research (and thus achieved a high level of listener loyalty, at any rate at the time of its initial release), created a link between classic radio and what podcasting is all about, and on a meta-level can certainly be seen as the birth of a "new human journalism" (Spinelli and Dann 2019, 194).

From a storytelling perspective, one of the most important effects is what Larry Rosin, president of Edison Research, describes in an interview with Martin Spinelli: "The most important impact he (Larry Rosin, SP) observed of *Serial*, he says, was that it left an enormous appetite among listeners for more high-quality narrative podcasts" (Spinelli and Dann 2019, 177). Years later, however, there still seems to be disagreement about how exactly Sarah Koenig and her team actually did all that: How did *Serial* maintain the tension over twelve episodes? Why did so many people feverishly await the next episode? How did Koenig find this authentic, subjective tone? The answers to these questions are important because they give an idea of the techniques which can be helpful in telling a complex story in a captivating and emotionally appropriate way. It is, perhaps, a bit disconcerting how many different answers are circulating to these questions. Therefore, here comes my personal hit list of *Serial* misunderstandings that I have encountered again and again in the last few years.

Misunderstanding 1: This story tells itself. Um, no, it doesn't. Even this frighteningly general statement reveals more ignorance than insight. Stories never tell themselves (what was that about frighteningly general statements?!). For that you still need something like a narrator. Should you ever get feedback like this to a piece you have published, you can still consider yourself lucky: Obviously, listening was an entertaining experience. Unfortunately, lightness is almost always hard work.

Misunderstanding 2: The protagonist Adnan Syed is perfect. Wrong again. The protagonist of the series is not Adnan Syed. The word protagonist, which can be translated from ancient Greek as main or first actor, already makes this clear. Syed does not really act. He is in prison, cannot leave and hardly has any possibilities to actively fight for a change in his condition. What is true is that there is a lot at stake for Syed, and he is also multi-layered and has a complex personality, which is certainly good for the story. But he is not the protagonist. That is the 'investigative' journalist Sarah Koenig (which is why it makes sense that we as listeners are so intensively involved in her learning process).

Misunderstanding 3: Sarah Koenig is just so likeable. Yes, um no, or no idea. Dramaturgically speaking this sentence is not quite precise. As listeners, we don't know whether Sarah Koenig is likeable or not. But what we do know, and feel, is that Sarah Koenig stages herself as a likeable narrator. Perhaps this is close to her real personality (that would be rather nice!). But it is certainly a staging decision for her to appear humorous, thoughtful and not perfect. Because that serves the story. It makes her credible as a narrator and gives her the opportunity to develop. It also makes clear what kind of narrator we as listeners like.

Misunderstanding 4: Americans simply talk more emotionally than, for example, Europeans. See also the note on general statements from Misunderstanding 1. What is true is that this story is very emotional and sometimes told emotionally. What is also true is that objectivity is an important asset in many European and definitely German newsrooms. Or to put it another way, even in long stories the journalist or reporter is not so prominent and emotionally involved. How much this is culturally determined is not important (it probably is a factor). What is decisive is that the narrative style has a specific task in the story and is often used quite deliberately in *Serial*. This makes it a well-used narrative craft, no more, no less.

Misunderstanding 5: The story is so great because it deals with a real criminal case. Really? Is this story primarily a true crime story? Or an investigative research story? Or a relationship story (between Sarah and Adnan)? Or all at once? And is that even important (yes, it is!)? If it were a true crime story, the core of the story would have to be that Sarah Koenig wants to solve the murder of Hae Min Lee. It might seem to be splitting hairs, but that is not Koenig's primary goal. Koenig checks whether Syed is wrongfully convicted. If she finds the real culprit, fine. If not, then it's not decisive for the story. If you understand *Serial* as a true crime story, there is a danger of getting yourself involved in a criminal case as well. With the aim of telling a similarly gripping story.

All five misunderstandings have been deliberately exaggerated to make a point. Clean analysis is important in order to recognise the central narrative principles. The arguments and theses don't just come out of thin air, but they are not spot on either. The great danger, and often the consequence, is that as editors, reporters or authors, we copy the factors that we recognise or think we recognise. But perhaps these are not the decisive factors. The result is then often somewhat unsatisfactory.

Serial has become an international reference point. For the first season, the production won a Peabody Award which honours outstanding radio and television productions. The Peabody nomination called *Serial* an "audio game changer." And that is true. There seems to be a pre-*Serial* and a post-*Serial* era. On the European market, too. Editors and authors are looking for material to tell series. Stories should be as exciting as *Serial*, as authentic as *Serial*, as relevant as *Serial* and told like *Serial*. But the omnipresent comparison poses at least three problems of its own:

1. The comparison is of little help if it is not clear which dramaturgical and manual techniques were used in Serial. Only they can help to create and narrate a similarly good series.

2. The comparison wears thin at some point. Or it hangs like a threatening cloud over the production: it better be as good as Serial. But hey, no pressure!

3. The duration comparison takes away freedom of design. Does everything now have to sound and be told like Serial? No, of course not. But Serial is a good example of an outstanding, touching and complex story. And it is based on good craftsmanship. You can understand that, filter out the narrative principles and thus learn something in addition to the great listening pleasure. The principles behind it can, of course, also be implemented in other, exciting narratives.

One thing is certain: *Serial* was not a lucky break; it was the result of a long development or another step along the way. And it was an important trigger for the second big podcast wave, which ultimately had a significant influence on developments in Europe. Furthermore, one can also claim *Serial* is a logical consequence of the American audio narrative universe of at least the last 20 years.

Several programmes and shows had a considerable impact on the development of storytelling in American podcasts, above all, *This American Life*, from whose philosophy and way of working *Serial* and *S-Town* would eventually emerge. *This American Life* originally launched in 1995 under the title *Your Radio Playhouse* (co-founded by Ira Glass and Torey Malatia). Over the years, the show has evolved into what it is today: One or more stories (often referred to as acts) woven together into an overarching theme or motto of sorts. The personal narrative style, the build-up of tension in the stories and the alternation between action and reflection are some of the hallmarks of *This American Life*. These elements have inspired many other formats and storytellers.

In 2002, another show premiered that would greatly influence audio storytelling in America: *Radiolab*. The show is dedicated to scientific and philosophical topics. Part of its brand is its elaborate sound and the interplay between its two hosts, Jad Abumrad and Robert Krulwich. Krulwich has now stepped down as host; the last edition featuring him was released in January 2020. Since then, the show, which is produced and released in seasons, has also been presented by Latif Nasser and Lulu Miller. There have been several successful and remarkable spin-offs from *Radiolab*, which now sees itself as a platform for long-form journalism and storytelling: June 2016 marked the launch of *More Perfect*, the first spin-off. The podcast series features important Supreme Court decisions. In 2019, the *Dolly Parton's America* podcast was released, focusing on American country singer Dolly Parton. 2020 also saw the addition of *The Other Latif*, a multi-part story about a Guantanamo detainee.

In the years following the founding of *Radiolab*, the first wave of podcasts took off. Early shows included *Matt Schichter Interviews*, Christopher Lyden's *Open Source* and Adam Curry's *Daily Source Code* (on the milestones of podcast development cf. Nuzum 2019, 232ff). Finally, shows that were already successful on linear radio, such as *This American Life* and *Radiolab*, were also offered as podcasts.

Additional inspiration to engage with personal stories came from other formats, as well. One example is *StoryCorps*, a special oral history project launched in 2003. The idea is that two people have a conversation with each other about the issues that really move them: their relationship, life, their fears or hopes. This conversation is recorded. Founder David Isay wants to capture and share the stories of Americans in a kind of collective audio memory.

During the years of experimentation after the first podcasts of the three *Serial* seasons until finally today, at least three major strands of development emerged: Firstly, exciting stories were told in a personal way and the range of topics expanded. The podcast *99% Invisible*, for example, is about design, about the 99% that are not visible or hard to grasp. Secondly, the special audio strengths such as intimacy and inwardness were brought into focus, especially for the podcast market (we will come to the advantages of the audio medium in detail in a moment). This can be seen in such formats as *Love & Radio, Terrible, thanks for asking* or *Invisibilia*. And thirdly, of course, numerous talk and interview formats were launched, with the founding of *The Daily* in January 2017 marking yet another milestone (whereby it is particularly exciting that *The Daily*, a *New York Times* podcast, does not have a great in-house audio tradition to draw on). The forms are not clearly defined: *The Daily* works with storytelling techniques just as *This American Life* may include interview sequences. Naturally, there has also been a focus on the celebrity factor, as *The Joe Rogan Experience* demonstrates. In recent years, various news formats have been added, too.

Once again, this is only a small and highly subjective selection, which illustrates that great podcast and audio productions with a storytelling focus existed in the US before *Serial*. The programmes were perhaps just not noticed to the same extent, at least not in Europe and certainly not in Germany (although many European countries with their public service systems have a great feature tradition).

Dramaturgically speaking, the success of *Serial* was thus a triggering event. European editorial offices also developed and broadcast similar formats shortly afterwards. The series often dealt with real-life criminal cases: *The Nobody Zone* (*RTE* with *Third Ear*), *Death in Ice Valley* (*BBC World Service* with *NRK*) or *Ringbinds-Attentatet* (*Third Ear*). Often, though not always, these productions were created by or in cooperation with public broadcasters' feature and radio drama departments. This is no coincidence as these series are relatively complex and require a certain amount of know-how in conception and realisation. This is available in the editorial departments. In Europe and in Germany in particular, there is a decades-long tradition of telling stories in features and radio plays (Krug 2003). The German author Peter Leonhard Braun founded the *International Feature Conference* in 1974—a mixture of conference and festival where feature makers come together every year to listen to productions, give feedback and share ideas.

The radio drama tradition, at least in Germany, goes back even further to the 1920s. Even today, many children, young people and adults fall asleep to radio plays (which is not a reflection on the suspense issue!), from *The Three Investigators* to *Professor van Dusen*. These fictional stories take us to another world, to Rocky Beach or to America and Europe at the beginning of the twentieth century. Radio plays are more or less clearly defined as fictional stories.

The feature, on the other hand, almost as traditionally eludes clear definition. The *ARD radiofeature* (one of the most important feature productions in Germany), for example, claims that it "is quality journalism and radio art all in one."[2] Wikipedia states: "A radio documentary, or feature, covers a topic in depth from one or more perspectives, often featuring interviews, commentary, and sound pictures."[3] And the standard work, *Das Radio-Feature*, lists seven different characteristics of "this dazzling form of radio," amongst them the use of real material, an artistic dramaturgical design, the utilisation of all creative possibilities and a fundamentally subjective narrative attitude. As a final criterion, the whole thing is then summarised again: "The feature does not have a clearly defined form: Every piece seeks its own form in a figurative sense, every programme is 'recreated.' There are no universally valid templates, no enduring ideology, no immortal school"[4] (Zindel and Rein 2007, 22).

Over the decades, however, three core characteristics have probably emerged which are decisive for the feature:

- Firstly, the feature deals with documentary material, not fiction. It therefore wants to depict and interpret reality, as in outstanding productions such as *Papa, we're in Syria* (2016, by Christian Lerch),[5] which documents a father's search for his two sons who have left Germany for Syria to join the Islamic State. Another example is the feature *After The Celebration* by Lisbeth Jessen (originally a production for Danmarks Radio 2002).[6] In the feature, the author sets out to find Allan whose radio interview in the mid-1990s was the inspiration for the first Danish dogma film *The Celebration* (1998). In the radio programme, Allan had talked about a family celebration where he had uncovered years of abuse within his family. When the Dogma film becomes a big success, everyone asks: Where is Allan? And is his story even true? Lisbeth Jessen sets out on a search.

    It is precisely these documentary productions that show that the feature is the non-fictional counterpart to the radio play and in this sense forms its own genre. The boundaries between the two forms are fluid, which has something to do with the next point.
- Secondly, in audio features, the how is just as important as the what. In-depth research and thematic understanding are just as important as the acoustic staging. This is why productions such as the one by Peter Leonhard Braun entitled *Chicken* (a production for Sender Freies Berlin 1967) are particularly remarkable. With this production, stereophony entered

the feature. But even modern productions experiment with new forms and ideas again and again, such as the feature *Nobody gets out of here alive* by Albrecht Kunze (a production for WDR 2011), in which the subject is the Love Parade catastrophe (which happened in summer 2010 in Duisburg, 21 people died and hundreds were injured), and language and techno music are condensed into a rhythm. Ideally, content and form fit together. They become one.

- Thirdly, openness. In theme and style. There is no topic that cannot also become a feature. And there is no acoustic implementation that must not be tried out. This is another reason why the boundaries to the radio play are fluid.

A rather open definition of this kind has advantages and disadvantages. The disadvantage is that when everything is possible, criteria and common vocabulary are sometimes missing. So, what makes an exciting story? What belongs in a concept? And what is the story? The big advantage is that nothing is set in stone. Everything can be tried out. This tradition of "anything is allowed" also ensures that, currently, a lot is being tried out in terms of storytelling and series. And that is good.

It is not only at the major broadcasters, however, that things are moving, but on the podcast market, too. Podcast labels have been established. A look at the German market indicates how transformative the business is right now. In 2016, *Viertausendhertz*, based in Berlin, was the first podcast label on the German market. Also, in 2016, both *Audible* and Bayerischer Rundfunk (BR) called for concepts for new formats to be submitted. The podcasts *The Moment* at *Audible* (in which people talk about particularly decisive moments in their lives) and *A Man for Mama* (at BR, where journalist Magdalena Bienert and her mother are looking for a new boyfriend for her mum) are just two of the results of these developments. In addition, numerous other podcasts were produced independently of these, from *The Anachronist* (the journalist Nora Hespers delves into her family history: Her grandfather was active in the resistance against National Socialism) to *Mummy and me* (motto: stories from the suburbs, told by a daughter). And Spotify has also moved into the podcast market with all its might, for example by buying the American label *Gimlet Media* in February 2019.

In the above-mentioned productions, it is more a matter of a very personal view of a topic than of elaborately told documentary stories. Just as in the US, Europe naturally had a podcast scene even before current developments. To this day, however, the two spheres podcast and feature still seem to be much more separate than in the US, which is not always helpful.

All in all, it is still a time of departure, trial and error and experimentation even though market structures in particular are gradually developing. Numerous new material and formats continue to emerge. At the same time, however, European productions do not seem to be able to match the American successes. And this is not only, but also, a marketing problem. There also seems to be a good deal of uncertainty about the craft sector which is sometimes even the reason for rejections. This then manifests itself in sceptical questions: Is it easy to transfer from America to other markets and countries, or are the cultural differences too great after all? Is that what we want at all? Does everything have to sound the same now? Do we only need series? And: Is this American emotionalism still journalism at all? The debate is somewhat reminiscent of the debate on New Journalism which entered the journalistic stage in the US in the 1960s and 1970s. The idea was to use literary techniques to tell elaborate stories that were as exciting as a novel, only true. The founder of *This American Life*, Ira Glass, was very much inspired by this school.

This book is an anti-insecurity book. It answers questions about craftsmanship: to achieve the central goal, namely to tell a real story as excitingly and as appropriately as possible—a story that does not artificially over-dramatise or neglect important aspects (just because they may not fit into the narrative as well as they might). From beginning to end. This is more about narrative principles than rules. The book shows which dramaturgical techniques help to fulfil these tasks. It is not directed against other forms of narration. Those who have mastered the techniques can also recognise where they are not helpful. And those who know the principles and rules can also choose to ignore them. The key questions in this book are the following: How do I tell a real story from beginning to end in an exciting, touching and appropriate way? Which dramaturgical techniques from other narrative forms such as cinema, theatre, TV or novels can help me to do this?

In the search for answers, one basic insight helps. That is, we humans have always been fascinated by stories and have been telling them to each other for a long time, around the campfire or at the cave entrance. But why is this actually so? Those who understand this will learn something about the basic attitude of storytellers. And this is the basis for all good storytelling.

The reasons why we hear these pleasurable stories are all related to the fact that we want to feel emotions, understand the world and sense our connection to it. This may sound somewhat pathetic, but it is very often exactly that. The techniques of narrative audio help to deliver this kind of experience. And audio, both radio and podcast, is particularly suited to telling stories. There are, however, a few differences between radio and podcast. That is what is coming up next.

1.3   Narrative Audio: Create a Sonic Experience

One notion has had a great career in journalism in recent years. And not for the first time: storytelling. It is mainly associated with the upswing in the podcast market, which many call the second big podcast wave or even the golden age of podcasting. And many use the term storytelling in that context, reporters, authors, directors and editors alike, sometimes with an enthusiastic undertone, sometimes with an air of mysticism and glorification, and sometimes rejection. It is a fashionable word (or retro word because it is not really new) as well as a kind of umbrella term. Such terms tend to have the advantage that you don't have to define them too precisely. On the other hand, this unfortunately makes a topic much harder to discuss because it is often not quite clear what exactly is being talked about.

What storytelling actually means is using dramaturgical techniques to tell a story scenically and make reality tangible. This neither defines the technique that is used, nor how it is done. Many other terms belong in this cosmos: tension, suspense, hero, protagonist, developmental arc, act structure, plot points, hero's journey, cliffhanger and many more. Often these terms are all mixed up together. To get a grip on them, you should start by asking a simple question: What exactly is a story and what elements does it comprise? Only when this is clear can the appropriate techniques help to tell the story. In documentary narration or journalism, the term 'story' is often equated with theme or headline. But "America's economic policy" is not a story in the dramaturgical sense, nor is "man bites dog." One is a theme, the other a singular event. In everyday journalistic life, however, both are subsumed under story. In addition, the term 'story' is more readily associated with fiction, a story is something that is invented and not something suitable for documentary narration.

In terms of craftsmanship, a story usually consists of three basic elements: active/acting person, goal and obstacles. To put it more precisely: In a story, a hero—let's call the main character that, even if it is a little bit pathetic— wants to achieve something but encounters obstacles. That is a starting point. If these elements are not present, it becomes difficult to tell the kind of story we are talking about here. For it to be a narrative, it must also consist of scenes. These scenes are the backbone of the story. So, we can witness what a hero experiences, and it is not for nothing that "drama" also means action. In addition to this classic dramaturgy focusing on a protagonist, I have developed further dramaturgies which should make it possible to tell stories when there is not one central character who carries the story.

For journalists, this usually means looking at their own story anew and sorting the material, not according to importance, relevance, novelty or thematic affiliation, but according to dramaturgical criteria. A topic must become a story. This is a great challenge, and the following questions can help: Which scenes can I narrate? How can I create suspense? What information should I still withhold? And perhaps most importantly: How can I make an event so tangible that someone who hears the story relives it?

For many journalistic formats, these questions do not provide meaningful answers. News communication still often assumes that the news or most important results come right at the beginning (even though there are now news formats that work with narrative techniques). Narrative audio, by contrast, delivers an experience. However, this is contrary to the classic journalistic approach because journalists usually do their research and then present their results, in the form of news, reports, discussions with colleagues and so on. The American author and Pulitzer Prize winner Cormac McCarthy is cred-ited with the quotation: "Where all is known, no narrative is possible" (Hart 2011, 27). The aim of a narration is therefore to let the listener participate in a process of cognition. To bind them to the narrative in this sense. Narrative audio thus means a dramaturgical narrative or story.

It makes sense to consider and use the particular strengths of the medium. In his standard work *Story*, the American script expert Robert McKee describes the corresponding media differences. "In the twentieth century we now have three media for telling story: prose (novel, novella, short story), theatre (legit, musical, opera, mime, ballet) and screen (film and television)" (McKee 1991, 365). All three have their own original storytelling strengths. It helps to be clear about what these are.

Prose allows us to participate most intimately in the inner life of a character. For this purpose, an inner monologue is often used. Dramaturgically speaking, a character's inner conflict is best staged. We can look directly into the mind of Harry Potter. We know what fears he faces as he approaches Lord Voldemort for the final duel. When we have finished a great book, we put a good friend aside, usually with a mixture of satisfaction, sadness and longing. We wanted to know how the story would end, but actually it wasn't supposed to end yet.

The theatre presents a plot live, unfolding it before the eyes of the audience. When the potential perpetrator approaches his victim on stage from behind, a whispered warning can sometimes be heard in the theatre (at least at children's performances): Watch out! Behind you! At the latest since Bertolt Brecht's epic theatre we know that this wall of illusion can also be broken down. Above all, the theatre stages a character's personal conflict with other characters, for which the main means is dialogue. The stage design options are concomitantly limited.

This is exactly the strength of the screen. It can show the world in all its colours and potentialities. Cinema and television have got much closer together in recent decades, as illustrated by many glossy series such as *The Queen's Gambit*, *Game of Thrones*, *Sherlock*, *Downton Abbey* and *Breaking Bad* (again a very subjective selection). The big or small screen strongly reveals the characters' conflict with the world, the extra-personal conflict, the action and the plot (hence the many lavish car chases and pursuits). In this respect, it is even consistent when the main character Frank Underwood breaks through the wall to the viewer in the series *House of Cards* because he has a conflict with everyone, including those watching him (which is very much like Brecht's epic theatre)!

Each medium therefore has its own personal strengths. McKee focuses on three conflict possibilities (conflict with the rules of the world, conflict with other people, conflict with oneself, see Sect. 4.2 for conflict levels) because they are the driving force of a story. This way of thinking in the respective media logic is not foreign to journalists. Sometimes, for example, topics are considered more suitable for print. A press conference just delivers boring pictures for television. But these are pragmatic arguments rather than dramaturgical reasons.

What is remarkable is that audio narratives are missing from Robert McKee's analysis (even though radio documentaries at least were already huge when McKee was writing the book). Radio and podcast narratives also have particular strengths. And those who know them can make use of them. That is why it is particularly important to know the strengths of the medium. Audio has at least five unique selling points.

1. Audio provides a scenic sensory experience. The action unfolds directly in the listeners' ears. This allows them to immerse themselves quickly and completely in the scene; they are close to the events being narrated. And with more sensory impressions than with written text and more directly than with moving pictures. The listener can and should use their imagination to experience the scene before the mind's eye. In this way, they are drawn into the story. Of course, this does not work with the same old street ambience from the archive, but the cry of seagulls and the noise of waves can sometimes have a stronger effect without pictures. In the second episode of the podcast S-*Town*, there is a telephone conversation between reporter Brian Reed and character John B. McLemore. In the middle of the conversation, John tells us that he just peed in the kitchen sink. An image of that might just be too much…

2. Audio creates proximity and intimacy. Each of us probably knows our inner voice. It sometimes torments us, does not let us fall asleep or quietly comments in our head (or did I say that out loud?!). It is something very personal, close and intimate. Audio stories get nearest to this feeling, especially when we listen to them with headsets on our smartphones (so it's with us most of the time). When very special voices penetrate directly into our ears, we cannot and do not want to switch off. In 2013, the BBC adapted the novel *Neverwhere* by Neil Gaiman into a six-part radio play. Lady Door was played by Natalie Dormer and Angel Islington by Benedict Cumberbatch. What these two actors can do with their voices alone is fantastic!

3. Audio really tells a story. It sounds so banal, but an essential feature of audio stories is the narrator or host. They lead us through the story, put it on a firm footing. We are completely immersed in the thoughts of the narrator and "their" characters. In doing so, we can get as close to the inner life and inner conflicts of the characters as in a novel (e.g. in the personal first-person narrator). As listeners, we always build a relationship with the narrator or host. They are a point of reference for us and can be a figure of identification. Sarah Koenig fulfils this role as narrator magnificently—just like Ira Glass in *This American Life* or Jad Abumrad and Robert Krulwich in *Radiolab* (although the latter co-hosted his last episode in January 2020).

4. Audio dissolves space and time. It is the classic amongst the media advantages: In narratives, all levels of space and time can be quickly connected or switched. This not only provides for possible variety, but also creates even better dramaturgical possibilities than on screen. Our characters can encounter and come into conflict with everything imaginable. This also makes the conflict with the outside world easy to portray.
5. Audio delivers reality experiences. This has something to do with the production logic of the medium. Even relatively high-quality recording devices and headphones do not take up much space these days. The earlier reporters introduce them as a normal object in the recording situation, the greater the chance of getting authentic material. People forget that this strange object is a foreign body recording everything, and this is more likely to happen than when I am taking notes on a block or have a camera running. In this sense, audio is a minimally invasive medium.[7]

In principle, both forms of listening, radio and podcast, can use and play to these strengths. But there are a few differences between these two forms of audio. One of the biggest differences is probably listeners' reception behaviour. While radio functions as a secondary medium, podcast is more of an active switch-on medium. Listeners consciously decide to listen to a particular podcast (this can, of course, also happen with radio programmes, but is much more usual with podcasts). This kind of reception has a direct impact on the attitude that prevails in the respective medium. Radio presenters must always expect to gain or lose listeners. Constant localisation (time, programme, location) is part of the basics of classic radio presentation. Podcast hosts can allow themselves much more freedom, flexibility and thus also individuality. With podcasts, intimacy and privacy are not only a question of the subject matter, but also of the approach, the attitude with which a host meets their community.

In this sense, radio is a medium flowing by—which certainly has its advantages, because it can surprise us. "If radio is a 'flow' medium, podcasting is a 'beginning-to-end' medium. In radio we speak of programming; in podcasting we talk about a program" (Spinelli and Dann 2019, 78). This does not mean, of course, that listeners do nothing apart from listening to podcasts and focus their attention exclusively on the story. But the active choice of a product ensures that people create the environment or listen to it in a situation where they can follow or want to get involved in the story (from cooking or cleaning to sitting on a train). The chance of immersion is therefore significantly higher with podcasts than with radio.

This active shaping of the listening experience (whereby listeners play a part in making podcasts an experience) is further enhanced when a podcast is heard through headphones. "Podcasts (…) facilitate a radically different engagement with the body, opening the way to a more immersive sonic experience which could be exploited dramaturgically" (Llinares et al. 2018, 198).

This special privacy and intimacy are also reflected thematically in a raft of podcasts. In recent years, a great variety have been developed revolving around psychology and sexuality (*Terrible, thanks for asking*, *The Heart* and *Invisibilia* are just three examples).

From a storytelling perspective, this leads to a key insight: If people consciously decide in favour of podcasts and actively shape their listening experience, then podcasts are particularly suitable for complex stories. Narrative podcasts are the format of the moment. "Therefore podcasting, which offers a completely different manner of listening experience, requires its own mode of dramaturgy" (Llinares et al. 2018, 191). This means that anyone who turns complex stories into narrative podcasts requires a dual skill set, dramaturgical and acoustic, in order to create a special experience through dramaturgy and sound. This book shows how stories and sound conception fit together. At least in Europe, it should be remembered that there is a long tradition of experimental stories on the radio as well, especially in the sound and dramaturgical field.

What is special is that the sound of podcasts in all its diversity is developing in different directions, from acoustically complex productions like *Radiolab*, *S-Town* and *Quarks Storys*, which exhaust almost all acoustic possibilities, right through to a sound that sometimes consciously uses the somewhat rocked-out authenticity of the respective situation. Through all three seasons, *Serial* also made use of this element. Especially, the unclean sound of the telephone calls between Sarah Koenig and Adnan Syed during the first season, for example, emphasised the authenticity. This real sound is also adapted by radio plays and radio drama as shown by productions like *Limetown* and *Homecoming*.

These factors together have a strong impact on the dynamics between transmitter and receiver. While radio still tends to talk about 'presenter' and 'listener,' podcast productions prefer the terms 'host' and 'community' (the latter being the more important distinction). What at first glance appears to be just a linguistic distinction actually emphasises the special bond that people form with 'their' podcasts. Trust and affinity play a major role, which is a key reason why native ads in particular could be a problem when podcast hosts transfer their own credibility to a product they advertise in their podcast (although there seem to be big cultural differences in acceptance of native ads, meaning it seems harder to establish them in Europe than in the US). Podcasts are no longer a one-way street, but a give and take, which means that identification with and loyalty to products is sometimes immensely high on both sides, maker and recipient. Neither is this difference altered by what are often radio broadcasters' obtrusive calls to listeners asking them respond to everyday questions, by whatever channel (e-mail, phone, voice message). The bond between a podcast and its community seems to exist on a deeper level. This is also demonstrated by the great success of live events such as *Welcome to Night Vale* or the productions of the Danish production company *Third Ear*. It remains to be seen to what extent this special character will be maintained as the market continues to develop according to the logic of the big platforms.

Back to storytelling, one thing is certain: Those who know the media strengths and effects of audio productions can use them. They show how many possibilities are open. It will not always be possible to exploit all the strengths of real material. But that is not necessary either because documentary material has a great advantage over fictional stories. With real stories listeners always have the wonderful feeling that this is really true and really happens or happened! And this feeling should not be underestimated.

1.4   THE TEN MOST COMMON STORY PROBLEMS

In my work as a writer, director, producer and story consultant, I repeatedly encounter similar problems when it comes to creating journalistic stories. I once tried to summarise these problems in a meaningful way. I have exaggerated them for better understanding. But only a little:

- The hell of the second act. Without story planning, it usually works like this: You might come up with a good beginning for your story at some point, and if you're lucky, you'll have something for the end. So, you'd better get started. But then you'll notice that once you've started, you won't really know what to do next. What happens then? As an author, you often fall into old patterns and line up different paragraphs of information (which of course are all important). That's when the problem arises, which is also called the hell of the second act. How can I maintain the suspense over the longest and most difficult part, the middle section? As an author, I suddenly notice that the order of the thematic blocks is somehow arbitrary, but some transitions always come to mind in the end. The rule of thumb is: If info blocks fit in several different places, then something is surely wrong with the structure of the story.
- The two-story or parallel strand problem. This often emerges when everything is to be told in one story and it is all mixed up together. Many things are somehow implied, but not explored. There is no identification with the characters. And there is no real ending either. It is a bit of something and nothing.
- No triggering event. This is usually the main reason when a story starts fraying after the opening and somehow peters out. Without a triggering event, the story does not really start properly and cannot be driven forward. The dynamics are missing.
- Results are anticipated: the exposition problem. One of the most common and biggest mistakes: too many facts too early on. It is the classic exposition problem. Too many facts make the beginning far too long. If everything is known, no tension can arise. Narrations are not breaking news. Remember what Jon Franklin wrote: "You could, of course, set aside a dozen paragraphs or so at the top of your story and give a mini-lecture on the subject at hand. You could… but you won't, not if you want to sell your story" (Franklin 1994, 151).

- No true-to-scene recordings. The original sounds are recorded here, there and everywhere. A topic is also discussed several times, so that you can select the best excerpts later. A frequent and annoying mistake because it causes many complications in the production. Once the mistake has happened, it is often not possible to remedy it satisfactorily afterwards. If sound bites have different acoustics, it is almost impossible to combine them in one scene (despite ever improving audio repair and sound tools).
- There are no scenes/no action at all. Sometimes the following question sounds slightly desperate, sometimes sad, sometimes defiantly reproachful (depending on the subtext): "But what do I do if I don't have any great scenes?" Without scenes, unfortunately, there is usually no action in the story either, so that it quickly becomes boring and in the worst-case arbitrary.
- Weak and boring tape and original sounds. Experts make classic expert statements and functionaries wallow in vagueness. The story thus seems empty and official. As a listener I am barely able to identify with the characters.
- Multiple breaks in the narrative: the lost perspective. Frequently an indicator of a lack of story planning. While listening we often ask ourselves: Why is this passage coming now? Often such passages begin with positively threatening phrases: "It all started..." or "Another problem was..." The next expert is then introduced and explains to listeners any general conditions or aspects (political, legal, historical).
- The omniscient narrator. The narrative attitude seems a bit distanced, but at the same time, rather condescending. Leads to rejection on the part of the listener.
- The narrative problem: stories not so well told. For me, this is the element that sums up the other problems to some extent. We often have good stories, but we just as often tell them badly. We don't get the best out of our stories, so to speak. We are satisfied with (too) little. This includes the typical things that kill tension: texts of original sounds that already reveal what the sound will actually say. It is not told as part of a process. And there are hardly any sequences in which anything happens.

Some of the problems may sound familiar. But you just haven't found the right solutions yet. We will work them out together in this book and summarise them specifically at the very end. Because this book is about how audio stories can really unfold their potential. Narrative audio aims to achieve the goal of telling exciting stories employing two approaches:

1. Dramaturgical techniques are transferred from other media and fields to acoustic narrations.
2. The strengths of the medium audio are consciously exploited.

A narration is defined as a scenic narrative that makes reality tangible. It delivers an experience. Scenes always form the backbone of the narration or story. How the path to such a narrative and its implementation works is explained in the following chapters. We will address all aspects of the story cosmos, from plot (Chapter 3), characters (Chapter 4), tension techniques (Chapter 5) and scenic narration (Chapter 6) to narrative attitude (Chapter 7), staging in the studio (Chapter 8) and debate on ethical norms (Chapter 9). Particular attention is also paid to the development of entire series (Sect. 3.10). The end of the book summarises the essential findings for the everyday life of the narrative reporter (Chapter 10). The reporter's working process also serves as the book's main thread. At the beginning of every major story, almost all reporters ask themselves the following questions (or at least they should): Is my material really suitable for a narrative? How can I develop my material or get to grips with a confusing set of facts? Or simply: What is my story? How to find answers to these questions is something we will tackle now!

NOTES

1. It is crucial, especially for journalistic products, that no spurious corrections are claimed. Cf. also the second episode of the first season of *The West Wing* entitled 'Post Hoc, Ergo Propter Hoc' ('Afterwards, so that's why').
2. https://www.ard.de/home/radio/Was_ist_das_ARD_radiofeature_/2425436/index.html.
3. https://en.wikipedia.org/wiki/Radio_documentary.
4. Translation by the author, unfortunately there is no international version of the book.
5. Audio with English subtitles: https://www.radioatlas.org/papa-were-in-syria/.
6. Audio with English subtitles: https://www.radioatlas.org/after-the-celebration/.
7. If I remember correctly, Sandra Müller (https://www.radio-machen.de/) was the first to use this term in connection with *The Hitchhiker*. Thanks for that!

BIBLIOGRAPHY

99% Invisible. 2020. Accessed 20 December 2020. https://99percentinvisible.org/.
A Man for Mama. 2020. Accessed 20 December 2020. https://www.br.de/mediathek/podcast/ein-mann-fuer-mama/563.
Franklin, Jon. 1994. *Writing for Story*. New York: Plume.
Hart, Jack. 2011. *Story Craft*. Chicago: The University of Chicago Press.
Homecoming. 2016. Accessed 20 December 2020. https://gimletmedia.com/shows/homecoming.
Invisibilia. 2020. Accessed 20 December 2020. https://www.npr.org/podcasts/510307/invisibilia.
Jessen, Lisbeth. 2002. *After the Celebration*. Accessed 20 December 2020. https://www.radioatlas.org/after-the-celebration/.
Johnstone, Keith. 2013. *Improvisation*, 11th ed. Berlin: Alexander Verlag.

Krug, Hans-Jürgen. 2003. *Kleine Geschichte des Hörspiels*. Konstanz: UVK.

Lerch, Christian. 2016. *Papa, We're in Syria*. Accessed 20 December 2020. https://www.radioatlas.org/papa-were-in-syria/.

Limetown. 2015. Accessed 20 December 2020. https://twoupproductions.com/limetown/podcast.

Llinares, Dario, Neil Fox, and Richard Berry, eds. 2018. *Podcasting. New aural cultures and digital media*. Cham: Palgrave Macmillan.

McKee, Robert. 1991. *Story. Substance, Structure, Style, and the Principles of Screenwriting*. New York: Harper-Collins.

Mummy and Me. 2020. Accessed 20 December 2020. https://www.mutti-podcast.de/.

Müller, Sandra. 2014. *Radio machen*, 2nd ed. Köln: Herbert von Halem Verlag.

Nuzum, Eric. 2019. *Make Noise. A Creator's Guido to Podcasting and Great Storytelling*. New York: Workman Publishing.

Radiolab. 2020. Accessed 20 December 2020. https://www.wnycstudios.org/podcasts/radiolab.

Serial. 2014. 'Season One'. Accessed 14 April 2020. https://serialpodcast.org/season-one.

Shaw, Julia. 2016. *The Memory Illusion. Remembering, Forgetting and the Science of False Memory*. London: Random House.

Spinelli, Martin, and Lance Dann. 2019. *Podcasting. The Audio Media Revolution*. New York: Bloomsbury.

Storr, Will. 2019. *The Science of Storytelling*. London: William Collins.

Story Corps. Accessed 20 December 2020. https://storycorps.org/.

Quarks Storys. 2019. Accessed 20 December 2020. https://www.quarks.de/quarksstorys/.

S-Town. 2017. Accessed 20 December 2020. https://stownpodcast.org/.

Third Ear. Accessed 20 December 2020. https://thirdear.dk/.

The Anachronist. Accessed 20 December 2020. https://www.die-anachronistin.de/.

The Listening Project. Accessed 20 December 2020. https://www.bbc.co.uk/programmes/b01cqx3b.

The Moment. Accessed 20 December 2020. https://www.audible.de/pd/Der-Moment-Original-Podcast-Hoerbuch/B07931LZJL.

The Nobody Zone. 2020. Accessed 20 December 2020. https://www.rte.ie/eile/podcasts/2020/0211/1114553-the-nobody-zone/.

The Untold. Accessed 20 December 2020. https://www.bbc.co.uk/programmes/b06wkdzd.

This American Life. 2019. 'The Out Crowd'. Accessed 20 December 2020. https://www.thisamericanlife.org/688/the-out-crowd.

This American Life. Accessed 20 December 2020. https://www.thisamericanlife.org.

Viertausendhertz. Accessed 20 December 2020. https://viertausendhertz.de/.

Welcome to Night Vale. 2012. Accessed 20 December 2020. https://www.welcometonightvale.com.

Wolfe, Tom. 1975. *The New Journalism*. London: Picador.

Yorke, John. 2014. *Into the Woods. How Stories Work and Why We Tell Them*. UK: Penguin Books.

Zindel, Udo, and Wolfgang Rein, ed. 2007. *Das Radio-Feature*, 2nd ed. Konstanz.

CHAPTER 2

A Good Story: Delivering an Experience

2.1 MORE DRAMA: WHAT ARISTOTLE AND AARON SORKIN HAVE IN COMMON

Sometimes it is worth playing a round of bullshit bingo in newsroom conferences. This works like a real bingo game, only instead of the numbers, the 25 boxes (arranged in 5*5) contain the classic, rather meaningless phrases of a typical current affairs conference. As soon as one of the phrases falls, the box may be crossed out. The first person to complete a row or diagonal is the winner (if you dare to shout "Bingo," that is). In the boxes, phrases like the following could be found: "We still need a regional approach," "We have to break this down to Europe / country / region / city (depending on the programme)," "What are the other programmes / newspapers doing?" or "We still need a top story!" All of us—myself included—have probably already said these sentences more than once. In editorial offices that are more concerned with background reporting, other sentences exist, more along the lines of: "We should do something about Brexit / Trump / Fridays for Future" or "What are the big events coming up next year?" After all, long-term topics can be planned ahead, that goes for national elections as well as for Olympic Games. What these examples show is that we think in topics, not stories. From a journalistic point of view, this makes sense, but unfortunately not so much from a dramaturgical point of view. These questions and thoughts are a starting point for research, but nothing more—a direction we want to take to look for stories. To be as clear as possible about this: A subject is not a story. Often, however, the two terms are still used interchangeably.

This fundamental misunderstanding is one of the greatest dangers for nonfiction narratives: From the very beginning, a standard has been established that obstructs a dramaturgical view. We try to get a grip on the subject, not

© The Author(s), under exclusive license to Springer Nature Switzerland AG 2021
S. Preger, *Storytelling in Radio and Podcasts*,
https://doi.org/10.1007/978-3-030-73130-4_2

the story. That is why we do not ask the necessary questions about the material. We ask: Are the facts correct? Did we report in a balanced way? Did we miss anything? This is necessary, but not sufficient. Moreover, we also choose stories according to their themes. Topics from major news internet-portals or big newspapers or TV shows are taken up earlier and faster; there is hardly any time left for researching one's own approach. We constrain ourselves. In his workbook for the online course *Masterclass Screenwriting*, the screenwriter and director Aaron Sorkin writes: "The rules of drama are the only ones you need to be concerned with" (Sorkin 2016). Of course, Sorkin is talking about fictional stuff. But the rules or principles of drama apply to documentary narratives just as much as journalistic principles. And the rules of drama have hardly changed over the millennia. Sorkin, for example, refers to Aristotle's *Poetics* as the most important source to this day. So, what can we learn from Aristotle and Aaron Sorkin? We can learn to ask the right questions about our idea. In order to develop a real story.

2.2   MAKE IT PRIMAL: DOES IT TOUCH ME IN MY INNERMOST BEING?

A colleague of mine occasionally tells the following anecdote: A reporter comes to her and tells her enthusiastically and vividly about a piece he is currently working on. In the course of the day, she listens to the piece on air and nothing of the enthusiasm and emotions is to be found in it. It is simply boring. The reasons for that? Perhaps anything else would violate the journalistic principle of objectivity. And besides, all these emotions are superfluous, inappropriate and distract from the subject anyway. The only problem is that the report ends up being so boring that we listeners may not even finish listening to it. And unfortunately, nothing sticks in our minds. Pity.

Many story consultants, script agents or other professionals trust their gut feeling when they first address a subject. When I first read about this approach, it was far too vague and subjective for me. Today I know what it means (at least, I think so). It is simply a matter of whether a story touches me, that is, whether it arouses an emotion in me. Initially, it does not matter whether it is joy, anger, surprise, lust, sadness or any other emotion. The only thing it should not be is superficial. The umpteenth comedy making fun of Donald Trump might make me smile, but it won't touch me. The same applies to the next Brexit piece, news of the latest traffic jams (even though it can of course drive you crazy to be stuck in the same traffic jam over and over again) or reports about the UN Security Council. This is why news and reports are the appropriate form of presentation for these types of topics and events. However, we will see that storytelling techniques can also be used for short pieces (see Sect. 3.9).

We are probably more likely to be touched inwardly if the event is significant, something that shakes our very foundations. It is not for nothing that one of the most fundamental story principles reads: It should always be a matter of life and death. In his *Poetics,* Aristotle expresses this in slightly more sophisticated terms. Aristotle names two components of stories: reversal and discovery. "A third component is suffering, which is an action involving pain or destruction, such as murders on stage, extreme agony, woundings, and so on" (Aristotle 2013, 30–31). How someone deals with such drastic events is much more instructive for us as listeners than a pure success story. In the WDR documentary series *The Hitchhiker,* my colleague Stephan Beuting and I tried to touch something fundamental in our audience right from the beginning. The starting point of the story (or, in dramaturgical parlance, the inciting incident) is that we both independently met the same hitchhiker at a petrol station in the south of Cologne (which is of course a surprise in its own right). But that alone would not touch anything fundamental. This only happens because Heinrich Kurzrock (that's the hitchhiker's name) is on his way to Zurich where he wants access to euthanasia (which is legal in Switzerland under certain circumstances, for example at an institution called Dignitas). At least, that's what he says. Stephan and I both try to help him reaching Zurich. But when we tell each other about it and find out that we met the same person about a year apart, we start looking…

"Make it primal" is therefore not a clearly defined criterion. What touches some people in their innermost being may be of no importance to others whatsoever. Two factors are therefore important:

1. Be strict. Is it really something fundamental? And if so, what? The more precisely I can define it, the more I can use it for my story and work with it. In the first season of *Serial,* Adnan Syed may be wrongfully imprisoned for life. If I want to work with this guiding theme, it is crucial that I make it possible to experience what it means for Adnan. That is exactly what Sarah Koenig does. For example, we are confronted again and again with the restrictions of his everyday life, such as the constantly interrupted telephone calls.

2. Trust your own gut feeling and reflect on it. Does the story really touch me (or am I just saying it does because I would like to put it on air)? What is it that touches me? Or what doesn't yet? An answer to the last question may give me an indication of what I might need to elaborate more—as long as it is true. The mere fact that Adnan Syed may be wrongfully imprisoned may not be of any concern to me. But if I like the person, this can change quickly. Clearly, Sarah Koenig is quite aware that convicted murderers are not necessarily the most trust-inspiring and sympathetic individuals in the audience's estimation. She therefore establishes herself as an emotional anchor in the story. We like Sarah, trust her and want to hear what her research brings to light. It may have very concrete implications, which brings us to the next point.

2.3   HIGH STAKES: WHAT IS AT RISK?

Question: What is worse than a criminal who gets off scot-free? Answer: An innocent person who has been convicted. Imagine for a moment: Adnan Syed did not kill his high school sweetheart, Hae Min Lee. He is wrongfully imprisoned. Life sentence. US-life sentence. Till death. All his wishes, dreams, plans—gone. Of course, it is debatable whether this thought process is legitimate at all. Firstly, Adnan has been lawfully convicted. Secondly, what should Hae Min Lee's family say? But Sarah Koenig has decided not to focus on the victim's family in *Serial*, but on the doubts about Adnan Syed's guilt. Ethically, by the way, this is not a very easy position for Sarah Koenig to take because her work draws renewed attention to a closed case, possibly more attention than ever before. This also means that all those involved, including Hae's family, will be confronted once again with the memories—and the requests from Sarah Koenig and other journalists. This only seems justified if Koenig and her team, after extensive research, actually come to the conclusion that they have reasonable doubts about Adnan's guilt (for the ethical debate, see also Chapter 9). Dramaturgically, it is important that Sarah Koenig manages to quickly and plausibly establish what is at stake. She does: Adnan Syed may have been wrongly convicted.

So, the question is not whether something is at stake. But what is at stake. And here, for once, the rule applies: A lot helps a lot. The more there is at stake, the better the story. It must be credible and convincing—as in Adnan's case. The important thing is that it must not be anything abstract. It must be concrete. From the very beginning of *The Hitchhiker*, we establish that a great injustice may not have been atoned for. Hitchhiker Heinrich tells both Stephan and me about his childhood in a child and youth psychiatric institution where he was allegedly abused. We establish this right at the beginning of the series and follow it up. It quickly becomes clear that if this kind of injustice really was perpetrated, there are numerous victims who have not received any recognition or compensation to this day.[1] This also means that the arc of suspense has been established.

To sum up, three factors are important to show what is at stake:

1. It needs to be something concrete. Money, health or a free life.
2. This something must be comprehensible, plausible and credible.
3. This something must be established very early in the piece.

The audience should feel and understand what is at stake. If this something is missing, an important dramatic component is missing. It is not clear to listeners what is actually being fought for or why they should get involved in the story. And this knowledge also helps the author to lay out the story and design the plot. When it is obvious what is at stake, it is also clear where the story must lead. In *The Hitchhiker*, the end of the series must be about the issue of recognition and compensation. Furthermore, if it is clear what is at stake, a logical link to the third important story principle can usually be established.

2.4   BIGGER IDEA: WHAT'S THE STORY BEHIND ALL THIS?

It's a must for the stories in *This American Life*. This is what *TAL* founder Ira Glass describes. For the editors, searching for the bigger ideas behind the story is an important part of the selection process: "(…) if the story doesn't lead to some interesting idea about how the world works, then it doesn't work for radio" (Glass 2017, 70). In other words, the narrative must point beyond itself, reveal something greater. This satisfies the listener's need to learn something. The story about Adnan Syed, for example, is tragic enough in its own right, but it also points beyond itself because it deals with another, more fundamental question in addition to the specific one (Is there reasonable doubt about his guilt?): What does it say about the US justice system if innocent people are convicted?

For me, there are two types of "bigger ideas": One is more concerned with gaining insight and understanding something that is functional and important for society (like the US judicial system). The other tends to address the debate on values that are relevant to society—detached from concrete institutions. In a *ZeitZeichen* documentary (a WDR documentary history programme I am involved in) about the first intercontinental flight in a solar aircraft, Bertrand Piccard first describes the great resistance he had to overcome in order to realise his plan (to fly around the entire world in a solar plane). Finally, the documentary illustrates why the project goes beyond itself: For him, it is about leadership, i.e. the question of what role models we need in our society and how we deal with dreams and big goals.

So, the bigger idea provides social relevance. As such, it is not only a category that makes dramaturgical sense, but also journalistic sense. That should sound familiar. After all, in many journalistic stories, there is this famous transition from the specific to the general, often employing the perhaps somewhat overused sentence: "The fate of Mrs, Mr or the so and so Family is not an isolated case; there are dozens, hundreds, thousands." The idea behind this is very similar: The dimension of a problem should become clear. Or in other words, the social relevance. There is one crucial difference: The dimension alone does not illustrate what exactly the core issue is and thus reveal the "bigger idea." An example: There is a *Radiolab* story called *On the Edge*. It tells the story of figure skater Surya Bonaly, who spent her whole active life as an athlete struggling to fit in with the image of the elegant, filigree figure skater. Bonaly was athletic and strong. The story therefore begins with the question: If you want to be the best at something—your idea of what is best—but it doesn't fit the idea of those who judge you, what do you do? So, *Radiolab* opens with the big question and then illustrates it with the story of Surya Bonaly. Even the accompanying online text explicitly refers to this dimension of the story: "This week, we lace up our skates and tell a story about loving a sport that doesn't love you back, and being judged in front of the world according to rules you don't understand" (Radiolab 2016).

The idea behind the story thus helps in three ways:

1. It satisfies the listener's need to learn something. After listening to the story, they understand how the world works a little better.
2. It creates an additional dimension of relevance. The story thus points beyond itself.
3. It lends the argument a leitmotif and thus structure. The bigger idea helps to choose which parts of the story are emphasized more or told in greater detail. Cleverly constructed, the actual story can thus be interrupted again and again at exciting points to debate the bigger idea. There is a high probability that the audience will continue to listen (we will come to plot design and tension techniques in Chapters 3 and 5).

This trio of story principles—make it primal, high stakes and bigger idea—helps in two ways. On the one hand, they are the operationalised criteria for why we listen to stories. On the other, they sharpen the focus for all those involved. The story principles thus help to find answers to the question of what exactly should be told and how. With real stories, these factors are particularly important at the beginning of the work process because they help to filter out the essential facts, events and discussion partners from the many researched facts, events and discussion partners. For fictional stories, the trio is often supplemented by a fourth story principle, which can appear in two forms: the premise or deeper moral. The terms actually derive from different perspectives. The moral is often made clear to us at the end of the story. It's the take-home message. In fables, it often comes across as didactic. The premise, on the other hand, tends to help develop a story piece by piece, for example in the theatre. In his standard work *Dramatic Writing*, Lajos Egri writes that every good play must have a carefully formulated premise (Egri 2011, 24). The premise consists of three elements: character, conflict and resolution. For Shakespeare's tragedy *Romeo and Juliet*, for example, the premise could be: Great love (points to the character of the central figures) defies (points to the conflict) even death (points to the end or solution). The whole piece then serves to prove the premise. This approach is particularly difficult for journalists because there is a danger of no longer depicting reality appropriately, but only telling the story one wants to tell.

But real material can also be examined to see whether a premise can be filtered out, which in turn helps to tell the story. Taking the first season of *Serial*, the premise could be: Persistence leads to special responsibility. After all, Sarah Koenig has immersed herself so deeply in the story that she simply cannot turn her back on it again. She has taken responsibility, also for Adnan—on a moral-human level. This finally becomes a central conflict for her. But the example also shows that premises are not always helpful for real stories because *Serial* is so much more than this one, albeit important, statement. Both elements, the moral and the premise, are also in danger of being presented in a patronising way, along the lines of "Here comes the message for you, dear little listener." This attitude can and probably will generate rejection.

Of course, real material cannot always completely satisfy all these factors (primal, high stakes, bigger idea, premise or moral), but they give us a dramaturgical handle on our material. They make us realise what we need and what we don't. And they help us to turn our own story into a pitch that is clear and unambiguous, the kind that simply increases the chances that freelance reporters or producers will be able to convince commissioning editors, production companies, labels or publishers to buy the piece. If you have your story principles clear and verified, you should be able to summarise your story in just a few sentences.

2.5   One-Liner: How to Pitch and Convince in just a Few Sentences

Unfortunately, many pitches are not very convincing. They are either unspecific ("I have the following ingredients..."), a little confused ("Then we can consider this, this and that...") or, to put it mildly, half-baked ("We can make something..."). Even tips from editorial staff don't always help but seem more like a minor knowledge marathon ("What still interests me about the topic is this, that and that...!"), along the lines of "What I also know." The examples and sentences described here are of course exaggerated, pointed and would never really occur, ever. Podcasters, on the other hand, have another challenge to face: They frequently still work alone. With all the advantages and disadvantages this implies. They have a lot of freedom, but sometimes hardly anyone who can share their thoughts or be a critical mirror. For everyone, there is a simple tool that has reached us from places like Hollywood (not all bad there, after all!): the one-liner.

The one-liner or logline summarises the story in one phrase, or just a few sentences, and gives an indication of the plot. The idea is that anyone who can get straight to the point of their story not only has a better chance of convincing others, but also gains clarity for themselves. This, in turn, can help you to get a grip on your own story and develop it. Screenwriter Blake Snyder (2005, 16–17) has defined four functions of the logline:

1. The logline expresses surprise or at least draws emotionally into the story. It works as an appetiser to create the impression: I would like to see or hear more of the story. The logline is what is classically called the hook. It lures me in and makes sure that the story hooks me faster than I realise.
2. The logline gives a convincing picture of the story. I can imagine what the story is about, what a possible plot might look like and what happens.

3. The logline provides an idea of the target audience and the costs. This is especially important for authors or producers who want to sell their story. But it certainly never hurts to have an idea about it. After all, the imagination of the target audience also influences the attitude with which I tell the story (for the narrative attitude, see Chapter 7).
4. As the icing on the cake, the logline delivers a great title—or at least a convincing working title. Then, the story has a reasonable label.

Snyder has, of course, tailored these elements primarily to the needs of Hollywood. The one-liner is an elementary component of what is called "high concept," the idea that a film can be summed up in a few words or sentences. Gladly combined with the question, "What if?" plot and possible marketing strategy are immediately obvious: What would happen, for example, if we could really clone dinosaurs? *Jurassic Park*. What would happen if an unconventional teacher came to a traditional boys' boarding school and inspired the students? *Dead Poets Society*. Or what would happen if a Stasi Captain developed sympathy and understanding for the people he was spying on? *The Lives of Others*. Typically, the Hollywood "high concept," which focuses attention strongly on pitch, plot, audience and marketing possibilities, differs from films that concentrate more on character development (which are known as "low concept"). For a good story, it's best to have both.

The idea of the one-liner is directly transferable neither to the market worldwide nor to audio narratives or complex realities. Moreover, it is also questionable whether Hollywood is always and everywhere such a desirable and meaningful role model. But the idea behind it is crucial: The one-liner forces us to think the story through and get to the heart of it—without distorting or oversimplifying it. Incidentally, experience has shown that journalists who also work on current affairs find it a little easier than reporters or producers who only tell stories for long formats.

Effective loglines and titles are especially important for podcasts. A good example of this is again the *Radiolab* story about Surya Bonaly. The logline could be something like: "A figure skater wants to be the best in the world but is not recognized by juries. This motivates her to develop a very personal style, but it also drives her closer to the edge." The title of the story is appropriate: *On the Edge*. The logline already suggests a complication in the story, illustrated by the word "but"—and this brings us to an element that is even more important for documentary narratives than the logline. If the logline gives us an idea of the story, then this element goes one step further. It helps us as reporters to develop our story.

2.6   The Narrative Sentence: Four Elements for a Story

This is usually how it goes: As reporters, we define a topic, work through the various aspects of it (usually with the help of more or less capable people, whom we like to call experts or protagonists (both of whom, by the way, are usually not completely accurate or at best exaggerated), then pick out the best sound bites (whatever exactly that means) and then start to build the reporter's text around it). As a result, we find it difficult to keep our focus when writing, we create long explanatory passages (because the information has to go in and is also important) and the whole process feels rather random and tedious. But that need not be the case.

There is one tool that helps us to maintain our focus at all times: I call it the narrative sentence. It is, so to speak, an extension of the logline, maybe a little less pointed, but clear. It helps us to decide whether a story can really be told as a story. It provides orientation for everyone involved during the entire work process. Ira Glass describes this story line for *This American Life* in the wonderful graphic novel *Out on the Wire* (by Jessica Abel). For him, it consists of three elements: "Somebody does something (A character in motion. Doing something.) because (A motivation for doing that thing.), but (A challenge to overcome.)" (Abel 2015, 52). I would like to add something and differentiate a bit, to help develop the idea of the story even better and set a benchmark for the narrative.

The narrative sentence introduced here consists of four elements. Three of them are a must, the fourth an optional extra:

1. The protagonist. This should be a real protagonist. The mere fact that someone drives to work, goes shopping or has something happen to him, does not make him or her a protagonist (see also Sect. 4.1). A protagonist needs to be active. Because he's chasing.
2. A goal. The protagonist wants something. This also means that the story arc is formed by that goal. If someone wants something, then it is clear what the story will be about, namely the path to this goal (or the attempt to reach it). It is important to note that the more specific the goal is, the better the story arc can be stretched towards the climax. However, this is relatively boring, unless another element is added.
3. The obstacles. Our protagonist pursues a goal but encounters obstacles in the process. Only then do conflict and tension arise. If figure skater Surya Bonaly rushed from victory to victory and always got the top scores from the jury, it would be a pure success story that would quickly bore us. It only gets exciting when Bonaly encounters obstacles. The story gains depth when a fourth element emerges.
4. The protagonist's motivation. Why does anyone do what they do? The more we are interested in a person, the more we want to understand their motives. Then, we can feel close to that person and identify with

them even better. Or vice versa: If it is clear to us why someone acts the way they do, we understand the actions—even if we ourselves would act differently or do not approve. The protagonist's motivation is not always clear from the beginning. But at some point, the motivation, if it is researchable, should become clear.

A narrative sentence thus takes the following form: A (the protagonist) wants B (intention/goal) because he or she C (the motivation), but encounters D (obstacles). The protagonist must overcome these obstacles, or at least try to do so. The narrative sentence is thus the compass on which the story is based.

So, for the *Radiolab* story *On the Edge*, the narrative sentence reads something like this: The figure skater Surya Bonaly (A) wants to be the best in the world and therefore an Olympic champion (B as precisely as possible), but she is always up against the experts and juries of the figure skating world (D). The story shows how Surya Bonaly gradually overcomes the obstacles or suffers setbacks—until the all-decisive competition. The reasons why she does this and accepts all the burdens and setbacks may be various and diverse. Perhaps she is particularly ambitious, under pressure from her parents or simply enjoys the competition (C). The longer we follow the story, the more the question of motivation arises: We want to understand why the hell Surya Bonaly exposes herself to all these privations and burdens. And whether she will achieve her goal. The story provides answers to precisely these questions.

The narrative sentence is therefore the answer to the question: What is the story? If the narrative sentence is missing, it is not (yet) a story. Of course, overall, this has a somewhat formulaic and regulated effect, according to the motto: We always have to tell everything about protagonists. One argument against the narrative sentence could be that some abstract or complex topics do not initially involve people doing things (such as the debate about weighing up two basic rights) or demand a level of abstraction beyond specific events or people (such as the question about different gradations of infinity in Georg Cantor's set theory). Many debates, no matter how abstract, usually have a tangible connection to reality, either because certain events or persons have triggered the debate (e.g. if two national football players are photographed with the president of another country, a debate on the relationship between top-level sport and politics may ensue) or because the debate has a definite impact on reality. The narrative sentence is therefore not an argument against abstract argumentation. On the contrary, if you take the narrative sentence to heart, you open up a space to conduct precisely such debates and to inspire listeners to do so (I will revisit this in a moment when covering the ladder of abstraction).

What the narrative sentence does not want: to treat people as empty shells and simple placeholders. Unfortunately, this happens frequently. We show people only in very specific situations and roles (preferably as victims, rebels, oppressors). As a result, many journalistic products seemed stereotyped and lack credibility. This is another reason why the protagonist's motivation is so important. It depicts the person in their complexity, making them appear more credible and real. The problem is that making this a tangible experience takes time.

One decisive question remains: What do I do if I can't form a narrative sentence? For example, if I am dealing with the current developments surrounding the TTIP free trade agreement or the consequences of a hurricane in Florida? If there is not one protagonist who naturally leads through the story? You then quite simply adapt the narrative sentence accordingly. I would therefore like to introduce alternative versions of the narrative sentence, which help to retain the focus with more abstract topics. In addition to the more classic protagonist narrative, there are at least two other forms of narration: An explanatory or analytical narrative describes how something works. An argumentative narrative explores a thesis. Perhaps this needs a bit of clarification.

Let us start with an explanatory narrative. This kind of story could deal, for example, with the question of how bananas from South America reach Europe. It could be a story that explains global trade and the carbon footprint. The elements of a narrative sentence therefore change slightly and could look like this: Bananas from Colombia (A, the bananas take the place of the protagonist) should reach Europe perfectly ripe (B, the goal, no change here) because that will ensure the best price (C, the reasoning takes the place of the motivation), but to make that happen many processes have to interlock perfectly (D, the obstacles which lay out the path to the goal). This narrative sentence gives you a very good idea of how the story is going to develop. From stage to stage. At each stage, there are new obstacles that have to be overcome. This generates action and tension. Enriched by the story principles (what is at stake, for example, if a cargo does not arrive on the European market in time?), an exciting story is created in the form of an explanatory narrative.

An argumentative narrative on the other hand could deal, for example, with the reasons for a crisis, let us say of the social democrats in Germany. A narrative sentence could then look like this: The Social Democratic Party SPD (A, the party takes the place of the protagonist) will be punished in the forthcoming national elections (B, the goal is thus formulated as an assertion or thesis, which must now be substantiated) because it has the wrong advisors, does not believe in itself sufficiently, is poorly managed (C, the motivation becomes various arguments, which together substantiate the thesis), but does not recognise this or know the way out (D, the obstacles). In an argumentative narrative, there is an important shift: Not only are there several obstacles, but above all, there are several arguments for the thesis formulated (that is why I call it an argumentative narrative).

Common to both explanatory and argumentative narratives, scenes remain the backbone of the story. They ensure action and excitement. In an explanatory narrative, the obstacles deliver the scenes; in an argumentative narrative, the different parts of the argument take care of that. Both forms therefore place high demands on the reporter. A purely abstract, analytical description is not sufficient for a narrative (see Sect. 3.8 for the structural models of all narratives). So, in the banana example, each stage (harvesting, handling at the port, on the high seas, etc.) ideally requires a thrilling scene with corresponding characters who try to overcome the obstacles and thus advance the story. And in the example of the social democrats, each argument should be supported by a scene, or the argument should result from a scene.

Consequently, for all narratives, the following applies: The narrative sentence helps me and others to focus on what I actually want to tell—it is like a compass guiding the entire working process.

Defining the narrative sentence is also a milestone in collaboration when different people are involved in a product. It marks the transition from an initial idea to a specified project. As a reporter or producer, for example, I should continue to do my research until I can formulate a narrative sentence. Then, I pitch it. As a commissioning editor or proofreader, I expect an author to be able to provide me with this narrative sentence. This protects both sides. If reporter, producer, presenter and editor, for example, do not agree on this sentence, it complicates their entire future cooperation. If, on the other hand, there is agreement, they are much less likely to encounter unpleasant surprises.

To avoid a common misunderstanding, the narrative sentence does not narrow my view, but rather sharpens it. That's why it is dramaturgically so important to have researched the story at least to the extent that the narrative sentence is actually plausible and realisable. It doesn't mean that I have to have completely researched the whole story and made all the recordings. For the serial *The Hitchhiker*, Stephan and I did research for several weeks to make sure that we could actually tell the story and assess it correctly. Two factors were decisive: On the one hand, we had to find the hitchhiker again. And on the other, we had to prove as far as possible that his childhood stories (abuse in psychiatry) were true. Only after we had verified these two points did we approach editorial offices. But that also means that we as reporters have already invested heavily in the story. How exactly the workflow for an elaborate narrative can be organised meaningfully is still to be clarified (see Sect. 10.2). But this kind of preliminary work has one big advantage: As a reporter, I have an idea of what my material can deliver. I also know, for example, whether it contains the two essential elements for creating plot and surprises. That's up next.

2.7   The Engines of a Good Story: Action and Revelation

The fifth episode of the first season of *Serial* has a title that doesn't promise much action at all: *Route Talk*. Nonetheless, the scenes in this episode are probably some of the ones you remember best because Sarah and her colleague Dana are checking out a crucial detail of the case: Is it possible to get from the car park of *Woodlawn High School* to the *Best Buy* shopping centre by car in 21 minutes—right after the end of school? So, the two journalists drive the route that Adnan and his friend Jay allegedly took on 13 January 1999, the day Hae Min Lee was murdered. As a listener you sit in the car with Sarah and Dana as they fight their way out of the school car park with the other students, drive down the road and finally approach the shopping centre car park. Along the way, the clock is always ticking: Are they going to make it in 21 minutes or not? Adnan claims that's not possible. The question is of great relevance to what exactly happened that day as well as Adnan's guilt. Now that the relevance of the question has been established, the listener wants to know whether they will make it or not. This little experiment would of course not hold up in court, but it works. These are not scenes from an action film, but situations in which something really happens. The two reporters encounter obstacles and acquire insights which Sarah in turn has to discuss with Adnan. The story thus gains momentum.

This is how the first of the two story engines works: action. As a reporter, even during the research for the narrative sentence, I specifically check whether there are any actions that advance my story. Of course, they must have something to do with the protagonist's goal, the phenomenon to be explained or the thesis to be proven. Otherwise, the situation makes no sense at all but just seems rather strange (see also Sect. 6.7 on the great danger of 'false' reporting). The answer at the end of the experiment also guarantees listener satisfaction. Together, we have understood something that was previously unclear. The *Serial* example already shows how a reporter can deal with the fact that material often does not offer an infinite number of scenes that can be recorded and broadcast. This example is a special case of a reconstructed scene (see also Sect. 6.6).

The other important story engine is revelation, which can also come in the form of an insight. The American (screenplay) author William Goldman is said to have exaggerated the famous quote attributed to Charles Dickens ("Make them laugh, make them cry, make them wait."): "Make 'em laugh, make 'em cry. But most of all, make 'em wait" (Iglesias 2005, 94). The idea behind it: Not all information needs to be delivered and presented immediately. The more a question forms in the listener's mind, the more they long for the answer. Patience should be rewarded at some point. It can be particularly satisfying when the listener and the journalist have the same level of knowledge and they both experience revelations together. An example: At the end of the second episode of *The Hitchhiker*, Heinrich is able to take a look at the admissions book of the child and youth psychiatric ward in Marsberg. From this admissions book, it is indeed clear that Heinrich was in the clinic as a child. He always told us that he had been admitted as an infant after the death of his parents. But the date of admission on the file shows that Heinrich was already eight years old when he came here. So, something's wrong. We let the listener experience this moment of revelation together with us. In this way, the information has a much greater impact than a mere description of the facts. The scene is a mixture of revelation and recognition. We reveal the fact that there really is still information about Heinrich's time in the clinic (not a complete medical file, but at least the admissions book) and we also recognise the contradiction between Heinrich's story and the facts in the admissions book. As a result, we learn something that generates new questions. The story gains momentum and takes its course.

Both story engines, action and revelation, are designed to keep the plot moving forward and create surprising twists. Ideally, a scene delivers both an exciting experience and a surprising result. We learn something by listening. That is why it seems to be a popular method in many current productions to use the investigating journalist as a guiding thread. If the journalist learns something, the listener learns something too. As long as this happens in the form of a stringent story, nothing can be said against it. But this approach harbours the risk of putting too much emphasis on yourself as a journalist and/or boring the listener with details that actually have nothing to do with the story. The learning effect in a crime thriller, for example, is usually quite high; after each scene, we are a little bit wiser. However, the problem here can be the non-existent action. The plot often consists of more or less exciting conversations (moving from one suspect to another), taking place in different places like offices, offices or even offices. Many crime novels therefore seem rather static and perhaps tedious. In addition, fictional audio stories easily succumb to the temptation to stage the usual places using typical acoustics (private investigator's detective agency, the gloomy bar, police station, the hipster bar, interrogation room). In many detective stories or crime thrillers not only the locations but also the dialogues are often rather tedious. The story will put you to sleep quicker than your favourite audio book. It often sounds a bit like the old Paul Temple radio plays (originally produced for the BBC between 1938 and 1968), just a little quicker and in a modern world. It is difficult to create new listening impressions. What helps are a few additional story stimulants like the following.

2.8   STORY PILLARS: NARRATIVE CHANGE MANAGEMENT

An old piece of story wisdom says: The hero does not have to make it, but he or she has to try. If the hero fails, then it's just a tragedy. As this mnemonic points out: At the end of a story something should be different from the beginning. Stories are, so to speak, change management, achieved in two possible ways: by making a decision and taking action. These are the two pillars of change. It is therefore worthwhile pinpointing the following elements during your research:

1. Obstacles: If there is a goal, then it should not be too easy to achieve—see narrative sentence. The obstacles should also get bigger rather than smaller over time. Then, there's a good chance that the entire action will come to a climax—like the one freestyle skating programme with figure skater Surya Bonaly.

2. Highlights or special situations: Are there scenes which reveal something important for the story? Then, we should use these scenes for our narration and make them tangible.

3. Development: From where to where does the story go? The first season of *Serial* brings about a change in us as listeners. At the end, we think it is possible that a convicted murderer is indeed wrongfully imprisoned (after Serial was broadcasted Adnan Syed appealed for a new trial. This was finally denied by the US Supreme Court in November 2019).

4. Change: the manifestation of development. Thinking in film terms: If you put the first and the last shot of the story side by side—what has changed? Do you happen to remember the last sentence in *The Lord of the Rings*? At least in the book, this sentence is spoken by Samwise Gamgee, Frodo's closest friend. When he enters his home at the end of the final book, he says, "Well, I'm back" (Tolkien 1991, 1069). We know that home may be the same, but Sam isn't anymore. He has changed. Thus, the story ends on a very wise, melancholy note.

These elements should sharpen our view of what we need to deliver an exciting and satisfying story. This view does not contradict journalistic values and quality factors but is a different perspective, which, unfortunately, we rarely take. This is probably connected with our self-image as journalists: We are used to research things and more likely to share the results of our research. But if you think like that, you can never make a process tangible. Of course, this also means not always being the omniscient journalist, but living with the fact that one day you may not appear very smart or competent. In the first episode of *The Hitchhiker*, there is a scene in the car with my colleague Stephan Beuting and me: We have actually found Heinrich and are on our way to meet him. A few minutes before we get there, we're just discussing our expectations. And I am convinced that Heinrich is not really interested in taking money from us. That's what I say. To put it cautiously: I was proven wrong on several occasions afterwards. But it was my level of knowledge or my hope at that moment—so it stays in the story.

2.9   Summary Example Analysis: Story Check *Serial*

The first season of *Serial* was successful for several reasons. The story about Adnan Syed hit a nerve, the long story from over twelve episodes was very detailed and kind of new—and the story possibly also hit the zeitgeist in the US. After all, it is about the big questions of law, justice and appropriate treatment of one another. But one reason was also the good dramaturgy. Sarah and her team didn't lay out the whole series in advance; that is, they didn't design the entire plot (neither for the series as a whole nor for the individual episodes, see Sect. 3.10), but partly developed it during the ongoing process—week by week. This approach is actually not ideal, as it makes the work much more difficult but gives listeners the authentic feeling of revealing new facts with

Sarah Koenig which glues people to the narrative. We'll see that suspense can also be designed if the entire storyline is developed at one time. This chapter addressed the question: Is my material even suitable for a bigger narrative? Do I have a real story here? And that's where the first season of *Serial* ticked the boxes all along the line:

***Serial,* Season 1: story check for narrative sentence and story principles**

- Narrative sentence: Sarah Koenig (a humorous, slightly self-ironic and very reflective protagonist) wants to check whether Adnan Syed is guilty (her goal) but encounters numerous obstacles in the process (there is a final judgement, it was a long time ago, not all the people involved want to talk to her). She does it for several reasons—at least they become transparent throughout the series. In the beginning, she is curious; maybe, the potentially investigative story also excites her. The longer she works on it, the clearer it becomes: She also thinks researching this story is the right thing to do, creating an even larger leitmotif: It's worth fighting for the right thing. There is even a premise or moral to it.
- Story principle "Make it primal": Adnan may be wrongfully imprisoned. So, for him, it is existential in any case. At the same time, his story touches many people's sense of justice and fear (Could I also be wrongly condemned?) and thus something within us listeners.
- Story principle "High stakes": There is a great deal at stake. Especially for Adnan. After all, it is about his freedom and the vague hope of regaining it or having to accept a life behind bars for good. At the outset of the story, Adnan Syed is convicted, which means that Sarah Koenig has to live with the possibility of raising false hopes coupled with the concomitant threat of a great human disappointment. This theme recurs at the end of the series—in a long telephone conversation between Adnan and Sarah. This also makes it clear that the longer the story lasts, the more important the relationship between Adnan and Sarah becomes. And Sarah can't just turn her back on the story.
- Story principle "Bigger idea": If someone has possibly been wrongly convicted, then this also says something about the judicial system. In this way, we as listeners learn something about an essential part of modern society beyond the case itself. The whole season delivers detailed insights into how the US justice system works.
- Story principle "Premise / Moral": Those who get involved also take responsibility. With all the advantages and disadvantages this implies. That's a moral. Another could be: It is always worth

fighting for good, even if it is exhausting. So, we find elements of both a premise and a moral. These messages are conveyed subcutaneously and are not explicitly named or didactically formulated from above.

- Story engine "Action": The starting conditions of *Serial* are rather difficult. After all, Adnan Syed is already in prison, a convicted murderer. He can hardly be active from there. Consequently, it is also a good and right decision to make Sarah Koenig the main character of the series. She can be active and is. Again and again, she involves us in her research. In order to introduce action into the story, for example, she conducts the experiment already described in the episode *Route Talk*. She and her team realised that they had to have some action—and did something about it.
- Story engine "Revelations / Discoveries": Sarah Koenig guides us through the story and its research so well that we as listeners are always aware of the relevance of the discoveries and revelations. We know why this information plays a role in the story—and which one. Sarah thus not only creates tension but also an emotional impact. We literally experience the story: from the discovery of the body to the interrogations with Adnan and the trial.
- Story pillar "Change management": There are plenty of obstacles (see narrative sentence above) as well as changes in the protagonist and the listeners (sometimes we think Adnan is innocent, sometimes we are convinced he is guilty) and developments (the relationship between Sarah and Adnan first gets closer, then more distant again). These changes make us, as listeners, ask ourselves: What will happen next?
- Sonic factors: At the end of the story check (although in practice it probably happens incidentally and continuously), one must of course assess whether the material can be turned into an audio story. One question, above all, is paramount: Do I have the original sound bites I need as a reporter, or do I at least have a realistic chance of getting them? *Serial*, for example, benefits from the fact that in the US both interrogations and court cases are recorded, and the tapes can be used by journalists. The material evokes highly authentic situations and scenes. In addition, the regular phone calls between Sarah and Adnan are very personal and intimate. They not only reveal two personalities, but also the dynamics of their relationship (which is something that is missing in the second season of *Serial*, by the way; there is no direct access to Bowe Bergdahl). This means that *Serial* scores particularly well with the audio advantages of "proximity" and "scenic experience." The technical quality of the audio (which, to put it mildly, is often not perfect) does

> not play such a negative role as one might think but underlines the authenticity of the story. Lastly, Sarah Koenig's special narrative style is also a striking audio factor.

The *Serial* material as such therefore has everything that a great acoustic narration needs. And where the material itself does not provide it the *Serial* team consciously develops strategies to compensate. And that's what it's all about: With non-fictional stories, it will never be possible to incorporate all elements perfectly. But the check gives you the opportunity to recognise the strengths and weaknesses of your own story. It provides clues as to where you need to work on the dramaturgy and what can be utilised well. You don't have to like *Serial* (because maybe you just don't care for the story), but the product is definitely well made. The strengths of the story have not only been recognised, but also exploited. The story always reflects reality appropriately and does not dramatise inappropriately or even incorrectly. At least as far as we as listeners can judge.

Yet another example illustrates the purpose of a story check. At *ZeitZeichen*, the authors are always faced with the challenge of how precisely to tell their story. Every day, the 15-minute documentary (broadcast on German public radio and a podcast channel) reminds us of a figure or event from the past. The reason for this is the date (birthday, day of death or anniversary of the event itself) five, 50, 500 or 5,000 years ago (if datable)—sometimes it goes back even further, for example to the extinction of the dinosaurs (then of course without an exact date!). Sometimes the event itself already suggests a dramaturgy (like the crash of the airship *Hindenburg*). But often the authors have to create one first. How exactly do I depict the life of the writer Michael Ende or the physicist Stephen Hawking? After the initial research phase of hunting and gathering (books, journals, archival work), the story check also helps to get a grip on the material. In the *ZeitZeichen* about the Austrian doctor Johannes Bischko, for example, I was able to form the narrative sentence in a fairly simple way. It reads roughly: The physician Johannes Bischko (who died in 2004) wants to introduce Austria to acupuncture because he is convinced by it, but meets with resistance (from his profession, the university). But problematic was the question of risk: What is at stake for Bischko? He has a secure job, is healthy, etc. The answer is: his reputation. He committed himself to acupuncture. If it doesn't work, his reputation is ruined. So, the documentary begins with a reconstructed scene (told by a former colleague who is still alive) that addresses and clarifies this very point. In the scene, Bischko tries to perform an operation in front of a live audience, only using acupuncture as the anaesthetic.

To sum it up: On the one hand, the story check shows whether your idea or topic is basically suitable. And on the other, it helps isolate the elements that need more work done on them. However, one thing the story check does not do is tell you how long the piece should ideally be (apart from format requirements) or how exactly the plot should develop. That comes in the next chapter!

NOTES

1. At the time, 2015, abuse victims in psychiatric institutions have not been compensated in Germany.

BIBLIOGRAPHY

Abel, Jessica. 2015. *Out on the Wire*. New York: Broadway Books.

Aristotle. 2013. *Poetics*. Oxford: Oxford University Press.

Biewen, John, and Alexa Dilworth, ed. 2017. *Reality Radio*. Durham: The University of North Carolina Press, second edition.

Egri, Lajos. 2011. *Dramatisches Schreiben*. Berlin: Autorenhaus.

Glass, Ira. 2017. Harnessing Luck as an Industrial Product. In: *Reality Radio*, ed. John Biewen and Alexa Dilworth, 64–76. Durham: The University of North Carolina Press, second edition.

Iglesias, Karl. 2005. *Writing for Emotional Impact*. Livermore: Wing Span Press.

McKee, Robert. 1997. *Story. Substance, Structure, Style, and the Principles of Screenwriting*. New York: Harper Collins Publisher.

Preger, Sven. 2017a. 'Interkontinentalflug mit Solarflugzeug endet'. Accessed 20 December 2020. https://www1.wdr.de/radio/wdr5/sendungen/zeitzeichen/solar-flugzeug-100.html.

Preger, Sven. 2017b. 'Johannes Bischko, Pionier der Akupunktur'. Accessed 20 December 2020. https://www1.wdr.de/mediathek/audio/zeitzeichen/audio-johannes-bischko-pionier-der-akupunktur-geburtstag–102.html.

Radiolab. 2016. 'On the Edge'. Accessed 20 December 2020. http://www.radiolab.org/story/edge/.

Snyder, Blake. 2005. *Save the Cat. The Last Book On Screenwriting That You'll Ever Need*. Studio City: Michael Wiese Productions.

Sorkin, Aaron. 2016. Masterclass 'Screenwriting' (online-course comes with charge). Accessed 20 December 2020. https://www.masterclass.com/classes/aaron-sorkin-teaches-screenwriting.

Tolkien, J.R.R. 1991. *The Lord of the Rings*. London: Harper Collins Publisher.

CHAPTER 3

No Story Without Structure: Plot Development

3.1   IF YOU WANT LISTENERS, YOU NEED A PLOT

There is hardly a sentence I consider to be as true as that of story consultant John Truby: "Plot is the most underestimated of all the major storytelling skills" (2007, 258). I am firmly convinced that he has a point. In shorter audio pieces, we often solve the problem quite simply: In a report without sound bites, we find our structure very easily, by different topics or headlines. First the news, then the reactions of different people to that news, supplemented by opinions on the topic, genesis of the conflict and finally outlook. This is an easy way of filling one to four minutes. Of course, the whole thing also works if sound bites are included. If I interview all the groups in parliament, for example (there may be a lot of them!), the mere assessment of the groups alone can lengthen the piece no end. Alternatively, as reporters, we collect the three, four or five sound bites that we need or that we think are best and build our report around them.

With one of these methods, something broadcast-worthy will emerge. After all, that's what a lot of people do, and it has worked well for decades— so why change it? At least two reasons speak for change: Firstly, the craft rules of dramaturgy are helpful even with short stories and, secondly, this approach doesn't really work properly when I'm dealing with a longer and more complex story. So that no misunderstandings arise: Of course, I can also achieve a journalistically good result in the classic way. The problem is that these pieces often sound like expanded reports and are probably more boring than they need to be.

The longer and more complex my story gets, the less the tried and tested strategies for short reports help. Authors immerse themselves in the material, somehow allowing the story to emerge while writing and structuring it

S. Preger, *Storytelling in Radio and Podcasts*,
https://doi.org/10.1007/978-3-030-73130-4_3

purely thematically. If the plot only emerges when I have finished my research (along the lines of "I'll go out first, get the sounds and then I'll see…") or while writing the manuscript (along the lines of "Well, let's see how it goes …"), then it's usually much too late; the plot doesn't emerge purposefully, but somehow just happens.

That is why the first plot draft is crafted after completing your basic research. It is the first step after determining the narrative sentence.

The most common counterargument is that this moment is much too early: I don't even know how my story is going to end. Besides, as a journalist, I'm no longer open-minded, but pinned down. So the procedure does not follow journalistic rules. That's true—except for two small things. Firstly, it says, "…the first plot draft is created **after** completing your basic research." But experience shows that even with long stories, many authors start by heading out, making recordings and even like to use recorded interviews for extensive research. This not only extends the length of the interview immensely, but also determines the kind of sound clips you get (see also Sect. 6.5). And secondly, my openness as a reporter is not really curtailed. For example, as an author, I can anticipate that an event will appear in my plot without knowing how that event will turn out. A more specific example to illustrate what I mean: Imagine a story about a patient who is waiting for a new heart he needs. Clearly, this story will develop at some point in the future. When the crucial call for a new organ comes, the operation may succeed, fail or there may be complications. If the call doesn't come for a long time, the patient will eventually realise that he or she will not get an organ at all (whether through personal reflection, talking to relatives, friends or a doctor)—tragic though it may be. So, as a reporter, I do not know exactly what will happen and how people will deal with the situation. But I can plausibly assume that there will be a decisive event in the future which is crucial for my plot. It is important to identify this event as the point where a story takes a new direction (and to make sure I can wait until this point till I tell the story)—otherwise, I will lose control of my material. It won't be me in control of my material, but the other way round.

If I don't plan the plot of a story early, I lose control of the whole working process. Unfortunately, it often happens that authors (have to) start writing a manuscript at some point. They then have to deal with hours of recordings and a blank page and don't really know where to start or which way the story should go. A very unsatisfying moment. And yet perhaps this is not describing it precisely enough: Often you find a beginning at some point (Phew, what a relief!). The first one, two or three minutes of a longer story are like fireworks going off. But when that dies (usually indicated by music that fades out and reverberates slightly), then the big problem begins. How to continue? Due to my lack of ideas (I've just managed to create a great introduction), the first step is usually an info block, on the principle of here come the most important names, numbers, dates, facts and definitions. Just to be sure, the listener understands exactly what it is all about. These are permissible considerations—but they make pieces very predictable and relatively hard to digest.

Furthermore, it is immensely difficult to find your way back into the story. Many paragraphs (especially at the beginning of stories) are excessively long; they drag on for minutes on end and present listeners with every bit of information imaginable—even the ones that are totally unnecessary at this point. Nevertheless, the information is there anyway because it somehow fits thematically. As a result, the piece sounds like an entry in an encyclopaedia. So that that doesn't happen here, too, let's only look at the most important definitions and characteristics of a plot!

3.2   Audio Plot: Logical Sequence of Scenes

The founder of *This American Life*, Ira Glass, puts it relatively simply: "There's the plot, where a person has some sort of experience" (2017, 70). So, the plot is the action, what a person does, lives through or accomplishes. In a little more detail: If an audio narrative is a scenic narrative in which someone wants something for a reason and encounters obstacles, then the plot establishes the causal sequence of these scenes. Just to make it absolutely clear once again and counteract an existing misunderstanding, a plot is not a sequence of thematic paragraphs however logical they may be. The topic and information must be subordinated to the plot—facts are woven into the story at the point where they serve the story. The actual structure of the story, the causal sequence, the plot, is shaped by scenes. The following three guidelines help with this:

1. The plot is the sequence of the scenes. It describes how the action develops. This maxim is partly responsible for the fact that most stories are still told chronologically. Films like *Memento*, which use a different order, are likely to be very difficult to realise on the radio or in a podcast because listeners only have acoustics to orientate themselves in time and space. This does not mean, of course, that you can only work with one timeline. The fictional series *Homecoming* by *Gimlet Media* works with two timelines in the first season. On the one hand, it tells how the main character Heidi Bergman takes care of war veterans in an institution, apparently in the form of talking therapy. Then, there is a second timeline in which we experience Heidi as a waitress. The second timeline is apparently years later—both lines are linked and necessary for the story. Little by little, a coherent picture is formed by both lines. And both strands finally unite; they are components of one and the same story.

   This example can also be used to briefly discuss how to deal with flashbacks, i.e. the short temporal return to a previous event. A common mistake when working with flashbacks is to employ them merely to supply information that has not yet been accommodated. Used in this way, flashbacks are of little dramaturgical use, and they slow down the story. Flashbacks make sense when they provide the answer to a question that has slowly built up in listeners' minds. In movies, this technique is still often used to finally reveal a key experience in the past that has special meaning for the main character. Or when a person finally regains their memory (we will discuss flashbacks in more detail in Sect. 5.10).

2. The plot follows the principle of "cause and effect," not chance. A frequently quoted example illustrates what is meant by this. "First the king died, then the queen died." This sentence alone is a chronological sequence of events. The following sentence links these events logically: "First the king died, and the queen died of grief shortly afterwards." The two events are now connected by cause and effect (which, of course, has to be true to become a part of a journalistic report). This is what the plot does. This logical connection is also important because it lets us decide whether we really need a scene for our story or not! If the scene is not a logical part of the narrative, it won't make it into the story.

3. The plot is an entity. This is a somewhat difficult principle to implement, but nevertheless easy to illustrate. It has to do with Chekhov's gun, amongst other things. The Russian writer Anton Chekhov is credited with the following idea: "If you say in the first chapter that there is a rifle hanging on the wall, in the second or third chapter it absolutely must go off. If it's not going to be fired, it shouldn't be hanging there." What he meant by that was that everything that happens on stage also has a place or meaning in the play. There is nothing superfluous. Transferred to plot, this means that everything that occurs in the story must also have something to do with the story that is being told. In this sense, the plot is an entity. What Chekhov did not actually mean by this is the dramaturgical technique of insinuation, hinting or foreshadowing (see Sect. 5.5). But the example with the rifle can also be understood in this sense: As a spectator, I already have an inkling that the rifle will be used at some point if it has been prominently displayed on stage since the beginning of the play.

Right back in Aristotle's *Poetics*, we are introduced to the demand for unity of action, time and place (2013, 27–28). Aristotle states that parts of the events must be brought together in such a way that the whole is changed and disarranged when any part is moved or taken away. One key thought is that what may be present or absent without visible consequences is not part of the whole story at all. The unification of the plot is a kind of compass: What is part of the narrative gets in. What isn't, stays out. That's why the narrative sentence is so important. It helps to make this decision. For me, this principle is also particularly helpful when revising manuscripts. It shows me which passages I can still trim—however valuable or exciting I may find them. But, hey: kill your darlings!

3.3   SELECT AND CHANGE YOUR POV: THE LADDER OF ABSTRACTION

Many people love the personal tone of Sarah Koenig in *Serial* (especially in the first season): the way she narrates, and with it the feeling of sharing her very thoughts. There is something personal and intimate about it. There are frequent passages in *Serial* lasting several minutes in which Sarah reflects on what she has experienced, and debates with herself and others. These passages radiate a similar narrative power to the passages in which the actual action is driven forward. And this is no coincidence, but classic *This American Life* school. The Ira Glass quotation from the beginning of the previous section goes even further: "There's the plot, where a person has some sort of experience. And then there are moments of reflection, where this person (or another character in the story or the narrator) says something interesting about what's happened" (2017, 70).

This precise change between level of experience and level of reflection can be illustrated by the ladder of abstraction. The more specific an event is, the lower the rung of the ladder on which it occurs. The more abstract something is, the further up it is to be found (see Fig. 3.1 Ladder of Abstraction). What Ira Glass proposes is a continuous alternation between the lower and the upper rungs, between the specific events that drive the plot forward and the debates about what he calls reflection or the bigger idea. Anyone who consciously listens to *This American Life* will recognise this structure in many stories.

For storytellers, the ladder of abstraction is also a good means of establishing their own point of view (POV). How close do I get to the story? Or how much distance do I build up? The further down the ladder I locate myself, the more I immerse myself in the situation, the more emotions unfold and the

LADDER OF ABSTRACTION

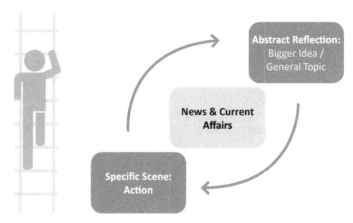

Fig. 3.1 Ladder of Abstraction

more I map the process and deliver an experience to the listener. The higher up I locate myself, the more distanced I am, the more I summarise results. Normally, as journalists and reporters, we instinctively locate ourselves in the upper middle segment: We talk about a topic, present results and create the impression of objective distance; we are not too close to people (although we often claim to be), but we don't take the whole thing too seriously either. After all, we only depict the event. This is a very good solution for news or current affairs reports. But for a narrative it's the wrong point of view. In this context, the American editor and author Jack Hart also speaks of two different types of narrative, which have a direct effect on the reporter's use of language (2011, 54): "When the distance is great, when you step way back from the action, you write in *summary narrative*. When you shrink the distance, you shift into *scenic narrative*." One delivers results (as in news), and the other delivers an experience (as in a story).

The problem is that as authors or reporters, we don't usually think about our position and automatically locate ourselves where we always locate ourselves: in the upper middle segment. "Usually, choosing stance isn't rocket science. The important thing is that you do *choose*" (Hart 2011, 52). Just remember: you don't get half-length versions of films! If anything, this intermediate stage is a transition—don't hang about there for too long. It is the most boring place. Only by consciously changing my point of view can I repeatedly establish a journalistically appropriate distance to my story, reflect on what I have experienced or debate the bigger ideas behind the actual story. Ideally, a new thought emerges from this debate which leads to a scene that, in turn, drives the action, from which new questions and thoughts develop and so on. You get the idea.

It is the leaps on the ladder of abstraction that are the great challenge for authors. It is what I call narrative transmission. It should take place as naturally and quickly as possible, without a break. Ideally, the bigger question is generated by the scene directly; the listener asks himself the question before the leap up the ladder of abstraction happens. An example: The first season of *Serial* starts with the poll moderated by Sarah Koenig (a good example, by the way, for the handling of a vox pop, see Sect. 6.5). She wants to know if young people remember what they did on a certain day six weeks ago: "Now imagine you have to account for a day that happened six weeks back. Because that's the situation in the story I'm working on in which a bunch of teenagers had to recall a day six weeks earlier. And it was 1999, so they had to do it without the benefit of texts or Facebook or Instagram. Just for a lark, I asked some teenagers to try it".[1] The survey begins. Koenig very humorously makes us experience how badly we remember certain activities on certain dates. The narrative transmissions, the leaps from the specific situation to the abstract level and back, happen quickly and efficiently, just as here, from the survey and the insights gained from it to the actual case: "One kid did actually remember pretty well, because it was the last day of state testing at his school and he'd saved up to go to a nightclub. That's the main thing I learned from this exercise, which is no big shocker, I guess. If some significant event happened that day, you remember that, plus you remember the entire day much better. If nothing significant happened, then the answers get very general. I most likely did this, or I most likely did that. These are words I've heard a lot lately. Here's the case I've been working on". In just a few, concise sentences, Koenig summarises the lessons of the survey and puts them in context ("which is no big shocker, I guess") and then addresses the question that has built up in the listeners' minds: "Why is this important for the story?" Koenig again comes to the point with a very brief transition: "Here's the case I've been working on." This pattern will run through the whole story and shows how concrete scenes and abstract debates are always meaningfully linked together. In this way, the feeling of a dense story is created over a long narrative. In the process, the listener is repeatedly and almost imperceptibly led up and down the ladder of abstraction. Flow is created. Should a transition not occur dynamically of its own accord, the following rule of thumb applies: Bad transitions should be fast. Anyone who consciously draws attention to their own weak points with long, elaborate formulations only has themselves to blame.

The ladder of abstraction is therefore a simple tool for designing the plot in more detail. A first approximation. But it does not help you to determine the exact order in which scenes are created and why. This requires rather more complex tools and models into which we can integrate the ladder of abstraction.

3.4   ACT STRUCTURE: CREATING ORDER

Every story needs a beginning, a middle and an end. This sentence is correct, but perhaps a bit hackneyed and still too general. Therefore, it is not very helpful. The following sentence is a little better: At the beginning, the conflict is created; in the middle, the confrontation unfolds; in the end, the conflict is solved. But that is not really specific either. As an author, for years, I have been pondering one question above all: How do I manage to make my story gripping from beginning to end? At some point, I realised I am not the only one asking this question. On the contrary, this problem is so familiar that it can almost boast its own proverb: He who works in three acts knows the hell of the second act. Oh yes! After all, the second act accounts for about half of the story, with one quarter each going to the beginning and the end, i.e. the first and third acts.

The three-act structure (to start with this structural model) can help us, above all, to roughly order our story. It allows us to sort our material, assigning a place in the story to content and situations. An act is a self-contained section in which a part stage or an intermediate goal (on the way to the big goal) is reached. Each act thus has a minor climax. Let's take a medium-sized story as an example: a 15-minute documentary in the history programme *ZeitZeichen*, which is broadcast daily by German public broadcaster WDR. Every day a person or event is remembered.[2] Fifteen minutes is a good example for length because each of the acts has a length we are familiar with from shorter audio pieces. The first act is about three and a half to four minutes long, so is the third act. That leaves something between seven and eight minutes for the second act. The idea behind that is to divide the long story into portions that you can handle well. The topic (not yet the story) in the following example is the birthday (5 August 1922) of Austrian physician Dr Johannes Bischko (broadcast date: 5 August 2017). Let us recall once again the narrative sentence (see Sect. 2.6) which gives an idea of the story: The physician Johannes Bischko (who died in 2004) wants to introduce acupuncture into Austria because he is convinced by it, but meets with resistance (from his profession, the university). The three-act structure now helps us to get a grip on the subject.

Act One (target length: three to four minutes): exposition. In the first act, all essential elements of the story must emerge. Both the characters and the central conflict. At the same time, listeners should be given a good reason to tune in. Since it is supposed to be a narrative, there should be a scenic introduction in which the listener experiences Bischko and the central conflict. Research and interviews on the topic have suggested one scene in particular: Bischko's attempt to perform an operation (the removal of tonsils) under acupuncture anaesthesia. Originally, the operation was supposed to take place in secret, but someone spilt the beans. So, in the end, Bischko performs this operation in a lecture hall full of journalists. I had just one big problem with this scene: There is not a single recording, neither video nor audio, of the whole event. The scene must therefore be completely reconstructed (not re-enacted, for real and reconstructed scenes see also Sect. 6.1). Here, this is done by a close friend of Bischko's who retells the scene. The beginning of the documentary thus reads like this:

Music: Driving, underscore.
Author: Some ideas really do sound crazy: An operation without classic anaesthesia.
Tape: (Manfred Richart, studio) Naturally, there was an anaesthetist standing by in case of emergency. Of course. Bischko had not conducted this procedure before.
Author: Removing the tonsils is not a difficult operation for a surgeon. Even if several journalists are watching.
Ambience: Cameras and murmuring voices.

Here comes the next problem: There are only very few original recordings of Johannes Bischko. Nevertheless, listeners should have an opportunity to hear his voice. That's why it's necessary to include a sound bite that doesn't actually have much to do with the scene. This is done here by briefly opening the scene up to establish the bigger idea of the piece. Directly after that sound bite, the listener is led back into the scene. Bischko is thus introduced as a character who is tangible:

Ambience: Cameras and murmuring voices.

Tape: (Manfred Richart, studio) The whole thing was supposed to be kept completely secret. We still don't know how it was leaked. Suddenly there were huge headlines in the newspapers: The first tonsil operation to take place in Vienna.

Author: This is an operation, the likes of which the western world has never seen. In Vienna, in 1972, Dr Johannes Bischko wants to attempt the unthinkable.

Tape: (Johannes Bischko, archive) Because people in Europe are dominated by fear they don't want to know anything about the events surrounding the operation. That means people are perhaps less afraid of the pain than the whole trappings of the operation.

Author: Especially with an audience like that.

Ambience: Cameras

Tape: (Manfred Richart, studio) They couldn't even do it in the operating theatre at the time because such a flood of journalists had announced their presence that they did it in the lecture hall of the general polyclinic.

Author: Failure at this point is no longer an option. Wobbly nerves are taboo. Fortunately, this is not Bischko's problem anyway, says his long-time colleague and close friend Manfred Richart.

Tape: (Manfred Richart, studio) Never. Bischko has never been afraid. He was always sure of himself and never afraid of anything.

Author: Self-confidence or show? Bischko wants to remove a patient's tonsils. Acupuncture alone is supposed to eliminate the pain. If it works, it's a possible breakthrough for a new method. If it goes wrong, it is not only Bischko who will be pilloried, but acupuncture as well.

Music ends.

The scene is only narrated to the point where it becomes clear what is supposed to happen here. Whether Bischko will really succeed is not revealed yet, of course. So far, about 1:40 min have passed. So, there is enough time to establish more central questions that seem important from a journalistic point of view in this context: Does acupuncture work? How does it work? Is it evidence-based? These are the questions behind Johannes Bischko's attempt. And there is no reason why the answers to these questions should not also be scenic. The next paragraph of the manuscript reads like this:

Tape: (Valerie Arrowsmith, treatment room) Well, it's not very big.

Author: A treatment room in Bonn.

Tape: (Valerie Arrowsmith, treatment room) Now the colour. You can clearly see that it is very pale.

Tape: (Sven Preger, tongue sticking out, treatment room) Aha...

Author: And I'm allowed to stick my tongue out at Valerie Arrowsmith...

Tape: (Valerie Arrowsmith, treatment room) Just put it out! Okay, and back in again.

Author: I enjoyed doing that as a child. But Dr Valerie Arrowsmith is interested in different things from my paediatrician. Because she is not only a general practitioner but has also studied acupuncture and Traditional Chinese Medicine.

Tape: (Sven Preger, tongue sticking out, treatment room) And?

Tape: (Valerie Arrowsmith, treatment room) And...

Author: And my tongue speaks to her.

Tape: (Valerie Arrowsmith, treatment room) It's a bit swollen. And if it wasn't, it would probably be rather small.

Tape: (Sven Preger, treatment room) I have a swollen tongue...

Tape: (Valerie Arrowsmith, treatment room) Yes ...

Author: I am here for the pain-relieving effects of acupuncture. Tension, neck pain, sometimes extending to the temples. I've had it again and again for years. Since 2007, acupuncture for chronic back and knee pain is a service that, under certain conditions, has been covered by health insurance providers. German studies on acupuncture were partly responsible for this. One result was that for chronic knee and back pain, acupuncture was better than standard therapy. The needles help. And acupuncture is one of altogether five pillars of Traditional Chinese Medicine, which aims to understand the human being holistically.

Tape: (Valerie Arrowsmith, treatment Room) The patient's entire state of health is paramount, not so much the actual diagnosis.

Both action strands are created at this point: Bischko's specific challenge, whether he really will master the operation. And the journalistically necessary questions about acupuncture. Both strands should be brought together at the end. Also, the main characters and their goals are established (Johannes Bischko wants to do the operation, I as a reporter want to get rid of my afflictions and Valerie Arrowsmith wants to help me), and the conflicts are emerging. End of Act One. Timing so far: about three minutes.

Act Two (target length: seven to eight minutes): confrontation. The second act is determined by the attempt to achieve the goals set. Obstacles appear and must be overcome. Ideally, these obstacles get bigger over time, so that listeners have the feeling of a story becoming more intense. Dramaturgically speaking, *ZeitZeichen* has an inherent problem that is typical of many long audio narratives: The person or the event should be depicted appropriately—with all the necessary information. In the *ZeitZeichen* about Johannes Bischko, for example, this means that the second act should feature all the information that is important for his life and work so that an appropriate image of his character and activities emerges. To exaggerate just slightly, the journalistic appropriateness of the story tends to get in the way. In order to accommodate all the necessary and important information, an exciting plot design is essential; otherwise, the piece will very soon get boring.

So, the first thing to do is to establish the obstacles. For Johannes Bischko, there are at least three:

- Firstly, his overriding self-confidence (from the outside it could almost look like arrogance). If the planned operation goes wrong, his reputation may not recover. This character obstacle is already established in the exposition, which also makes sense dramaturgically because it shows the potential for character development.
- Secondly, the military. Bischko is drafted as a young man and can't go to university immediately (not mentioned in the first act). This obstacle is particularly well suited to conveying Bischko's most important biographical data (date of birth, upbringing) because the obstacle reflects the circumstances of the time. The connection to Bischko's life is easily made.
- Thirdly, the planned operation. There are even several sub-obstacles: The secretly planned operation will be made public. At first, Bischko cannot find a volunteer patient. And he cannot practise the operation beforehand. It must work first time.

Using all these obstacles, this strand of the second act can be well designed, while also portraying Bischko's life and work. At the same time, it is possible to foresee where the final conflict in the third act will lead.

The same way of thinking and planning is now applied to the second thread of the story (let's call it "self-experiment acupuncture"), which is supposed to address the issues revolving around the effectiveness and success of acupuncture while building a bridge to the present day. There are two major obstacles here:

- Firstly: The reporter's neck pain, which is supposed to get better—with the help of Valerie Arrowsmith. This conflict was already introduced in the first act. But what listeners don't know yet is that there is another obstacle looming which has to do with the reporter's character.
- That is, secondly, the reporter, i.e. me, does not particularly like the small, sharp acupuncture needles. This makes the treatment more difficult, of course. Can acupuncture even work under these circumstances? At the same time, this obstacle gives us the opportunity to talk about the functioning and success of acupuncture. This part of the narrative thus also provides essential information and lays the ground for further developments. Just like the main narrative strand, it is about hopefully successful treatment. In this way, it is always possible to switch between the two strands, leading—best of all, of course—to a minor cliffhanger.

End of Act 2. Timing so far: about ten minutes (so approximately seven minutes for the second act).

Act Three (target length: approx. 3:30 minutes): final confrontation, climax and resolution. The third act is where everything is heading. It contains the final confrontation or climax and resolution of the conflict, whichever way it turns out. If it ends badly, it is more likely to be a tragedy. Terms like "final confrontation" or "climax" are a bit woolly. What they mean is that the narrative is heading towards a central event (which could be anything from an election to a wedding or a boxing match). This event takes place in the third act and determines whether the story ends well or badly, whether the protagonist achieves his goal or fails.

When planning a story, this means that this event must be identified as early as possible—preferably in the conception phase. Otherwise, as a reporter, I can't properly align the story with it. Using the example of the *ZeitZeichen* about Johannes Bischko, the main narrative strand leads to the question: Will the operation be successful? A volunteer patient has finally been found (a colleague of Bischko's from another department) as well as a place where journalists can watch the operation (the lecture hall of the general polyclinic)—so it can start. We dive back into the scene with Bischko's close friend Manfred Richart. The scene is finally completed, as is the second narrative strand.

Music: Change to tension theme.

Tape: (Manfred Richart, studio) It was then that, of course, to be honest, hardly any patients were found who voluntarily wanted to undergo such a procedure. Then one in the ENT department of a polyclinic - a colleague, a doctor colleague, made himself available to have his tonsils removed under this acupuncture pain elimination procedure.

Author: And the international press watches live.

Tape: (Manfred Richart, studio) You have to imagine it: Today there are devices for this kind of thing, which means that they stimulate the needles with electric current. At that time, during the entire operation, an acupuncturist sat on each side, Bischko on one side, a colleague on the other, and had to stimulate the needles with an up and down and simultaneous left-turning movement during the entire operation. The operation lasted about 40 minutes. So, you can imagine, if you stimulate the needles manually for 40 minutes, what an effort it was.

Author: Bischko is hanging in there.

Tape: (Manfred Richart, studio) It worked, the patient was pain-free during the whole operation.

Music accent.

Tape: (Valerie Arrowsmith, treatment room) (comes in) So, Mr Preger, how are you? How are you feeling?

Tape: (Sven Preger, treatment room) It is easier for me to relax now, even in these few minutes. What do we do now?

Tape: (Valerie Arrowsmith, treatment room) Ok... ...I'm going to remove the needles, very carefully.

Author: Actually, I'm doing quite well. Despite or because of the needles in my body.

Tape: (Valerie Arrowsmith, treatment room) But I think it's good that you're so open about it and admit that you don't like the needles. This gives me a bit more information on what I have to look out for during the next treatment. I don't want you to come here feeling tense and anxious. You should enjoy coming here and feel good.

Author: Many people appreciate that. Taking time, listening, holistic. Two hours pass quickly this afternoon. In the evening, my shoulders actually feel lighter.

This narrative strand can also be brought to a positive end. The central conflict has been resolved as far as possible. It is important that the endings are credible. They must not only end positively because that's what makes for a better ending. That can quickly become unbelievable. If the report were to end here now, it would feel as though it had broken off before it was finished. It still needs some kind of an echo, a conclusion, a deeper level of meaning and, as far as possible, a merging of the two narrative levels (which do not really produce a single plot here—so much for unity, but that is often the case with journalism and non-fiction topics). But for them to work together credibly, they must be logically related to one another, answering questions that arise in the other part. The transitions, in particular, must be coherent. Let me remind you once again: If you can't find a really good transition, it should at least happen quickly. Every additional word draws attention to the weak point and puzzles listeners. So, the final fusion, as far as there can be one, happens in the last parts of the story:

Author: Many people appreciate that. Taking time, listening, holistic. Two hours pass quickly this afternoon. In the evening, my shoulders actually feel lighter.

Tape: (Valerie Arrowsmith, treatment room) Generally, I find it more fulfilling or satisfying when I have more time for the individual patient, which is what TCM[3] allows me to do. And overall, I am moving more and more towards using holistic methods. Nevertheless, I would not say that I would like to dispense with orthodox medicine completely.

Tape: (Manfred Richart, studio) Bischko has always postulated that every method has its potential, but also its limits. And he has looked for alternative methods for these limits that can perhaps support orthodox medicine in a meaningful way.

> *Author*: This is something we can use to advantage. And try to combine the best of both worlds. Conventional medicine and complementary methods. The debate continues to this day.
> *Music*: Sustained-melancholic.
> *Author*: In November 2004, Manfred Richart visits his close friend for the last time.
> *Tape*: (Manfred Richart, studio) And then we smoked a few cigarettes, drank a few glasses of wine. Then finally, I think it was about four or five, I said goodbye. And something happened that had never happened before when I visited him. He let me out in his wheelchair and waved to me until I got in the lift.
> *Author*: ...a few hours later Johannes Bischko is dead. He is 82 years old. All his life Bischko fought for acupuncture to be accepted by orthodox medicine in Austria. And that's exactly what he achieves. In 1986, the Supreme Medical Council recognises acupuncture as a scientific healing method.

Having Valerie Arrowsmith and Manfred Richart speak in direct succession establishes the connection between the two narrative levels. What Valerie Arrowsmith formulates fits in perfectly with Johannes Bischko's philosophy. The bridge to today has been built. At the end of the piece, Johannes Bischko's life story is told to the end. This can be done by his close friend Manfred Richart contributing a very personal view and anecdote. The concluding fact that acupuncture has been recognised as a healing method encapsulates Bischko's life's work in one sentence. The piece could stop here, but I wanted it to end on a cheerful note—after all, to some extent, the documentary was also about my fear of acupuncture needles.

> *Author*: ...a few hours later Johannes Bischko is dead. He is 82 years old. All his life Bischko fought for acupuncture to be accepted by orthodox medicine in Austria. And that's exactly what he achieves. In 1986, the Supreme Medical Council recognises acupuncture as a scientific healing method.
> *Tape*: (Valerie Arrowsmith, treatment room) Take a deep breath in and out.
> *Tape*: (Sven Preger, treatment room) Argh!
> *Tape*: (Valerie Arrowsmith, treatment room) It can be very intense!
> *Tape*: (Sven Preger, treatment room) Oh yeah?!
> *Tape*: (Valerie Arrowsmith, treatment room) I'm telling you now... (laughs).
>
> Music over.

End of Act Three. Total time: 13:54 minutes. The third act lasts just under four minutes. So, it's a little longer than the opening act. I often think that's a good solution, to dive into a topic really quickly. Once listeners are immersed in the story and stay with it, the story can wind up more slowly. Besides, you always need to take more time, especially for the climax in the third act. If the decisive scene is narrated too fast, the listener is often left with an empty feeling.

To wrap it up: The act structure helps us to order our material, to classify obstacles and to focus them on a goal. Especially for the beginning and end, the model is very helpful. However, the longer the piece, the longer the acts. Then, it can make sense to insert additional acts so that you end up with four or five.

Expanding the piece by adding acts means you need to have clear, intermediate goals and steps in the story. In Bischko's case, for example, the search for a volunteer patient would have been one possibility. But there is not always enough information and matching scenes to really justify another act. If you work with a five-act structure, the second act is classically where the situation becomes aggravated, i.e. where the conflicts escalate. The fourth act, on the other hand, delays the final catastrophe and acts as a retarding moment. In Bischko's story, the search for a suitable operating room (in which the audience can also be accommodated) could have provided such a moment. However, both the aggravation and the retardation ideas did not work out. Neither the interview with Manfred Richart nor other research yielded enough information for a reconstructed scene. And perhaps that was not a bad thing after all. Sometimes the dense, but shorter piece is also the more exciting one. Longer does not automatically mean better. In my experience, three acts up to a length of 30 minutes are sufficient and easy to handle. Anything longer requires a somewhat subtler structure.

Robert McKee (1997, 221) mentions two further arguments against the five-act structure. Firstly, he points out the danger of clichés. The more acts there are, the more climaxes you need (in every act). But, in real life, there are usually simply not that many highlights. And secondly, multiplying the acts weakens the effect of climaxes and can lead to repetition (McKee 1997, 222). This can quickly become unbelievable or boring—or both. If there are stories that deliver or offer enough acts, the five-act model can be just as helpful and powerful as the three-act one. It can also help to break up the long second act and thus get a better grip on it. But there is another model that gives us yet further (structural) access to our material and it should not be omitted from any book about dramaturgy. Especially not when it comes to oral narratives— because this model is based on the stories and myths of our world.

3.5   The Hero's Journey: Learning from Old Tales

Can this really be true? Is there a structure inherent in every story? The American mythologist Joseph Campbell asked himself this question and compared the myths of the world. His answer: Yes, this meta-structure does exist. Campbell has given it a name: the monomyth or hero's journey. If there is one single narrative model that can help us tell stories, then it really should be the hero's journey. The title of Campbell's standard work, *The Hero with a Thousand Faces* (first published in 1949), already answers one of the most frequent questions about the hero's journey: Must all stories be told in the same way? Of course not! Just like the act structure, the hero's journey is supposed to help you get a grip on the material, put it in order, create a plot. Just as language is always composed of grammar and vocabulary, stories are perhaps always composed of elements of the hero's journey. Sometimes all of them, sometimes only a few. Especially with real stories, it will not always be possible to portray all elements. And that is not even necessary (Fig. 3.2).

The hero's journey is two things: a structural model and a philosophy of life. This double meaning helps you order your own material. The structural model is useful for putting the events and thoughts into a dramaturgically meaningful order. And the philosophy of life lets us identify the aspects that are particularly important for character development. If you look at the stages of the hero's journey, you get an idea of what I mean. Campbell originally identified 17 stages of a story. The American screenwriter and author Christopher Vogler later condensed them into twelve (Vogler 1998). They are the ones that are still common today. Let's illustrate them with excerpts from a 15-minute radio documentary about Joseph Campbell (first broadcast on *Zeitzeichen* on 30 October 2017, the 30th anniversary of Campbell's death):

Fig. 3.2   The Hero's Journey

Stage 1: Ordinary world. Two core thoughts are important here. One: Every story has to start somewhere. Any place, any moment can be a starting point. Two: Something in that specific situation should be amiss. The hero is dissatisfied with the here and now, the world is too familiar, too ordinary:

> *Author*: Joseph Campbell's birth in White Plains, New York on 26 March 1904 is unspectacular. His parents are Irish Catholics who move to the countryside soon after his birth.
>
> *Tape*: (Martin Weyers, apartment) Where he spent his time as a little boy looking for arrows, Native American's arrows, and got so enthusiastic that he then read all the books in the children's library. And was so thrilled that he became a researcher on the spot, so to speak, as he later explained.

This passage depicts a world that is obviously not big enough for the young Joseph Campbell.

Stage 2: Call to adventure. In the inadequate world presented here something happens that sets the whole story in motion. In other dramaturgical models, it is also called the starting point or inciting incident. In Campbell's case, it was his first contact with mythical stories—as already indicated in the excerpt above, which comes immediately before the following passage in the documentary:

> *Author*: These are Campbell's first myths, says Martin Weyers, a visual artist who works with the Joseph Campbell Foundation. Campbell is fascinated by the stories of the indigenous peoples of America - even if that doesn't quite conform with the zeitgeist.
>
> *Tape*: (Martin Weyers, apartment) When he was a little boy a lot of Westerns were shown at the cinema…

Stage 3: Refusal of the call. A brief delaying moment, a hero's pause: Should I really dare to leave my comfort zone? A feeling familiar to many of us which makes the hero human and relatable. This is exactly how Joseph Campbell felt during his lifetime:

> *Author*: Perhaps Campbell already senses that myths and stories give him energy, and interest him more than anything else. Nevertheless, he initially studies mathematics and biology. But that's a great trial for him because what he learns there is not compatible with his upbringing.

> *Tape*: (Martin Weyers, apartment) It triggered the collapse of his religious belief. He suddenly discovered there was a completely different biological story of creation or evolution.
> *Author*: Campbell transfers to Columbia University. And begins a new course of study there: English literature.

Of course, this denial cannot last long— otherwise, the story would grind to a halt. But maybe the hero can be given a little help.

Stage 4: Meeting with the mentor. We do not have to accomplish everything alone. There are people out there who inspire us or offer advice. They can help us to find our way (into adventure). It doesn't have to be the great Jedi Master Yoda, it can also be shorter encounters with other personalities. Campbell had such an encounter:

> *Author*: In 1924, his family takes him to Europe. On the way back, Campbell meets a man who will inspire him, the Indian philosopher Jiddu Krishnamurti. He awakens Campbell's interest in Indian philosophy, in stories and symbols. Back in the US, Campbell begins a master's degree in mediaeval literature.

Stage 5: Crossing the first threshold. Now the adventure really begins. The hero sets off, he dives into a new world. In fictional stories, this is often marked by a spatial change. The Hogwarts Express brings Harry Potter to Hogwarts, a train also brings Katniss Everdeen and Peeta Mellark to the Capitol in *The Hunger Games*, and the Titanic sets off to cross the Atlantic. Joseph Campbell also crosses a threshold— in his case more figuratively. He enters a new intellectual world of myths. And what he wants to achieve there is already apparent:

> *Author*: And slowly an idea is maturing within him as to what he actually wants to do with all these myths and his life:
> *Tape*: (Martin Weyers, apartment) He wanted to make the myths readable, understandable and experienceable again. And sharing this discovery, I think that's the central thread running through his work.
> *Author*: Mythology as something specific...

Stage 6: Road of trials, challenges & temptations, friends & allies. Once the hero has immersed himself in the new world, he must first find his way. Who is his friend? Who is his enemy? And how can he get closer to his goal? We are familiar with similar questions from the second act with its obstacles.

Depending on how serious the first obstacles are, this can also be quite a fast and humorous part. Blake Snyder (2005, 80f) calls it the "Fun & Games" part. Campbell also tries to find his way around the new intellectual world and is confronted with numerous challenges:

> *Author*: Campbell's story continues in Europe, with the help of a scholarship from his university. He studies the archetypes of C.G. Jung and the works of Thomas Mann; he even learns German. When he returns to the US, he has a plan: he wants to write his doctoral thesis. But the faculty turns him down. And world history has an additional unpleasant surprise in store for him: in 1929.

Stage 7: Approach to the inmost cave. Once the hero has orientated himself in the unknown world, he knows which path to take to reach his goal. On this path, a final big obstacle is awaiting him. And to make the whole thing a bit more exciting, the path leading there is intentionally long drawn out. Campbell only has a short way to go in terms of distance, but in terms of time, he has to prepare himself for a long dry spell:

> *Author*: …When he returns to the US, he has a plan: he wants to write his doctoral thesis. But the faculty turns him down. And world history has an additional unpleasant surprise in store for him: in 1929.
> *Tape*: (Martin Weyers, apartment) There was the big stock market crash, which meant no-one had any money at all. And then he went into the forest for five years. Near Woodstock.
> *Author*: There is not much to do here. And Campbell doesn't have a job…

Stage 8: The ordeal. The hero is already exhausted from his long journey, but he still has to pull himself together to pass his greatest test of all. Of course, it looks as though he won't be able to pass this one. For years, nothing changes in Campbell's life. He has to accept that he is destitute, and that won't change for the foreseeable future. The situation seems hopeless. So, the biggest test for him is to come to terms with this situation. And to try to make the best of life anyway:

> *Author*: … So, he just continues to spend his time reading.
> *Tape*; (Martin Weyers, apartment) And then he lived there for years. And if this is the way things are, that life offers no chance of earning money, or the circumstances are such that I might not be able to study at Stanford, then I'll just go into the woods, without running water and without electricity. And then I can read books. That might not be ideal

> or what you would choose, but you have to make the best of it. That
> can also be a hippie time. And that can teach us as much as studying at
> Stanford.

Stage 9: Reward. Anyone who perseveres this long and wins the final battle against themselves or others can expect a reward. The reward might be material goods (money, sword) or ideal goods (love, knowledge). In most cases, it is both. Campbell is rewarded three times over: with a job, a partner and an answer:

> *Author*: Campbell finally uses his extensive knowledge to pursue one
>   particular question:
> *Tape*: (Uwe Walter, apartment) Is it possible that all these religions, all
>   these heroes, perhaps have the same core in them everywhere? Maybe
>   even an original core?
> *Author*: Campbell really does find an answer. But before that, he returns
>   from the forest to civilization. From 1934, he teaches at Sarah Lawrence
>   College, a private college for girls. In 1938, he marries a former student,
>   Jean Erdman.

Stage 10: The road back. Anyone who has been so successful as a hero in the foreign world must or may at some point return, go home. Campbell finally finds his place in the academic world by writing what is probably his most important book:

> *Author*: Joseph Campbell finds an answer to his question. He compares
>   myths and narratives from all over the world, searching for a pattern
>   that is common to all stories. He finally describes this meta-structure
>   in his book, *The Hero with a Thousand Faces*. This basic structure of
>   all mythical tales is given a name: the monomyth or the hero's journey.
>   For Uwe Walter it is not an invention, but a discovery.

Stage 11: Resurrection. On his return journey, the hero begins to realise that after all these experiences, life is no longer the same. Something has changed significantly. The hero not only becomes aware of this change, but he can use it for himself. Campbell's book has changed storytelling. Later, a director and screenwriter will use the hero's journey as a blueprint for a story he is currently working on. It takes place in a galaxy far, far away and will eventually be shown in cinemas near you. The director's name: George Lucas. The name of his story: Star Wars. Campbell not only inspired others, but also understood what was important to him in life:

Author: Campbell has developed and reinvented himself. It was always important to him to live in the here and now. That's also the reason why he continues lecturing - as in this 1970 recording of the Joseph Campbell Foundation in New York. At the end of his lecture on myths and kangaroos he tells another mythical story from Hinduism - about a guru and a young disciple...

Stage 12: Return with the elixir. No place like home. Like many other people, the hero is pleased to return home at the end of his adventures. But home feels different now because the hero has changed. The elixir he brings back from his journey can be symbolic, material or idealistic, or all three. Remember one of the most famous homecomers of all, Samwise Gamgee. Although he is Frodo's closest friend, he is not allowed to leave the Shire with Frodo at the end of *The Lord of the Rings*. He stays in the Shire and says that famous final sentence, 'Well I'm back' (Tolkien 1991, 1069). Joseph Campbell gives a long, multipart interview shortly before his death, which is broadcast on American television afterwards, and moves many people. But Campbell no longer experiences it:

Tape: (Martin Weyers, apartment) He'd just started to become successful and then actually just before he became known to an audience of millions in the US, he died. By the way, best possible scenario for the hero: on the way from his bed to his desk. He dropped dead as he was about to get to work.

Author: Joseph Campbell dies on 30 October 1987 in Hawaii. He is 83 years old. His great love, Jean Erdman, is still alive today. She is now 101.[4]

Music fades in.

Author: Joseph Campbell researched myths, saw connections and understood that stories give us courage, explain the world, maybe even heal. Campbell transferred the hero's journey to real life.

Tape: (Martin Weyers, apartment) And it goes on like that and I think the smartest thing to do is to give up and stop thinking about it: At some point, I may have managed one hero's journey, but it's not so bad to make the hero's journey again and again. Because as long as we have problems, we are still alive.

Author: The twelfth and final stage is therefore returning home. A little bit smarter than before and ready for a new adventure.

Tape: (Uwe Walter, apartment) And I believe that the hero's journey never ends.

Music fades out.

**HERO'S JOURNEY
AND ACT STRUCTURE**

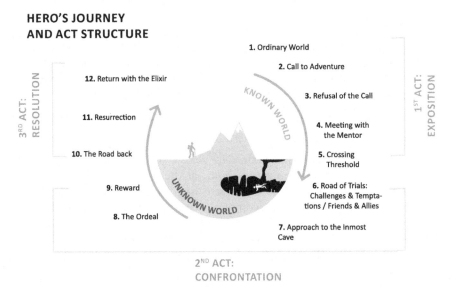

Fig. 3.3 Hero's Journey and Act Structure

Above all, the hero's journey emphasises the development of the hero, his path and his personal growth to serve society or the greater good. This perspective is immensely helpful in building the big arcs of a story: What does the story boil down to? How does the hero change? Through what? The model of the hero's journey is thus, in contrast to the act model, somewhat more hero-centred than plot-centred. However, a comparison shows that essential elements occur in both models (Fig. 3.3).

For audio narratives, the hero's journey is especially useful because it helps us find the narrative perspective. And because it divides the plot into smaller sections. It overcomes the problem of the long second act. Ideally, as a listener, I have the feeling that the story is flowing all the time—one thing results from the other. To achieve this, a reporter must pay attention to special elements: the transitions. Be they the transitions from one act to another or from the stages of the hero's journey. The good news is that there is a model that pays extra attention to these elements. It helps us every time to come up with surprises and special moments in our sonic narratives, even if it derives from script writing school.

3.6   Screenplay Paradigm: Designing Dynamic Transitions

Every story needs these moments of plot development in order to create dynamics, pace and density. Listeners should feel that something special has just happened, as in the following excerpt from a documentary about the

English theoretical physicist and cosmologist Stephen Hawking I did for his 75th birthday in January 2017 (Hawking was still alive then, he died in March 2018). The longer paragraph is placed at the end of Act One: "In October 1962, Hawking starts at Cambridge, reading modern cosmology, mathematics and the theory of relativity. He is fascinated by the idea of finding a formula for everything, the very big and the very small. But his health is not good. During the first Christmas holidays he finally needs to see a doctor. And receives a devastating diagnosis: motor neurone disease, an incurable disease of the nervous system. It damages the nerve cells that control the muscles. Hawking is just 21 years old. And the prognosis is bad: the doctors give him two or three more years. And what does he do? He writes: If I'm going to die, I can still do some good first– so he starts working on his PhD."

The diagnosis is not only a dramatic and incisive experience in the life of Stephen Hawking, but from a dramaturgical point of view, a classic plot point. I have already pointed out that weak transitions are best made quickly. Plot points are an even better option: They make transitions dynamic and drive the story forward. Instead of a break in the narrative, you give it pace.

The definition of a plot point is not that simple. According to German Wikipedia, a plot point is "a surprise that causes the plot to become more complicated over time". The English Wikipedia entry on plot point is even broader: "In television and film, a plot point is a significant event within a plot that spins the action around in another direction." The specific reference to television and film has something to do with the origin of the plot-point theory which was introduced into film and television theory for the first time by the American non-fiction author Syd Field. For him, the plot point is a core instrument (Field 1979). A plot point, Field says, intervenes in the plot and sends it in a different direction. It is therefore an event or incident that moves the story forward. Of course, we can also use plot points for audio narratives. They help us to structure long stories better and to design transitions—at least partially. I personally find the definition given by the American script consultant and author Karl Iglesias helpful: "The two most powerful categories of change in stories, and in our lives, are **discoveries**, which are changes in knowledge, and **decisions**, which are changes in actions. In a story, these moments are plot points" (Iglesias 2005, 83). For me, a plot point must fulfil three criteria:

1. Powerful: Whatever the event, it must make an impression. Emotionally, like Stephen Hawking's diagnosis. And/or because it has consequences. After an accident or a decision to break up, life goes on, but differently. The event itself can be triggered from the outside (like an accident) or from the inside (like a decision). The effect is even more important than the element of surprise. A plot point can also announce itself (like a crisis meeting, a doctor's appointment or court hearing). The event is naturally stronger when it breaks with expectations. The surprise then refers to the "how" of the event rather than the "if" Sometimes both.

2. Plot-related: A plot point is only a plot point if it also refers to the plot. This sounds trivial or self-evident at first, but this is not necessarily the case. There are certainly many outstanding events in Stephen Hawking's life (such as the birth of his children, his weddings, divorces or his meetings with various popes). All these events were certainly powerful and important to him and perhaps even surprising and formative. But which of them is suitable for a plot point? All? None? The answer is it depends on the plot of the story. Or in other words, the narrative sentence. This, after all, determines which story (and therefore which plot) I want to tell. In the documentary quoted above, for example, the narrative sentence reads like this: "Stephen Hawking wants to find the all-encompassing world formula because he is fascinated by the universe. But he falls ill in his early twenties - the doctors give him only a few more years to live." The main challenge of this plot is to find some kind of world formula. In relation to this goal, the chosen event must be a powerful and surprising event. This would be the case, for example, if Hawking's encounter with the Pope made him believe in God and therefore stop pursuing his original goal (which was not the case!). The narrative sentence is thus the yardstick for judging the plot point.

3. Irreversible: The plot cannot go back to a point before the plot point. This also sounds banal at first. What irreversible means is that if I find out that my partner has cheated on me, or that a loved one has died, or if I understand that deep inside of me, there is a longing for recognition—then I can't revert to the situation prior to this insight. I cannot ignore it, I can only integrate it. If a lamp falls off the bedside table and splinters into a thousand pieces, then I buy a new one—but if this lamp is an old family heirloom that means a lot to me, then I have to live with having destroyed it. After having a tracheotomy in 1985, Stephen Hawking is unable to speak—he has to use his speech computer. This is irreversible.

With his plot point model, Syd Field helps us, in particular, to make the transitions dynamic. In doing so, he makes targeted use of the three-act structure and extends it (Fig. 3.4).

In this model, the plot points are positioned just before the transition to the next act. They initiate the transitions. Field also introduces the midpoint, a kind of (negative) climax in the middle of the story, not to be confused with the final confrontation or resolution of the conflict in the third act. The midpoint is the moment of deepest crisis—we already know this from stage eight of the hero's journey. In fictional stories, it's the moment when the character realises that he has been striving for goals that are not good for him. He discovers his true goals, which he wants to achieve from now on. It's the difference between "what a character wants" (before the midpoint) and "what a character really needs" (after the midpoint). The midpoint is a great help in preventing the second act from getting boring.

PLOT POINT PARADIGM

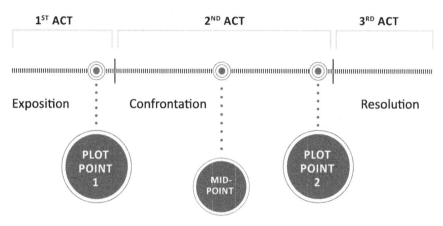

Fig. 3.4 Plot Point Paradigm

An example: In the documentary series *The Hitchhiker*, my colleague Stephan Beuting tells me about his encounter with hitchhiker Heinrich in the first act of the first episode (Stephan met Heinrich at a petrol station on his way home from Cologne to Bonn). When Stephan tells me about it, we realise that I know this person, too, and met him at the same spot, about a year before Stephan. This is the first plot point. As a result, we reach a decision: We want to find hitchhiker Heinrich. With this decision, the second act begins. In it, we systematically follow all leads. During this research, we realise that Heinrich's stories about abuse in a child and youth psychiatric ward may be true. From now on, it is no longer a matter of finding a hitchhiker and checking whether he has committed suicide, as announced, but also of possibly uncovering a major scandal. So, the story goes in a slightly new or more specific direction—this is the somewhat early midpoint. At the end of our extensive search, the phone finally rings: Hitchhiker Heinrich calls back (after we have left a message for him at a social institution for homeless people where we think he could be). This is the second plot point. We agree to meet and, finally, Stephan and I set off to find Heinrich (beginning of the third act). For the storyboard of *The Hitchhiker*, see also Sect. 3.10.

Plot points are particularly important in long stories. They give structure, surprise and, above all, drive the plot forward! To make sure the story does not get boring or lose focus.

In my opinion, the three models (act structure, hero's journey, plot-point paradigm) take a slightly different angle on a story. They have been developed for fictional narratives, for different media. So, we have to adapt them slightly for audio narratives. The great thing about all three models is that they can help us to make non-fiction stories exciting: The act-structure creates order, the hero's journey spans the developmental and suspense arc, and the

HERO'S JOURNEY, ACTS AND PLOT POINTS

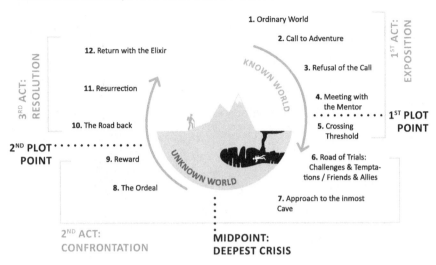

Fig. 3.5 Hero's Journey, Acts and Plot Points

plot-point paradigm provides dynamics and shapes the transitions. When you superimpose them, you also realise that they are not so different after all, but have a lot in common (Fig. 3.5).

There are, moreover, numerous other models, for four or eight acts, the original hero's journey with 17 steps or John Truby's 22 steps of a story (2007, 267f.). Some of them have been developed for specific formats, such as the typical American 45-minute TV series episode (four or eight acts) or a major motion picture. They all pursue two goals: to give the story tension and structure, but they do this using different perspectives. For me, the following elements and principles have proved to be the most effective. They are a mixture of different models, incorporating variations and additions, and optimised to design the plot for sonic narratives.

3.7   Sonic Narratives: Principles and Core Elements

So, we are now in the middle of the structural work. But how exactly do I design my plot as a producer or reporter? Preferably in two steps: Firstly, I recall a few principles and use them to sift through my material. In a second step, I then craft eleven specific plot elements. Let's start with the principles:

1. Find the narrative sentence. The narrative sentence is the yardstick for the course of the story. Whatever fits with the sentence gets into the story. What does not, is excluded. The fact that I want to demonstrate all the knowledge I have acquired as a reporter is no justification for a

boring script. Only bits and pieces of research make it on the air. When everything I know becomes part of my piece, then something is probably wrong. It's like an iceberg. The research is much more extensive, but it enables us to create precise sentences and statements that would not otherwise be possible.

2. Think in scenes. This is one of the biggest challenges for journalists—see the ladder of abstraction in Sect. 3.3. We are used to communicating results and appearing omniscient or neutral. When crafting a narration, we have to give that up. Look for scenes that advance your story. Where does your hero act? Where do obstacles appear? During my basic research, for example, I write down powerful situations or scenes I come across. Some of them always make it into the piece. That means that all the material is worked through twice, first thematically sorted (journalistically) and then scenically plotted (dramaturgically). In this way, I also make sure that all the important journalistic information and arguments also appear in my story.

3. Draw an arc of suspense. Where is the story heading? This is a helpful question to plot the story from the end. Because as an author, I have my sights firmly set on the goal. And always remember that tension or suspense is defined by the open question: what's next? Listeners should ask themselves this question; otherwise, they will switch off at some point, especially with long stories (for suspense techniques and scenic work, see also Chapters 5 and 6).

4. Draw an arc of development. How does the main character or hero develop? What is his or her task, what is the challenge? Which obstacles are in the way? The earlier the development is established, the more credible it is (we will also deal with character development in detail in Chapter 4).

5. Develop subplots. If possible. A helpful question here is: Are there other strands of action beyond the central challenges? In the case of cinema films, for example, there is what is known as "love interest." *Avatar* might have been successful as a purely science-fiction film and dystopia. But the love story between Jake Sully and Neytiri deepens the story immensely and becomes, in the famous final scene, the main plot (keep your eyes open when choosing a partner!). In real stories, sub-plots are very difficult to realise because they thrive on a complex character network. For longer series, however, this is worth noting.

6. Make a list of revelations. Does your research reveal information that shines a new light on the subject, that surprises or moves even you as a reporter when you first notice it? Make a note of this moment in any case. Your list of revelations will help you determine the right plot points. In the case of Stephen Hawking, it is likely that a lot of people know that he was seriously ill and possibly also that the illness was a serious nervous disorder. But what might not be known is when exactly he was diagnosed

and that the doctors only gave him a few years to live. Dramaturgically important in this context is the question as to when information has the greatest dramatic effect. Most of the time, it's a specific point in the story—normally not at the beginning. Therefore, it sometimes makes sense to withhold information and place it deliberately where it serves the story best. Under certain circumstances, it may make sense to mention information early on. In a documentary about the first intercontinental flight in a solar plane (I did for our documentary department on the fifth anniversary in 2017), it quickly becomes clear that Bertrand Piccard is the main character. He is a member of a family of explorers. Both his grandfather Auguste (first balloon flight into the stratosphere in 1931) and his father Jacques (first dive to the deepest point of the sea in the Mariana Trench in 1960) were great adventurers and pioneers. This information can be included at many points in a 15-minute narration. The crucial question is where does the information unleash most power in relation to the narrative? The answer in this case is, actually, right at the beginning. Because it increases the pressure on Bertrand Piccard. He is a member of a great pioneering family. Failure is therefore not an option for him. This information about his family background is used to raise the stakes, to put pressure on Piccard, dramaturgically speaking. That's why it comes right up front.

If you take these principles into account, you can create an exciting, specific plot which can then comprise the following eleven elements:

1. Captivating entry scene: It starts right away. No big speeches. The first scene draws the listener into the story. Something happens. Dynamic rather than static. In the first scene, we see the main character of the story in action, creating an impression. For example, the documentary about Johannes Bischko begins at the operating table.
2. The triggering event: Is embedded in the first scene or follows immediately after (depending on the total length of the piece). The story gets rolling. Joseph Campbell encounters the first myths; Bertrand Piccard decides to fly around the earth without fuel. The triggering event indicates the path of the story. The triggering event is always a specific event, not a conglomeration of impressions. Even today, many long stories still begin with a collage of different tapes, the reasoning being that it opens up the cosmos of the whole story beautifully. But it usually confuses listeners. They do not know the story-universe yet and are hardly likely to get to know it through sound snippets. The collage sometimes seems like the idea that was leftover when the author couldn't think of anything better. Of course, there are also stories where the collage makes sense at the beginning, especially if it is a moderated or more presented collage (by that I mean additional short sentences

from the reporter)—this form can provide much more guidance and orientation than the simple collage of sound bites. A different role is played by the catch-up collage ("Previously on..."), i.e. the intro at the beginning of series episodes, which briefly summarise what has happened and what point or conflict has been reached in the story so far.

3. Introducing characters: Save the Cat. In the introductory scene and in the triggering event, we experience the main character of the story in action. Blake Snyder (2005, 120ff.) says we must find the main character sympathetic in some way as a result of doing something all too human—like saving a cat, for example. Indeed, Snyder calls this 'Save the Cat.' Since the anti-heroes started conquering the cinema and television screens, this may have changed a bit. I don't have to like the main character, but I do have to be able to understand his actions. Viewers or listeners should feel that the hero deserves to achieve his goal. They can see where he's coming from and think it is justified: Empathy is more important than sympathy. Heroes must be relatable. There are many ways to make that happen (Storr 2019 and Kellermann 2018); for example, listeners and viewers root for people who have been treated unfairly, who reveal a part of themselves (even one we perhaps normally like to hide), who are very brave or a role model or who are great at what they are doing (even if they are not very nice)—Don Draper in *Mad Men* and Gregory House in *House, M.D.* are just two examples. I find the idea of portraying the main character so that you can at least like something about them—right from the beginning—still very helpful for non-fictional stories (but beware: just nice can get boring very quickly). This might be an element of humour, for instance, which also has the advantage that the story acquires a lighter quality—something that is still missing far too often, particularly in journalistic products.

4. Voice the narrative sentence: Don't be afraid of the explicit (at least in this case). By the end of the first act or exposition, listeners should know what the story is about. The task or goal may be named explicitly. Ideally, it should result directly from the first or second scene. This also helps to mark the transition to the second act. In order to include all the names and facts that are crucial for the story in the first act (and no more than that!), the scriptwriter and director Aaron Sorkin suggests a useful trick. At the beginning of every story, there should be one person who represents the audience. This person is just as uninformed and has every right to ask questions. In a workplace drama, this function is often taken on by trainees or new colleagues. But the idea is also transferable to non-fictional stories. *Radiolab*, for example, often employs exactly this division of tasks between the two presenters Jad Abumrad and Robert Krulwich (at least before Krulwich retired in January 2020). One of the two usually has no idea about the story at

the beginning and is allowed to ask all the necessary questions. A clever way of transferring Sorkin's idea to real stories.

5. Plot point 1: This is where the list of revelations comes into play. Can it provide a significant, perhaps even surprising event or insight that can act as a plot point? Then use it. The plot point is also the trigger for the transition into the second act.

6. Worsening crises: Look for the hurdles the main character has to overcome on the way to his goal. Try to find scenes that illustrate these hurdles, in which we experience the main character as an actor. Now put the hurdles into order, from easy through medium to difficult, and, if possible, work through them, one after the other. The plot thickens. Sometimes this is quite challenging for documentaries and non-fictional stories because the story is supposed to be told chronologically, but the hero encounters the most difficult hurdles quite early on. Then, you have to weigh up the pros and cons: Do I keep the chronology and relate the story in a logical progression, or do I find a structure in which the conflicts come to a head? In that case, it shouldn't be too confusing, should not, for example, contain too many jumps in the temporal dimension. Most of the time, you'll probably decide to use the chronological narrative after all.

7. Moment of crisis/insight: In fictional narratives, this is the situation in which the main character realises what he or she actually needs. Often this insight is triggered by a serious crisis. For non-fictional stories, the following questions are helpful: When was the hero furthest away from his goal? When did he have least hope of reaching his goal? I try to build this moment into the second act! This also helps to get a better grip on the longest act.

8. Plot point 2: Again, the list of revelations can help to mark the transition to the third act. The number of possible plot points often gives you a good idea of how long a piece can be without losing momentum and suspense. This is especially important for plotting a series (see Sect. 3.10).

9. Climax/Special moment: It's the moment of truth: Will the hero achieve his goal or not? It is the final confrontation. If the narrative sentence describes what the story is about, then the climax determines the outcome of the story. In the documentary about Johannes Bischko, it is the outcome of the operation. If a story does not have a clear climax, then, for me, a very special moment can replace the climax. Every piece should have one.

In a radio documentary about the aviation pioneer Hugo Junkers, for example, I included the following moment: A team from different trades has reassembled an old "Ju 52" (a plane that was used, amongst other things, to transport sick people during World War II). In a commented collage, the engineer responsible describes all the work steps that were necessary to accomplish that goal. Finally, the work is done, the moment has come, the "Ju 52" should fly again. Combined with music and ambience, the engineer in charge, Harald Claasen, finally says: "So I listened to the radio where my colleague said: 'Ju 52 ready for take-off for the first time'." This moment comes approximately three quarters of the way through the story. It is the emotional climax. If there are moments when life can be portrayed in such a concentrated form, listeners often feel they are experiencing something very special—it's a larger than life moment.

10. New Balance/Conclusion/Wrap-Up: The moment of taking a deep breath and taking stock at the end of the story. The climax reverberates and we, as listeners, recognise the change. In audio narratives, these are often the final sentences that summarise the story. Here, the underlying or bigger idea can also reappear.

11. Bouncer/Cliffhanger: Is there any information, an anecdote or an event that symbolically reviews the whole story again? In a series, this is the place for the cliffhanger. Important: A teaser, such as "next week we will deal with that and that aspect of our topic," is not a cliffhanger. A cliffhanger is a closed door I really want to open. It is a specific question that I would like to have answered. In contrast to the conclusion, it is about a specific situation or an experience. The documentary about Stephen Hawking ends with a classic bouncer; after all, it is a one-part piece, not a series or serial. The end is a kind of quotation that attempts to summarise Hawking's life and work in an anecdote, to get close to him one last time and leave the listener with a smile: "Whether he thinks time travel is possible, he is often asked. He wouldn't bet on it, Hawking once wrote. For the other might have the advantage of knowing the future."

Just to reassure you: It is only in the rarest of cases that all eleven elements of the narrative plot can be found in journalistic stories. But it's all about perspective. If you don't search, you won't find these elements—or you will miss their dramatic effect. The important thing is that all these elements are based on thorough journalistic research. It is about crafting an appropriate image of reality. Or in other words: telling a true and truthful story.

The eleven elements described here are most likely to apply to a purely scenic or scenic-reflective narrative (we'll deal with the meta-plots next). It is what feels like a real story. Here, too, the question remains: What do I do if I want to transport something journalistically and I don't have the one, outstanding protagonist? Does my subject die? And, again, the answer is no, of course not. That would narrow down the view of the world too much and completely distort it (even more than it already is). Depending on the theme and approach, I can adapt the structure and still use narrative techniques. The following five structural models, which I call narrative meta-plots, help me to do this. They go further than Hollywood and classic fictional plots. They are an alternative way of helping you structure your material.

3.8   FIVE NARRATIVE METAPLOTS

Meta-structures have the great advantage that they provide orientation. They point out the important aspects of a narrative. That said, they will never or very rarely offer the ideal template for the story in front of you. In terms of detail, non-fictional narratives are simply too different. Over time, I have developed the following five meta-structures. They help me to keep the essence of a narrative in view.

The scenic narrative: the real story. With protagonist, challenges, plot points and final battle. It is the story in which, from scene to scene, we as listeners become most immersed. The Danish podcast production company *Third Ear* uses this form very successfully. For example, in the story *Ringbindsattentatet* (roughly translated as *The Ring Binder Assassination*) by Tim Hinman and Krister Moltzen (Fig. 3.6).

The scenic-reflective narrative: also a real story. With protagonist, challenges, plot points and final battle. The information needed to understand the story is woven into the scenes as usual. But between the scenes there are also longer reflective passages in which the larger ideas behind the story are debated. Here, too, you can include the background information that is important for the story. Structurally, there is thus constant movement on the ladder of abstraction (see Sect. 3.3), between specific scenes and reflective debate. Hence the name of this form. As a rough guide, I work with a 50:50 rule. I try to keep the ratio between scenes and reflection more or less equal. If the scenic parts are too short, listeners may lose touch with the story and think they are hearing an entry in an encyclopaedia. The extent to which the story carries through the reflective and informative passages also depends on how exciting the scenic plot level is, how deep, personal and witty the thoughts are

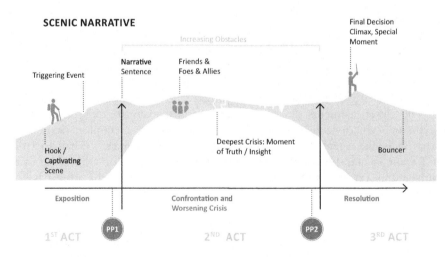

Fig. 3.6 Scenic Narrative

in the more reflective parts (Sarah Koenig gets away with very long passages because they are great) and on the strength of the minor cliffhangers. Productions such as the first season of *Serial*, *The Hitchhiker* or *The Nobody Zone* (a collaboration between *Third Ear* and Irish public radio *RTÉ*) are designed in this way (Fig. 3.7).

The explanatory or analytical narrative: Let us imagine that you want to approach a complex phenomenon. A topic rather than a story. That doesn't mean you have to dispense with narrative techniques and structures. The biggest problem with this kind of narration is that there is not one single protagonist whose challenge leads us through the story. Nevertheless, for a thrilling story, you need the classic elements like the triggering event, plot points, scenes etc., just as in the banana example (see Sect. 2.6). The narrative sentence was: Bananas from Colombia (A, the bananas take the place of the protagonist) should reach Europe perfectly ripe (B, the goal) because that will ensure the best price (C, the reasoning takes the place of the motivation), but to make that happen many processes have to interlock perfectly (D, the obstacles which pave the path to the goal).

This is an explanatory narrative. The big challenge here is how to glue the listener to the story. This, too, must be done via a strong introductory scene from which your leading question arises directly. In this case, the question would be: How do bananas get from South America to Europe? This question should arise from a scene which includes people who invite some kind of identification or relation-building. Furthermore, you need people like this (and others, too) at every stage of the story. In the banana story, these could be employees of plantations, logistics or shipping companies, food market or

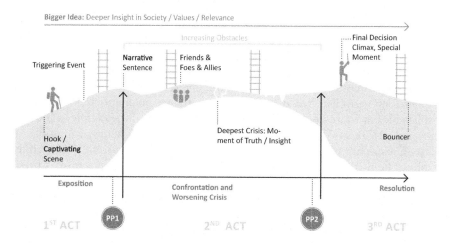

Fig. 3.7   Scenic-Reflective Narrative

dock workers. You don't need a protagonist who leads the way through the entire story, but you do need many individual characters who solve problems at the respective stages—ideally, they are all capable of sparking empathy. That's a big ask!

An example of an outstanding explanatory narrative is the *Invisibilia* episode, 'The Culture Inside,' which addresses the following question (NPR 2017): "Is there a part of ourselves that we don't acknowledge, that we don't even have access to and that might make us ashamed if we encountered it?" Specifically, the question is how strongly racism is embedded in each of us and what we can do about it. It is an extremely multifaceted and complex issue. The great challenge is to combine the various content aspects and make them tangible at the same time. The plot of the narrative therefore always involves strong scenes. The story begins in a hospital with a woman who has had an operation for epilepsy. Suddenly, she can no longer control one hand. The hand develops a life of its own. This scene is used as a kind of analogy to develop the central question of the piece: Is there an unconscious part of us that we don't recognise and accept? This builds a bridge to the topic of racism. Again and again, the story manages to open up astonishing and exciting scenes, in the middle of the story, for example, about half an hour in: It's all about what is known as "implicit bias," the kind of bias or prejudice that we're not aware of. The previous scene throws up the question as to what we as human beings can do to fight this bias. How do we get rid of our bias? The story then jumps to a new scene. In it, we hear a woman apparently greeting a group of people. It sounds like a conference, seminar or group meeting. It is soon revealed that it is the weekly meeting of a group called "Racists Anonymous," a support group consisting of people who want to confront their prejudices. And, of course, we as listeners are enthralled because we want to know who these people are. The story constantly keeps changing levels: scene and reflection. And this change is not arbitrary, but logical. One scene leads to a question that is debated. This debate leads to a new question or a new phenomenon and thus to a new scene. And so on and so forth. In this way, an explanatory or analytical narrative can emerge—great, but also complex and challenging dramaturgy (Fig. 3.8).

The argumentative narrative: Structurally, it is very closely related to the explanatory narrative. But it is not about a theme or phenomenon which is explained, but more about a thesis that is explored. If, for example, a football club repeatedly wins the national championship (purely fictional example, at least in Germany), there will be reasons for it. As a reporter, I can either explore them (then it's more of an analytical narrative) or I can posit a thesis and play it through (then it's more of an argumentative narrative). It is a different perspective on a story. If topics are addressed for the first time or are relatively new, then an explanatory narrative is more appropriate; if topics have been on the market for some time, an argumentative narrative may be more suitable. But that also depends a lot on the publication and the audience.

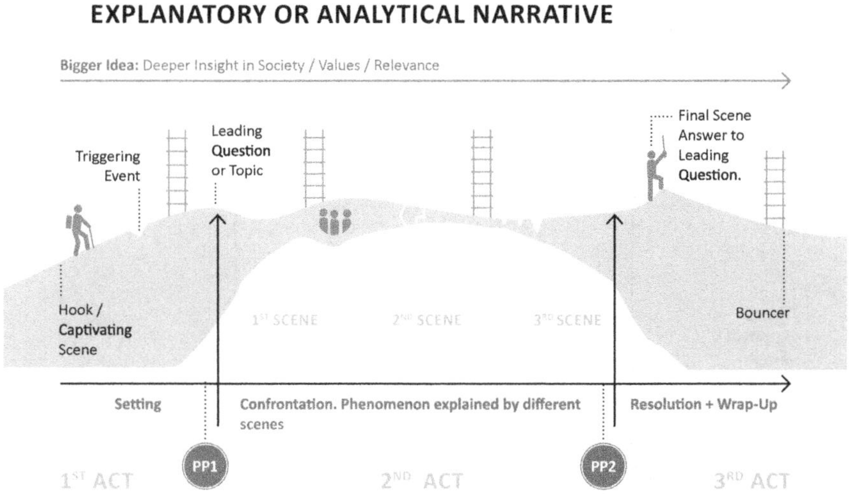

EXPLANATORY OR ANALYTICAL NARRATIVE

Fig. 3.8 Explanatory Narrative

Argumentative narratives struggle with the same challenges as explanatory narratives. The great suspense arc (the leading thesis) must be anchored in the listener's mind—preferably as the result of a strong introductory scene. Afterwards, for each new argument, scenes are needed that can be experienced tangibly. Stories in the German news magazine *Der Spiegel* often work in this way. At the beginning, a thesis is proposed, which is then substantiated—by debates and scenes. A major problem for such types of narrative is often the narrative flow. At the beginning of a new section, for example, it is very tempting to simply start from scratch somewhere else in terms of content. Unfortunately, this breaks the narrative flow. This is another reason why plot planning is important. As a meta-structure, there are many similarities between explanatory and argumentative narratives (Fig. 3.9).

The narrative anecdote: the shortened, scenic or scenic-reflective narrative. The one-act piece that uses an event to illustrate or narrate a phenomenon. Often these stories don't develop the depth of major narratives; there is not quite as much at stake, for example. But they are everyday stories that nevertheless draw attention to an important phenomenon or problem. As a listener, you often come away feeling the reporter has observed something really well in order to give a deeper insight into society by means of an everyday event or experience. In this respect, the bigger idea is more likely to be conveyed in the subtext. Structurally, the narrative anecdote often consists of just one act. The shorter pieces in *This American Life* frequently consist of this kind of narrative anecdote. "Mom Jokes" (*This American Life*, 2016) is a delightful story about a woman who can't stop laughing when she tries to tell her own joke. She herself finds it so funny that she is unable to tell it all. So, her daughter's friend asks her to tell the joke on stage. Another example: my colleague

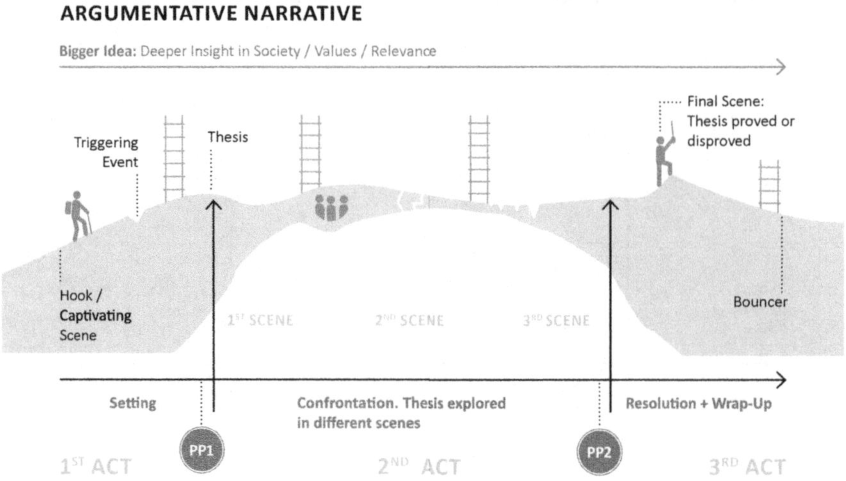

ARGUMENTATIVE NARRATIVE

Bigger Idea: Deeper Insight in Society / Values / Relevance

Fig. 3.9   Argumentative Narrative

Stephan Beuting once lent his tent to construction workers (Deutschlandfunk Nova 2015). The six of them were sharing a two-person tent and Stephan wanted to help. What then happened, he relates in a story entitled *My tent is gone*. It revolves around helpfulness and trust in everyday life and exemplifies how Stephan deals with his inner conflict: On the one hand, he wants to help, and on the other, he has to have the confidence to lend an object that is personally important to him. Both stories are fine narrative anecdotes, which focus on one central event (Fig. 3.10).

3.9   STORYTELLING FOR SHORT REPORTS AND REPORTER INTERVIEWS

Meta-structures and narrative techniques should help reporters and producers to focus and create suspense in their stories. One of the many great things about them is that they are appropriate not only for longer documentaries and stories, but also for shorter reports, presenter reads or two ways on air. This is especially true for current news reporting. Under time pressure, every reporter is dependent on many coincidences and pragmatic solutions. That's why no one can wait until they have everything to build a perfect, dense story. But even in shorter reports, editors and reporters often want too much (illustrative examples, entertaining survey, reaction level, outlook, service—and all this in 2:30 minutes, including the host's part, of course). That's why focusing is useful even when creating shorter pieces. I found it helpful to distinguish between three different types of shorter stories:

NARRATIVE ANECDOTE

Fig. 3.10 Narrative Anecdote

- Mapping an event. This includes all classic news situations for current affairs. Something has happened somewhere, and a reporter maps the event. The retelling of the event up to the present time can be the central theme. The greatest difficulty is that the host or the reporter's first few sentences usually summarise the result. Why should I bother to listen to the rest then? Do not, therefore, offer all the information immediately. It can help to discuss this explicitly with editors, hosts and colleagues beforehand, because this kind of narration breaks with usual habits. If the piece or conversation also explains what the event means, a short form of an explanatory narrative is possible.
- Executing a task. This narrative form is very close to a scenic narrative. A real protagonist takes on a challenge. The story tells how he does it and whether he succeeds. But beware: A baker who has been baking bread rolls for 30 years is rarely a suitable protagonist for a piece about the profession of baking (for protagonists see Sect. 4.1). Perhaps he is suitable as a protagonist in another story; let's assume he wants to pass on his business to the next generation but cannot find a successor. Then, he will face a real challenge.
- Exploring a thesis. This is the short form of an argumentative narrative. For example, the report or talk explores the thesis: City X is particularly bicycle-unfriendly.

Often, the reason why short contributions or discussions with colleagues seem boring is because they have not been sufficiently agreed upon beforehand. The assignment might be to do something about the situation of cyclists in our city. This makes the work process more difficult for everyone involved, even when discussing the script or product later. In addition, of course, not all story ideas can be implemented in every situation. The time pressure is much too great for that. But there are a few aspects and questions that help to add narrative value even to short current affairs stories. The following questions help to add that value:

- Can I map a real process? Process here means something like a task, obstacle or goal that adds up to change. The best way to do this is to tell these kinds of story through people. If this is not possible: Do I at least have a clear focus? Have I established my guiding question, thesis or task and am I working through them? In this way, even short pieces get a better structure.
- Can I experience a scene? A scene means more than just an example. A scene consists of an intention and obstacles, i.e. a mini story (see also Chapter 6). Maybe, it is suitable for the introduction.
- Do I have not only talking heads and experts, but scenic tape or even real dialogue? Dialogue is the linguistic means of resolving conflicts. This is why dialogue on tape can be so powerful (see Sect. 6.5). Dialogue can also take place between an expert and the reporter—if it makes sense for the story. If it is not a scene or dialogue on tape, try to record genuine or special moments. They normally confer another tone on the whole piece. Such sounds are especially good for the introduction. They can, for example, already be incorporated into the host's part.
- Is there a real protagonist? A protagonist is more than an illustrative example. He needs a real challenge. What often helps is a 'Save the Cat'-moment: It makes people seem much more approachable.
- Is there any surprising information? Listeners can often guess right at the beginning of the report how it will run and end. Unfortunately, this is boring. A remedy for this is to introduce information that is unexpected. If reporters use it in a targeted fashion, it generates momentum. If you employ it at the end of your piece, you ensure that the story is more memorable and ends on a punch line.
- Is my piece heading for a genuine ending? Is there anything at stake if the task is not completed or the thesis proves to be false? Often, even shorter current affairs reports or conversations with reporters gradually peter out. After the usual topic blocks covering the actual event, reaction level (often of different political parties) and service for the listeners, there is the classic outlook ('remains to be seen')—that too is pretty boring! But if you establish a task or thesis at the beginning of the piece, you must pick it up again at the end: Has the task been completed? Is the thesis correct? Thus, even short contributions get a real ending. Alternatively: intentionally hold back a sound, information, a minor revelation or scene as a bouncer and put it at the end.

- Does the story have a relevance beyond the mere event? If a deeper problem or pattern is revealed, make it a theme. This gives the story more relevance and depth.

In addition, it also helps to experiment with perspective and form in current affairs pieces: report, poll/vox pop, solo, two ways with or without sound bites and everything in between. But don't play for the sake of playing. The form must serve the story. It doesn't usually work the other way around and creates more confusion than anything else. Remember, too, that the host's introduction is an elementary part of the story. If it anticipates all the results, the story will hardly be able to develop tension. A good introduction does not anticipate any results, but ends, for example, on the triggering event or ignition point. It works more like this: "In the centre of Dortmund, a beggar has fainted. Passers-by have called an ambulance. But the ambulance hasn't taken the beggar away." And then the actual report begins, or the first question follows. The triggering event often functions as a cliffhanger or hook in the introduction.

To have structures under control means you can freely develop your own creativity. There is one very special structural challenge left here, the multi-part form. Everything I have mentioned so far applies to it, as well. And even more so. That's why it's worth taking a look at what has given storytelling a new dynamic: serials.

3.10   SERIALS: NEXT TIME…

There are certain sentences that authors usually don't like hearing editors say. The editor of the WDR documentary series *The Hitchhiker*, Leslie Rosin, contacted us during the broadcast of the series and said, "Listeners have called the station's hotline and complained about *The Hitchhiker*." "Really?" "They weren't happy about having to wait another week for the next episode!" Whew! These moments are very rare. That's why we enjoyed it so much.

Ideally, an audio serial should engender exactly this feeling in listeners: "I really want to hear the next episode now. I don't want to leave the story universe." I myself joined the first season of *Serial*, for example, sometime around November 2014, when it was first broadcast. That meant I could listen to the first episodes all at once and then had to wait. It was a mixture of torture and anticipation. Remarkably, *Serial* was not fully structured and plotted beforehand. "That structure wasn't completely by design," says Sarah Koenig (Koenig and Snyder 2017, 77). "We plotted out a bunch of episodes, anywhere between, I don't know, eight or nine?" In the end, there were twelve episodes. "We really, truly did not know where we were going to end up until we got there." It was precisely this feeling that also captivated many who listened to *Serial* at the time of its first broadcast: What else would Sarah and her team find out in just one week? In this context, co-producer Julie Snyder sums up a key secret of success that also applies to audio series: "Well, I just think that serialised storytelling is very popular because people like consuming stories in this way. You know, coming back to the same characters, with an intimacy and a deeper understanding. And more nuances and contradictions, that kind of stuff" (Koenig and Snyder 2017, 78). People love to immerse themselves in stories and return to the story's (sound) universe. The really big bonus of such stories is that they can reach and touch listeners particularly deeply. If listeners have followed several parts of a story, they are bound to care about the characters. The chance of leaving an emotional impression is thus greater than in one-part narratives. Series are especially successful when they provide the listener with answers to very personal questions in addition to a thrilling story. For example, *Serial* touches on our sense of justice, and *The Hitchhiker* triggered one question in listeners right from the start: How would I have behaved towards Heinrich, would I have taken him with me, as well?

It is possible that at a certain age one likes to hear, read or watch certain stories. Some narratives are also particularly successful and gain momentum because they answer an urgent social question. The American podcast *More Perfect* is not a serial, but a series. It deals with basic questions of justice and law at a time when many Americans are questioning exactly that. Especially for multi-part formats, to move people like that and inform them at the same time is both an opportunity and a special mark of quality. Formally, it is expedient to differentiate between three formats:

- Serials. The main feature: Basically, one plot is pursued and developed. This includes fictional audio productions like *Neverwhere*. More in this category are also productions like *The Hitchhiker*, *S-Town*, *The Nobody Zone* and *Serial*. Formally, *Serial* is a bit on the brink, so to speak. The episodes are clearly thematically oriented (which actually speaks for a series)—but the main question is always the same: Is Adnan guilty? Furthermore, reference is made to previous insights. If the listener has to go back to the beginning to listen from the start, then it's more like a serial.
- Series. The main feature: A core theme, divided into several sub-themes or facets. The public radio station WDR 5 has a programme called *Tiefen-blick* (roughly translated as 'in-depth view'). It usually broadcasts series, often in three or four parts (30 minutes each) on broader topics like waste, female adventurers or yoga. Each episode stands alone and inten-sively explores one facet of the topic. As a listener, I don't necessarily have to start with the first episode.
- Serialised series. The main feature: Each episode focuses more strongly on a specific aspect. The episodes do not explicitly continue the big main plot. Nevertheless, they always revisit the core questions. It's a bit of an in-between format that includes German productions such as *The talented Mr Vossen*, *Who killed Burak?* or *Bilals path to terror*. From television, we are familiar with this format: classic crime thrillers work like this, be it

the German *Tatort* or British *Vera*. Every case is new, but the character development continuous.

The format says nothing about quality. One is no better or worse than the other—and the boundaries or transitions are fluid. A production like *S-Town* is probably harder to categorise (probably closer to a serial than a series as it makes sense to listen to all parts in order). Series and serialised series are conceived more journalistically/thematically. They tend to adopt the form: episode one—event/introduction; episode two—reactions; episode three—genesis. Real-life series pursue a main plot: Is Adnan innocent? Can hitchhiker Heinrich get justice? The strongest dramaturgical force, the addiction factor, is probably the real series—it draws the listener deeper and deeper into a story. Yet such a narrative must contain several characteristics in order to unfold this power:

- A unique (sound) universe. The series immerses listeners in a world to which they otherwise have no access. This experience is also carried by the sound. The podcast *S-Town*, for example, achieves this very convincingly. Even the first few minutes of the story tell us as listeners on all levels (language, music, sound bites) that the world we are about to enter is a bit weird or remote.
- Every episode is a story. Referring to *Serial*, Sarah Koenig puts it this way (2017, 79): "And then, like with any single radio story, it was just building an internal arc, an internal narrative for each episode." Each episode includes a narrative arc with a goal, and at the end each episode, a cliffhanger and a new question for the next episode arise logically. Until finally, the last episode also answers the very big question of the whole serial. To make this clear: Every episode therefore builds up suspense, with an inciting incident, plot points, complications and final confrontation (see below for an excerpt from the storyboard of *The Hitchhiker*). Each episode gives us an insight into a new part of the cosmos that was not apparent before. It is like the next layer of an onion. The number of layered insights also gives you an indication of how many episodes might be appropriate for a serial.
- One single protagonist is (probably) not enough. This does not mean that you as a writer need a second or third protagonist. But it does mean that a serial requires a complex network of characters: opponents, love interest, friends and shape-shifters (i.e. people who are sometimes friends and sometimes enemies or hard to pin down). These characters must interact with the protagonist, and the relationships must develop. That's how subplots are crafted that run alongside the main plot. The result is a complex story which spans several episodes. If you work with more than one protagonist, make sure each protagonist brings different qualities to the challenge (think of Harry, Ron and Hermione in *Harry Potter*).

- The sound conveys the story. If you are doing a complex series in several episodes, you need a sonic design that fits the story. You may or may not like the piano music in *Serial*, but it is a signature sound element that becomes instantly recognisable. One of the most elaborate musical sound designs in recent years was created by the podcast *S-Town*. The soundtrack was especially composed for it by Daniel Hart. The title song "Bibb County" defines the sound for the series with its partly playful, partly dissonant strings. Both sound elements—piano on *Serial* and strings on *S-Town*—are also used as the opener of each show. It is the gateway, the point of re-entry into the serial, which guides the listeners from their world into the world of the story. The opener is an acoustic narrative promise of what the character of the serial will be.

The design of the re-entries will always be a compromise—for different listening situations. It should provide enough orientation for listeners who, for example, follow the first broadcast week after week (as in *Serial* or *The Hitchhiker*). At the same time, it should not bore listeners who only listen to the series when all parts have been released. Generally, this will be most of the listeners in total. The rule of thumb is, therefore: Don't bore your binge-listeners. The podcast *S-Town* did not need to compromise because all the parts were published at once. Taking the example of *The Hitchhiker*, we always built the entry or re-opener around four elements:

- First: Previously on *The Hitchhiker*…
- Second: Transition to the first scene of each episode with an emphasis or minor cliffhanger.
- Third: Announcement of the serial and the respective episode.
- Fourth: Continuation of the first scene.

All four elements together never took more than 90s in order to get back into the story quickly. We always redesigned the first element (previously on *The Hitchhiker*…) to hit squarely on the central conflict of each episode. Within these collages, we also added elements that already connect with the first scene, such as the sound of a lighter or a telephone in the sound mix, often very subtle (for sound design, see also Chapter 8).

So how do you find the best form for a serial? How many parts are appropriate? How long are the individual episodes? At what point can I make all these decisions? A few aspects and questions always help me to find the answers:

- Ask yourself into how many smaller arcs the large narrative arc can be broken down? Be strict about this. Even the smaller arcs of tension must result in real stories; otherwise, the story will very quickly lose its momentum and power. The number of smaller arcs helps you decide on the number of episodes.

- Do not overdo it with the number of episodes. Rather a few good episodes than a lot of mediocre ones. Longer and more is not better.
- Find the scenes and plot points for the narrative arcs. The number of plot points shows you approximately the number of acts (two plot points = three acts etc.). The acts in turn need scenes. For example, the second act in a three-act story should have one scene per obstacle.
- Think from the end. It's an old trick but it's still helpful. If you can identify a situation in each episode that the episode is heading towards, there is a lot to be gained dramatically. This scene should answer the leading question or solve the main conflict in the episode and, at the same time, raise a new question.
- Identify cliffhangers. Ideally, at the end of each episode, you will have a real, strong cliffhanger that will draw listeners into the next episode. In a natural way. Artificially constructed cliffhangers feel empty and pompous. Remember: A cliffhanger is a specific question that listeners ask themselves, not a topic cue.
- Design the narrative attitude. A serial needs a narrative attitude (see Chapter 7). An omniscient, detached presenter is not a promising choice. The narrator is the most important figure next to the protagonist (if not identical). He or she guides listeners through the story and binds them to it by strength of personality.

It is very difficult to express all this in exact minutes, lengths, number of episodes and the like, assuming that you have a free hand in the first place and are not bound by the length of a specific broadcast slot. But the following formula is a very, very rough guideline: Number of narrative arcs = number of episodes. Number of plot points = number of acts in each episode. Number of scenes in the acts (if you calculate an average length of four to five minutes per scene) = length of the episode (and add some time for the reflective parts as well). Provided that, of course, everything fits together: the small arcs with the big arc, the plot points with the arcs, the scenes with the acts. Taken together, this indicates two essential aspects for the development of non-fictional serials:

- You need to plan. The more, the better. Work in progress is a very difficult undertaking for serials. The first season of *Serial* was an exception, and even they struggled with that. It worked because Sarah Koenig was such a strong, sympathetic narrator that people stayed with her, wanting to know what she would discover in just one week (which demonstrates again that Sarah Koenig is the protagonist). The potential problems of this approach can be witnessed, for example, in the second season of *Serial*. Basically, without a storyboard, there is no serial. If you have a storyboard, responsibilities can be clearly allocated even within a team of authors. Otherwise, you can hardly sort out who is responsible for which scenes, contents, sections and the associated sound bites. You need to manage your material.

- The more detailed the complete storyboard, the better. The clearer you are about the course of the entire story ahead, the better you can employ suspense techniques—for example, hinting early on at something you want to use later. If you don't know whether you will need a detail, an info or an item, don't introduce it or hint at it. This also means that, first of all, you need narrative sentences for the entire serial as well as each episode. This is the goal of your detailed research and fieldwork. Once these are almost complete, the final storyboard is created. Only then does the script work begin (on the narrative workflow see also Sect. 10.2).

To illustrate this with an example, here is an excerpt from the storyboard of *The Hitchhiker* (first two episodes). The storyboard illustrates the course of the story, including scenes as well as the essential dramaturgical elements of the plot. Here, the storyboard of *The Hitchhiker* has been reduced to the essential aspects and I have removed comments that would probably only mean something to us as authors:

Episode length approx. *30 minutes*	*1: Last exit Zurich*	*2: Closed institution*
Central conflict/key question	Do we find Heinrich?	Was Heinrich really in a psychiatric ward for the young, and experienced what he claims?
Opener/Previously on...	Scene: Stephan meets Heinrich at the petrol station (establishing leitmotifs: existentiality/help/truth vs lies). Ends on question: Then you have to help, don't you?	Guiding principles: Suicidal intent/truth vs lie/moral conflict for us Action ends on: We find Heinrich
Act 1 Developing a key question	Stephan's and Sven's encounters with Heinrich as a parallel montage of real and reconstructed scenes (leitmotifs: psychiatric ward/help/truth vs lie)	Heinrich tells his story (reconstructed scenes as far as possible). From his narratives, the question arises: What is actually true and can be proven?
Plot Point 1	Stephan & Sven realise they have met the same hitchhiker, a year apart. Leads to decision to search for him	Stephan & Sven decide they want to prove that Heinrich was in a psychiatric ward. And show that his reports are true (as far as this can be proven)

(continued)

(continued)

Episode length approx. 30 minutes	1: Last exit Zurich	2: Closed institution
Act 2 Obstacles in answering the key question	Obstacles and places to search, e.g. authorities (telephone scene), online, petrol station (visiting scene), prison, Dignitas, social aid organisation, etc. Enquiries with the authorities occur at several stages. This lead finally produces results	Obstacles and places in the search for evidence: e.g. search for contemporary witnesses and responsible persons, visit to researchers (scene in archive), request for files, shooting festival (as far as possible)
Plot Point 2	Breakthrough. Heinrich is alive and calling back. Scene: Heinrich calls Sven => arrange meeting	Breakthrough: Message from archive => they have a file and we can see it
Act 3 Answer the key question	Scene: Stephan and Sven drive to meeting point. Summary, expectations, concerns	Scene: Inspection of files in the archive of the psychiatric ward
Cliffhanger Develop new question	Scene: Arrival at meeting point. Appearance of Heinrich: There you are! Cliffhanger: We want to hear his story, next time…	Date of admission in file later than expected => Why did Heinrich come to the psychiatric ward in the first place? Third episode follows Heinrich's family history

The overview shows the plot design and we worked our way along it. The plot draft doesn't show when we introduced which characters or made hints. A detailed storyboard should contain both! I left that out here for the sake of clarity. The plot draft should be designed in such a way that you always know what to do—and where the story is going. This principle can be used as a guideline for how detailed the plot draft or storyboard is. What the storyboard also illustrates is the action. It shows at which points which scenes appear, when we as reporters make which decisions, and which actions result from them. This ensures that the story moves forward.

There are two ways of approaching dramatic stories: via the plot or via the central characters. Characters carry the plot. They are a central (one could argue the crucial) component of stories. The next chapter belongs to them.

NOTES

1. You can find the whole manuscript here: https://genius.com/Serial-podcast-episode-1-the-alibi-annotated.
2. Disclaimer: I have been working for this programme since 2004.
3. Traditional Chinese Medicine.
4. Jean Erdman died 4 May 2020 at the age of 104.

Bibliography

Aristotle. 2013. *Poetics*. Oxford: Oxford University Press.

Beuting, Stephan. *'Mein Zelt ist weg'*. Deutschlandfunk Nova. Accessed 14 April 142020. https://www.deutschlandfunknova.de/beitrag/hilfsbereitschaft-entt%C3%A4uschtes-vertrauen.

Campbell, Joseph. 1949. *The Hero with a Thousand Faces*. New York: Pantheon Books.

Field, Syd. 1979. *Screenplay. The Foundations of Screenwriting*. New York: Dell Publishing.

Genius. n.d. 'Episode 1: The Alibi. Serial Podcast'. Accessed 14 April 2020. https://genius.com/Serial-podcast-episode-1-the-alibi-annotated.

Gimlet Media. 2016. 'Homecoming'. Accessed 14 April 2020. https://gimletmedia.com/shows/homecoming.

Glass, Ira. 2017. Harnessing Luck as an Industrial Product. In *Reality Radio*, ed. John Biewen and Alexa Dilworth, 2nd ed., 64–76. Durham: The University of North Carolina Press.

Hart, Jack. 2011. *Story Craft*. Chicago: The University of Chicago Press.

Invisibilia. 2017. *The Culture Inside*. Accessed 14 April 2020. https://www.npr.org/programs/invisibilia/532950995/the-culture-inside.

Iglesias, Karl. 2005. *Writing for Emotional Impact*. Livermore: Wing Span Press.

Kellermann, Ron. 2018. *Das Storytelling Handbuch*. Zürich: Midas Management Verlag.

Koenig, Sarah, and Julie Snyder. 2017. One Story, Week by Week. An Interview with Sarah Koenig and Julie Snyder by John Biewen. In *Reality Radio*, ed. John Biewen and Alexa Dilworth, 2nd ed., 77–89. Durham: The University of North Carolina Press.

McKee, Robert. 1997. *Story. Substance, Structure, Style, and the Principles of Screenwriting*. New York: HarperCollins.

Preger, Sven. 2015. Hugo Junkers, Flugzeugingenieur. Accessed 20 December 2020. https://www1.wdr.de/mediathek/audio/zeitzeichen/audio-hugo-junkers-flugzeugingenieur-todestag–100.html.

Preger, Sven. 2017a. Interkontinentalflug mit Solarflugzeug endet. Accessed 20 December 2020. https://www1.wdr.de/radio/wdr5/sendungen/zeitzeichen/solar-flugzeug-100.html.

Preger, Sven. 2017b. Johannes Bischko, Pionier der Akupunktur. Accessed 20 December 2020. https://www1.wdr.de/mediathek/audio/zeitzeichen/audio-johannes-bischko-pionier-der-akupunktur-geburtstag–102.html.

Preger, Sven. 2017c. Stephen Hawking, englischer Physiker. Accessed 20 December 2020. https://www1.wdr.de/mediathek/audio/zeitzeichen/audio-stephen-hawking-englischer-physiker-geburtstag–100.html.

Radcliffe, Damian. 2017. *Short-Form Audio Storytelling: 10 Format Ideas*. Accessed 14 April 2020. https://medium.com/audio-storytelling-winter-2017/short-form-audio-storytelling-10-format-ideas-c593187351d6.

Serial. 2014. Season One. Accessed 14 April 2020. https://serialpodcast.org/season-one.

Snyder, Blake. 2005. *Save the Cat. The Last Book on Screenwriting That You'll Ever Need*. Studio City: Michael Wiese Productions.

Storr, Will. 2019. *The Science of Storytelling*. London: William Collins.

S-Town. 2017. Accessed 20 December 2020. https://stownpodcast.org/.

The Nobody Zone. 2020. Accessed 20 December 2020. https://www.rte.ie/eile/podcasts/2020/0211/1114553-the-nobody-zone/.

Third Ear. Accessed 20 December 2020. https://thirdear.dk/.

This American Life. 2016. Something Only I Can See. Mom Jokes. Accessed 20 December 2020. https://www.thisamericanlife.org/577/something-only-i-can-see/act-two-0.

Tolkien, J.R.R. 1991. *The Lord of the Rings*. London: HarperCollins.

Truby, John. 2007. *The Anatomy of Story*. New York: Farrar, Straus and Giroux.

Vogler, Christopher. 1998. *The Writer's Journey*. Studio City: Michael Wiese Productions.

WDR 5. n.d. Tiefenblick – Hintergrund in Serie. Accessed 14 April 2020. https://www1.wdr.de/radio/wdr5/sendungen/tiefenblick/index.html.

Wikipedia. 2020a. Plot Point (German). Accessed 20 December 2020. https://de.wikipedia.org/wiki/Plot_Point.

Wikipedia. 2020b. Plot Point (English). Accessed 20 December 2020. https://en.wikipedia.org/wiki/Plot_point.

CHAPTER 4

Character Development: The Actor Drives the Story

4.1   THE PROTAGONIST: ACTIVE, FOCUSED AND FLAWED

Daniel's life changes very early on. He is only about a year old when both of his eyes are removed. The diagnosis: retinoblastoma, a malignant tumour in the retina. He has eye cancer. When we hear about such a fate, it immediately sets a film running in many of our minds. Name, for example, three things that Daniel will probably never be able to do in his life. Perhaps they include watching a sunrise, admiring famous paintings and riding a bike. But that's exactly what he can do—at least the latter. And that is not because Daniel was cured. He is still blind today. But already when he is still a boy, he teaches himself to ride a bike. By clicking his tongue and listening to the echo. Experts call that human echolocation. Daniel's story is told by the two reporters Lulu Miller and Alix Spiegel in 'How to become Batman,' an episode in the first season of their podcast *Invisibilia* in 2015.[1] Daniel Kish is a good example of a protagonist because he incorporates the essential characteristics that are important for a main character in a story:

1. **Active**. Those who do nothing cannot advance a story. Nothing happens. Neither tension nor development is possible. The result: The story seems static and quickly becomes boring. This is still a big problem in many long journalistic stories or documentaries today. There is just not enough happening in them. Simply collecting a load of facts and presenting them comprehensibly does not make a story—this only captivates listeners for a while. I cannot emphasise this enough: The hero must be active. Daniel Kish, for example, teaches himself to ride a bike as a boy—of course, he doesn't manage without incident. But he gets up again and again and keeps trying until he has mastered it. He is active!

© The Author(s), under exclusive license to Springer Nature
Switzerland AG 2021
S. Preger, *Storytelling in Radio and Podcasts*,
https://doi.org/10.1007/978-3-030-73130-4_4

Every now and then, you read or hear about the passive hero. What is meant by this is that while the active hero brings about change, the passive hero fights to maintain the status quo. He actively defends himself against external forces, for example social change or technical progress. The passive hero is not <u>for</u> something, but against change. Those in power who run the risk of losing their position are often passive heroes (whereby the word hero is used in purely dramaturgical terms here!).

2. **Focused**. We experience the hero as an actor pursuing a goal. This character is not simply described. Rather, we experience how he deals with situations, how he behaves and solves problems. In this way, we as listeners get a real impression of the hero's character—we get to know him or her as a person. After all, actions reveal character. With Daniel Kish, for example, we experience key situations along his path. We become close. How he overcomes all the obstacles on the way to his goal shows what kind of person he is.

3. **Flawed**. How is the hero supposed to grow if he is already perfect? A weakness in the hero's character is essential. This might mean accepting a situation that cannot be changed. Daniel Kish must accept his blindness. But he doesn't let this dictate his life. He wants to ride a bike and finally gets there. This development is even more satisfying for listeners because Daniel is not perfect at the outset.

Terms are often confused: protagonist, hero, main character, central figure. I have also used various terms so far. There are two reasons for this vocabulary-mix. First, many keywords are used simultaneously in everyday editorial work—without a clear distinction. Many newsrooms ask their reporters to include at least one protagonist in every piece. Often, even ordinary everyday people, experts, perpetrators or victims are called protagonists. This is not precise and therefore not very helpful. A restaurant owner whose premises are flooded by a river is first of all a victim, not a protagonist (of course, this is no reflection on the suffering he has experienced). If he has fought against the flood (piling up sandbags, securing valuable items, saving himself and others) or is now fighting the insurance company for compensation (by making a claim, maybe even going to court), he becomes a protagonist. It may seem a bit subtle, but this distinction makes a big difference because it sharpens our view of what story we want to tell and from which perspective.

Second, some terms are rejected outright in other newsrooms or by certain editors, along the lines of "We don't want a protagonist in every single piece, it gets boring. I must be allowed to explain the difference between private and statutory health insurance for 30 minutes without constantly letting ordinary people or victims have their say." This quotation is of course fictitious, but it indicates the problem: certain words come up against a brick wall for a variety of reasons. For example, as soon as some editor says "protagonist," another one replies, "We don't want or need one." It is therefore crucial to define what these terms mean.

The word 'protagonist' is borrowed from ancient Greek and actually means the main or first actor. The idea originates in Greek drama (where else?!). The first actor (on stage) was the main character. There are two important messages in this designation: One, the protagonist is active, he acts, and two, he plays the central role in the story—no surprise so far, I guess. Taking it a little further, there is perhaps another aspect to the term. If the protagonist is acting first, then this could also refer to an action that this person has never done before, which is really new for her or him. In this sense, the action must be a real challenge. Perhaps the restaurant owner has never sued his insurance company before or launched judicial proceedings? This means that even if someone is actively involved in something, if these actions are part of their normal everyday life, they are not yet a protagonist. A baker who has been baking bread for 40 years and does so on the morning a reporter is present, is an example, not a protagonist. Only when the plot contains something new do we speak of a real protagonist. We have already encountered this idea several times in dramaturgical structural models when we were considering the protagonist's developmental arc: only when there is a real challenge is development likely or even possible. For the mythologist, Joseph Campbell, development and change are two of the hero's most important characteristics. The means to achieve development and change are the journey.

The hero in this sense is someone who accomplishes an extraordinary deed or goes on a journey. Here, again, we find the two characteristics 'active' and 'real challenge.' Moreover, this understanding is close to our everyday understanding. In my experience, terms like 'protagonist' or 'hero' are often rejected for real stories for two reasons: One, the fear of exaggerated, i.e. inappropriate dramatisation. Second, the fear that the chosen character will not live up to the standard thus set. After all, both terms come from the world of fictional stories. Both concerns are justified but should not tempt us to be satisfied with less. If the idea of a hero helps to tell fictional stories, then we can learn something from it for real stories.

Regardless of whether one speaks of a protagonist, hero, main character or central figure—the person described should ideally have four characteristics: They are pursuing a specific goal. They are active. They are performing actions for the first time or in a new way. And they are flawed, not perfect. Real stories should make all four characteristics visible. How to do this? Read on!

4.2   STAGING CHARACTERS, NOT PEOPLE

This idea from the world of fictional stories opens up a completely new way of dealing with real people. Aaron Sorkin sums it up in his online masterclass: "The properties of characters and the properties of people have very little to do with each other" (Sorkin 2016). The idea behind it is that a person's character is revealed by the actions and problem-solving strategies adopted to achieve a goal. The characteristics that become visible in these situations define the character; conflicts therefore reveal character. Sorkin's view is an ideal complement to the narrative sentence. Let's recall that the obstacles are a central element of the narrative sentence. And the way someone overcomes these obstacles shows character. The greater the conflict to be faced, the clearer the character becomes. Fictional characters like Daenarys Targaryen (mother of dragons) from *Game of Thrones* show their true being especially under pressure. If Daenarys can only maintain her power by the most extreme means, she doesn't shy away from that.

Transferred to real stories, there is one key message here: It is important to show someone in the situations in which they encounter obstacles because that is where people will show their true face. In conflicts, we as human beings are confronted with our inner values, convictions and moral views. Is it acceptable, for instance, to lie to people in order to achieve your goal? How far would you go? All these questions are answered in conflict situations, through the behaviour of characters. An example: My colleague Stephan Beuting and I both independently met 'Hitchhiker' Heinrich in a similar situation. He approached us both at the same petrol station. He did so in a forceful way; he literally pestered us both with his story and challenged us. How do we react? Both of us are actually on our way somewhere else. But we both help, although in different ways. Stephan gives him money and even interviews him briefly (we will be able to use the recordings he did with his smartphone later on to shape the beginning of the story). I, on the other hand, take Heinrich with me and put him on a train to his alleged destination (and pay his train fare). The scenes clearly reveal a part of our character better than any description could. What this example also shows is that places help to tell stories. As reporters, we often visit places again with central characters to talk about certain topics or memories. If we consider beforehand what exactly the scene is supposed to show (what obstacles, actions, behaviour), this usually helps the story—provided the content corresponds to reality.

The following principles help to make central figures more recognisable in real-life stories:

1. **Separate intention and need**. It is the old distinction between 'what a character wants' (the intention) and 'what a character needs' (the real deep need, that is). The intention is the declared goal, the need the underlying reason; the latter is often closely linked to people's motivation. A person is not always aware of his or her own underlying needs. To grow an awareness can be part of the development. 'Hitchhiker' Heinrich, for example, begs almost every person for money. His intention is to improve his income. But behind this lies the great need for closeness and recognition of his story (which we found out gradually).

   Dramaturgically, therefore, it makes sense to start with the intention. Over time, the hero realises that they actually need something else. In many fictional stories, this moment of realisation or deeper understanding is the midpoint, also called the moment of deepest crisis (about halfway through the story). The hero realises that all the previous strategies and intentions are not really target-oriented. They recognise what they really need and how they can achieve it. In order to integrate this distinction between 'intention' and 'need' into real stories, one not only needs a real protagonist, but also has to spend a lot of time with him or her—otherwise, there is a great danger of staging not reality, but one's own wishful thinking. If, however, these elements can be depicted realistically, they can become a powerful element of the story. One of the things that help me keep the difference in mind is that an intention is something more specific (money, fast car, big house) while a need is something more abstract (recognition, the feeling of belonging). The intention is usually easier to recognise than the need because people are often better able to identify the intention, or it is a bit more obvious.

What can help to recognise need: the hierarchy of needs drawn up by American psychologist Abraham Maslow. In a nutshell, it describes what drives us humans and what our needs are—hence the name (Maslow 1987). Originally, the pyramid comprises five levels that build on each other:

- Physiological: includes breathing, food, sleep, sex and hygiene.
- Safety: includes employment, health, property, but also morality or religion (because religious guidance gives security).
- Love/belonging: includes friendship, family and a place in society.
- Esteem: includes self-esteem, confidence, achievement, respect of and by others.
- Self-actualisation: Maslow understands this to mean striving to fully exploit one's own potential. Includes creativity, spontaneity, problem solving, lack of prejudice and acceptance of facts.

The rule of thumb is that only when the needs of one level are met will the needs of the next level be awakened. The boundaries or transitions are of course fluid. In addition, major and minor regressions are possible, depending on the life situation. The pyramid of needs helps authors and reporters to recognise which needs a character in a story wants to have satisfied.

To return to the example of the flooded restaurant: The owner's intention could be to rebuild the premises. This sets the scene for a dramaturgically good story. The restaurant owner may, however, need the insurance money for the reconstruction, but the insurance company is not willing to pay. This conflict could be about more than just money, perhaps the restaurant owner also wants social recognition: "Yes, bad things have happened to you and you are entitled to get help." This need not be the case, but it could be and, anyway, it makes sense to check the hypothesis. If it is correct, a deep story may emerge. This line of thought also corresponds to the idea of looking for a deeper idea behind the story—this time on the level of the character. This holds true for the figure skater Surya Bonaly, for example. She has spent her entire sporting life trying to impress coaches, spectators and—perhaps most importantly—the juries until she gets to a point where she realises maybe that's not what it's all about. What about staying true to yourself? This realisation leads to a leap in what is perhaps her most important freestyle routine, which no one has performed before her—and which still bears her name today.

2. **Establish the protagonist's flaw**. We have already seen this in the plot design. A character flaw is essential for the hero to develop. Moreover, not being perfect increases the credibility of a character. Nobody is perfect, only good or evil.

3. **Escalate conflicts: with the world, with others, with oneself**. If the protagonist is equipped with a defect, this can lead to an inner conflict, consciously or unconsciously. The British screenwriter and creator of the BBC Writer's Academy, John Yorke, puts it this way: "Whether real or imagined, great characters are consciously or subconsciously at war with themselves" (2014, 128). It is the constant struggle to either overcome the existing defect or cover it up. The true character of a person is often not immediately apparent. Each of us has a facade: "A character's façade, then, is an outer manifestation of an inner conflict" (ibid., 141). In the course of a narrative, it becomes increasingly difficult and exhausting to maintain this facade. People under pressure will eventually show their true character. That is why it is so important that the pressure increases as the story unfolds. We get closer and closer to the true character. An example of this is the character revelation of Adnan Syed in the first season of *Serial*. In the conversations with Sarah, we learn more about the facets of his character, not least because she involves him in more and more difficult debates. In the end, we have come closer to both Adnan's and Sarah's true characters. So, there is a development within the narrative: away from the facade towards the true character, a development that partnerships and friendships, for example, also experience. That's why we are so familiar with this pattern.

To make the listener feel that the conflicts are coming to a head—as with the obstacles—it helps to follow the following three-step model. Stage 1: Conflicts with the world (e.g. with social norms through to laws). Level 2: Conflicts with other people (such as parents, close friends or partners). Stage 3: Conflicts with oneself (from the first inkling via acceptance to confrontation with one's own shortcomings). Each of the three stages of conflict can also be intensified and can overlap with others in a narrative. To manage all the different levels, it helps to have a clear definition of a conflict: A conflict is the choice between two equally good or equally bad options. The mother who has to decide in favour of one child because there is only one place left in the refugee boat experiences an existential conflict.

4. **Target the maximum**. In each of these conflicts, the protagonist should act as well as possible. The American author James N. Frey has coined an appropriate term for this, even though he refers to fictional characters: the maximum capacity: "Homo fictus always operates at his maximum capacity and it is never within a dramatic character's maximum capacity, when faced with a problem or a challenge, to do nothing unless the lack of action is being played for comedy" (1987, 24). In real life, of course, we only very rarely act at maximum capacity. After all, anything else would hardly be feasible or endurable. As reporters, this thought helps us to identify the crucial scenes and situations. It helps us to experience condensed reality. An example: In the very touching episode 'Entanglement' of the first *Invisibilia* season, the two reporters Alix Spiegel and Lulu Miller meet a woman named Amanda who has a rare condition: mirror-touch synaesthesia. This means that Amanda feels what people around her feel. It applies to touch, pain, but also to emotions such as joy or fear. This phenomenon has only been described in very few people so far. Amanda can hardly bear to be amongst people and has developed a strong avoidance behaviour. The last scene of the story shows Amanda attending her daughter's school leaving party, nevertheless. "For many parents going to a graduation would be unremarkable, but for her it represented a heroic act of love. In other words, the last scene shows Amanda - like the rest of us - struggling to be her best self" (Spiegel 2017, 53). She is therefore acting at the limits of her own maximum capacity.

5. **Relating the figures to one another and staging them**. People do not live in isolation. They have friends, helpers, perhaps even opponents and people they are not quite sure what they feel about them (dramaturgically, these figures are called 'shapeshifters'). Based on the story's narrative sentence, a reporter can consider which relationships are particularly relevant. And how they develop. This relationship development also requires triggers, motivations or obstacles. Granted, a big cast (i.e. many contributors) is always difficult for audio; with too many participants and voices, recognition clearly suffers. But central relationships are important for a good story. As reporters, we often still tend to interview people alone and in isolation, in the hope of obtaining particularly 'clean' original sound bites. But then almost no interaction can take place. In the last episode of the originally broadcast first season of *The Hitchhiker*, there is a scene that made it to the storyboard relatively late. Stephan and I meet Heinrich in the social housing where he's living. There we let a staff member, Wilfried Karrer, show us the facilities. It soon becomes clear that Heinrich Kurzrock has a good relationship with Wilfried Karrer. Heinrich respects Wilfried who, in turn, is very interested in Heinrich and wants to help him, though he knows all about his tricks. We record more or less the whole time because this is what we have done from the very beginning. So, we are still recording when the

four of us sit down together for a final coffee. A situation arises that is carried by the dynamics of all four of us. Wilfried Karrer asks Heinrich to finally stop lying to us (e.g. about his state of health). What follows is a big debate, which finally becomes the last scene of the first season (we broadcast a very last sixth episode and an epilogue about two and a half years later), because on this afternoon our relationship with Heinrich develops significantly (a script excerpt with this scene can be found in Sect. 6.1).

6. **Create recognisability**. How do I describe a person on the radio or podcast so that listeners not only see a picture in their mind's eye, but a picture that is so evocative that it can be recalled at any time? The picture should be so unique that it avoids confusion with other people in the story. This is a task that is much more difficult for us audio people to master than for our colleagues in TV, online or print. Because—if they want to—they can work with real pictures. In order to deal with this issue, many reportage courses, for example, suggest describing what the person is wearing and what they look like. Some editorial offices even make it an explicit requirement that every person who appears is described that way, including clothing. But how helpful is the following description: 1.86 metres tall, curly brown hair, watery grey eyes, stonewashed blue jeans and a khaki sweater? Or: black suit with a tasteless brown tie, black leather shoes, white shirt? Granted, these are somewhat unkind descriptions. But the danger is real: Clothing and appearance can seem rather random and not necessarily aid the listener's imagination. I am not saying that it is wrong to pay attention to these things. But the crucial question is: To what extent do clothes, hairstyle or jewellery represent a person's character? Or in other words: Which character trait do I want to emphasise by the description?

The American author Tom Wolfe (yes, THE Tom Wolfe, the gentleman of New Journalism, he of the impeccable white suits with matching tie and breast pocket handkerchief, who died in May 2018) once noted the following thoughts on observing and recognising people: "This is the recording of everyday gestures, habits, manners, customs, styles of furniture, clothing, decoration, styles of travelling, eating, keeping house, modes of behaving towards children, servants, superiors, inferiors, peers, plus the various looks, glances, poses, styles of walking and other symbolic details that might exist within a scene. Symbolic of what? Symbolic, generally, of people's *status life*, using that term in the broad sense of the entire pattern of behaviour and possessions through which people express their position in the world or what they think it is or what they hope it to be" (Wolfe 1975, 47). I find this thought quite helpful! The status symbol or status detail (after all, it can also be a small thing) may not replace the rest of the description altogether, but it complements it and can help recognition (e.g. the breast pocket handkerchief). Status details can also lend the story particularly deep moments.

In Aaron Sorkin's TV series *The Newsroom*, the head of the news section of *Atlantic Cable News* is Charlie Skinner. Skinner always wears a bow tie, it is his trademark, a status detail. When Skinner dies at the end of the series, at the funeral, his widow gives the bow tie to one of Charlie Skinner's staff members. The foster father leaves his editorial son a token of appreciation and closeness. It's the moment when the status detail becomes much bigger and takes on even greater significance.

Admittedly, such use of the status symbol is rarely possible in real-life narratives, but the guiding question behind it is important: Which detail says the most about a character? The bow tie, the watch or the absence of fashion conventions (the hoodie in the law firm)? In *The Hitchhiker*, we deliberately chose two status details: Heinrich's crutch and his cap (his trucker vest with at least a hundred pockets would have been suitable, too). Both elements indicate Heinrich's relationship to this world. At first sight, the crutch, for example, merely illustrates that Heinrich has difficulty walking. But it also says something about his self-image: The crutch is a visible symbol that Heinrich sees himself as a victim. Hey, world, look at what you have done to me! It is remarkable that there are numerous situations in which Heinrich can apparently walk perfectly well without a crutch. With his cap, Heinrich is more on the offensive. It usually covers quite a big lump on his head. Several times, it seemed to us, he intentionally took off his cap just as someone wanted to take a bite of their sandwich, for example. A brief moment of shock, which Heinrich triggered again and again—and rather enjoyed.

And then, of course, there is something else that we audio narrators can use better than any other media to make someone recognisable: their voice and the way they speak. But we don't make nearly enough use of this option. We exclude a lot of potential interlocutors because their voice or way of speaking does not strike us as broadcastable (for whatever reasons). A counter-example is the affectionate and extremely entertaining documentary by Ralph Erdenberger, which was broadcast on 16 August 2015, the 310th anniversary of the death of the Swiss mathematician Jacob Bernoulli. For this, Erdenberger interviewed Volker Nollau, Professor of Stochastic Analysis at TU Dresden. Nollau has lived and taught in Dresden for a long time, and that's how he speaks. There is no ignoring the regional influence. For people in North Rhine-Westphalia (the documentary was broadcast by WDR), the Saxon dialect may make the speaker sound a bit simple-minded (just as for many people in other parts of Germany the Ruhr area accent sounds, let's say, less intellectual). There are probably similar dialect issues in other countries, too. Erdenberger takes ideal advantage of this by making humour the main element of his piece! In this sense, he does not work against his expert but uses the potential inherent in his voice—without being disrespectful.

Of course, there are limits when it comes to comprehensibility. If I can't understand someone or the technical quality of a voice recording is so bad that I can't hear anything, then I will hardly be able to use this material for my piece. On the other hand, if it takes a moment to get used to a new voice—that's good. The important thing is that the person has something exciting to say. That's also the reason why in *Serial* we always accept quite poor telephone recordings. Yes, you do have to listen carefully to get used to it (especially if you are not a native speaker), but we finally accept the sound quality. Indeed, we actually like the intimacy of these moments.

In order to increase the recognisability of voices, we should also take care not to smooth out speech patterns too radically. In many audio productions, the original sounds are 'cleaned' or 'smoothed' rigorously; that is, verbal errors, 'ums' and 'ahs' are cut out, pauses are shortened, seemingly unimportant things are removed, and sometimes even breathers are cut out. Every second counts in the end. The result is highly artificial and uniform sounding people. Of course, the rationale behind this procedure is linked to what we actually consider to be a good original sound, recording or tape in terms of content and form (see also Sect. 6.5). In terms of recognisability, however, this is rather counter-productive. If someone needs a moment to develop a thought or, say, uses certain phrases again and again (something like "I always say..." or "at the end of the day"), then we quickly recognise them. Furthermore, these half-sentences convey something about the character of the person. Naturally, there are limits here, as well. The speech has to be understandable (unless I want to illustrate the fact that someone is not speaking understandably) and no-one should be made to look a fool. The point is to make the characteristics of the voice and the way of speaking audible!

It is important to characterise people to make them recognisable and unmistakable. But this does not yet mean that we like these characters or that we can build a relationship with them as listeners. Especially for longer stories, however, this is essential.

4.3   3D-Relationship Between Listener and Character

Have a go at describing other people. Often, we fall back on standard formats: Besides appearance and clothing, we talk about name, place of residence or birth, and age. Perhaps supplemented by hobbies, education and current profession. Of course, it is not wrong to create an impression or an initial picture of a person like this, but it is usually not enough to develop a connection between listener and character. The American story consultant and author Karl Iglesias explains why: "But it doesn't necessarily make us care about or create empathy for them, which is the key factor in holding the reader's attention from beginning to end" (Iglesias 2005, 50). Here, Iglesias speaks of the reader, but it applies equally to the listener. The goal is to build a lasting emotional connection. Amongst others, the following three factors can help to achieve it:

1. Empathy. Empathy is roughly defined as the ability to recognise and understand emotions, thoughts, motives or personality traits in others. Empathy lets us feel what the other person is feeling (compassion, on the other hand, makes us feel sorry for the other person, and we may want to help). Not all of us are equally empathetic. And it is not always easy to sense other people's feelings or motives. As storytellers, we don't know how empathetic our listeners are, which means we should regularly appeal to their empathetic skills. Empathy often works through recognition: "Ah, what this person is feeling now – I've felt that." That's how connections are built. At the beginning of the first season of *Serial*, for example, Sarah Koenig introduces the case featured in the series with an important detail: "For the last year, I've spent every working day trying to figure out where a high school kid was for an hour after school one day in 1999 - or if you want to get technical about it, and apparently I do, where a high school kid was for 21 minutes after school one day in 1999"[2]. And then comes a sentence, which is actually not necessary in terms of content: "This search sometimes feels undignified on my part. I've had to ask about teenagers' sex lives, where, how often, with whom, about notes they passed in class, about their drug habits, their relationships with their parents." If you are only considering content, the first sentence of this quotation could be deleted. But the decisive thing that Sarah Koenig creates here is a connection between herself and the listener. She admits that she is not the super-confident, all-knowing journalist. The phrase "undignified on my part" also reveals a good dose of humour—she doesn't take herself too seriously. She kills two birds with one stone: She ties in with our experience that as adults it can be difficult to establish a connection with teenagers, especially when it comes to topics like sex or drugs. Many people have probably experienced this themselves. Empathy works through recognition. And Koenig doesn't take herself too seriously. We usually find that sympathetic. So, already, after 30s, we really like this Sarah! Other empathy-builders usually include courage (the way we want to be, we see that a better version of ourselves is possible) or unjustified harm (Harry Potter lost his parents).

2. Fascination. Clive Owen as Dr John Thackery in the TV series *The Knick*, Emma Watson as Hermione in Harry Potter and, of course, Benedict Cumberbatch as a modern Sherlock Holmes. They all have one thing in common: They fascinate us, they are geniuses. Or at least that's how their characters are set up. They are all brilliant in their own way. Thackery as a drug-addicted doctor, Hermione as a hard-working student and Sherlock as a sociopath (drugs play a role for him, too). If we are fascinated

by characters, we like them. At least up to a certain point, Thackery can get a bit crazy from time to time, Hermione sometimes overdoes the striving for good grades somewhat and Sherlock occasionally seems a little too arrogant and not very empathetic. It is a fine line: The flip side of fascination is rejection. That's why it's good when these characters have a flaw. It makes them more interesting and credible. Therefore, an exciting question is, for example: What is my protagonist most afraid of? This is a decisive factor in real-life narratives because we as reporters often portray protagonists or heroes as too positive, too fascinating or too perfect. In stories like the one about the first intercontinental flight in a solar plane, it is important that Bertrand Piccard is not only recognisable as someone who succeeds at everything. We must also learn about the setbacks he has experienced and feel what they mean to him. He wants to show what renewable energies are capable of. He also wants to show what a Piccard can achieve (his father and grandfather were great discoverers and engineers). If we experience Piccard's fears, worries and setbacks, we not only accept his great achievement, but later appreciate it all the more. This also applies to his stamina.

3. Secret. If I like someone, I want to understand him or her—to feel close to the person. What exactly happened to Harry Potter's parents? Important: The secret must have something to do with the story. If not, it can be very disappointing when it is finally revealed. For real stories, I find the following question helpful: Is there something the protagonist in my story is holding back? The great radio feature, *Urgently seeking Willy* (Radio Bremen 2015), is about a Dutchman called Willy, who is on the run because he is said to have cheated farmers out of millions. He has promised turnkey dairy plants in the US—without any bureaucratic European structures. German and Dutch farmers, amongst others, have fallen for it. Feature author Rainer Kahrs travels to the US to find out more and look for Willy, accompanied by Bärbel, an aggrieved farmer. At some point, the narrator confesses that Bärbel is his sister. A wonderful moment and the revelation of a great 'secret' that would have developed much less power if we had known about it from the beginning.

All these factors help to shape the relationship between listener and protagonist or other characters. As listeners, we sometimes react directly: We suffer with people who are treated unfairly. We admire people who, under pressure or in conflict situations, do the morally right thing and behave humanely, and we look up to people who have (apparently) aspirational character traits: enthusiastic, smart, humorous, but also more superficial qualities such as sporty or attractive.

Real characters have a very big advantage over fictional characters: Real people are always three-dimensional or complex. This old distinction between two-dimensional and three-dimensional figures and stories is, incidentally, often helpful. A quick reminder: Two-dimensional figures are figures that function as mere types—without development. They are the stereotypical waiters, taxi drivers, CEOs, etc. Three-dimensional figures have depth, are more complex and therefore much more interesting. One big problem is that real people are often only shown as two-dimensional figures, as poor shop owners, pitiful victims of crime or evil perpetrators. This is not only an inappropriate reflection of reality, but also possibly reinforces existing prejudices or even racism. Real figures have always been three-dimensional. We just have to show them as such. Best done from the very first moment.

4.4   MAKING AN APPEARANCE: INTRODUCING CHARACTERS

When was the last time you consciously thought about how to introduce a person into your narrative for the first time? In what situation? Using what sound bite? What first impression should be made on the listener? Let's take the following purely fictional excerpt from any random manuscript as an example—let's say it's about a county's crime statistics. The report starts with a poor, old woman (let's call her Doris Williams) who has had a break-in. Of course, the number of burglaries has increased since last year (which is why there has to be talk of 'more and more burglaries' in the introduction, even if this is statistically nonsense. After all, an increase from x to y is not yet an increase in the growth rate, as the expression 'more and more' or 'evermore' implies. But what the heck …). Mrs Williams has unfortunately suffered a severe shock and cannot speak to the media. There is only one solution: The police must of course have their say:

> *Reporter*: …but Doris Williams is not an isolated case. Even the spokesperson for the police, Martin Schmitt, knows that:
> *Tape*: (Martin Schmitt, in front of the police station) Unfortunately, Mrs Williams is not an isolated case. Last year we had 1,268 burglaries in our district. That is 3.79 percent more than in the previous year. But this rate of increase is roughly on a par with the national average.

This example is purely fictitious and would never be broadcast by any station. Or would it? In current affairs, reporters often simply don't have a choice or the creative possibility to develop special situations or even scenes. And especially press officers representing authorities often speak like—well—press officers representing authorities (Who actually teaches them that? And why do they believe that it is good, and that such behaviour strengthens people's trust in the authorities? But I digress …).

But what is almost always possible, even in current affairs, is to introduce a person by content rather than function. Anyone who consciously listens to programmes like *This American Life* will often find passages in which tape is cut to tape directly. These passages not only break up the boring rhythm of reporter-tape-reporter, but are also ideal for introducing a person, as the *Invisibilia* story 'Entanglement' shows. It is the story of Amanda, the woman with mirror-touch synaesthesia. Amanda wants to explain how this particular form of synaesthesia feels to her and is currently telling the story of how she observed a child falling over and hitting the back of its head in a shopping store:

> *Tape, Amanda*: And I'm just like, this child, he needs help! And my head hurt so bad that I basically was crawling to try to get to the kid. Like, it was bad.
> *Tape, Husband*: I think there may be a lot of people who hear this sort of thing and think it's basically bullshit.
> *Alix*: That's her husband again.
> *Tape, Husband*: But, I mean, I see it, and there's something to this.
> *Tape, a person with a British accent*: Certainly. Yeah, no totally.
> *Lulu*: Alix, were you not just thinking it was about time for a British scientist?
> *Alix*: I was yearning for the authority of a British person right now.
> *Lulu (laughing)*: Well, here we've got one, this one's name is Michael Banissy, and he is a neuroscientist at Goldsmith's, University of London (Spiegel 2017, 50).

On both occasions, the characters are (re-)introduced through their content—only subsequently are we introduced to them or reminded of who they are. Namely husband and neuroscientist. The latter, for example, is the first to comment on what the husband has just said. The listener automatically asks the question: Who is speaking? And who can apparently confirm that there is actually something to the phenomenon described? We don't have to wait long for the answer either, and we now learn the person's name and function. In addition, the authors here use the scientist's British accent to introduce it lightly and humorously—a positive note that benefits the story at this point. Again, it becomes clear that it helps to make use of what the interviewee's voice and speech have to offer, in this case the British accent.

This kind of direct response or commentary on something just said is one of at least four strategies I have identified for introducing people directly and dynamically. The other three are: scenic, with a strong argument or as a co-narrator. Scenic means there is a situation that is introduced by the reporter. For example, the narrator could take us into a staffroom during the long break. In this situation, a character appears, obviously a teacher. He is rushing into the staffroom because he wants to make a few copies for the lesson after the break. The appearance of this figure thus results organically from the situation. Our serial *The Hitchhiker* also uses this method right at the beginning:

> *Stephan*: When someone stands in front of you, in total despair…
> *Tape*: (Heinrich Kurzrock, petrol station) I want to scream. Yes, I want scream.
> *Stephan*: …who wants to end his life…
> *Tape*: (Heinrich Kurzrock, petrol station) …if I knew that this was my last day, I would shout hallelujah.
> *Stephan*: … and who asks you for a last favour, for his last journey….
> *Tape*: (Heinrich Kurzrock, petrol station) I don't have anything more to hope for. The path to Zurich is clear. Now I only need a few little grains of sand, little stones, by which I mean money, to survive until I get to Zurich and the end. I don't need anything else.
> *Stephan*: Then you have to help, don't you?

Introduction via a strong argument, on the other hand, can often be used to start a new act or section. The argument must be strong, concise or provocative and designed to be realised. In the documentary about Joseph Campbell, just before the halfway point—we have reached the crisis in Joseph Campbell's life—the dramaturgy coach Uwe Walter is introduced. He is supposed to help shed light on the aspect of why people are fascinated by stories at all. Just a moment ago we were with Campbell in a forest hut, without money. From there, the story now moves purposefully upwards on the ladder of abstraction:

> *Author*: Campbell reads and learns. He tries to put into practice what he will later describe in one of his most famous sentences: Follow your bliss. That is follow your luck, your calling, or whatever makes you happy. This is what matters to Campbell, in stories and in real life.
>
> Music fades out.
>
> *Tape*: (Uwe Walter, apartment) We love the best athletes. We love competition. We love the Nobel Prize. We love it when people make something of themselves.
> *Author*: Uwe Walter originally studied directing at the Academy for Film and TV in Munich and is now one of the most important dramaturgy trainers in Germany. In his seminars you learn to tell stories.

Uwe Walter is introduced here via a strong argument, namely: We love it when people make something of themselves. This makes us, as listeners, want to get to know the person who says something like that. And, even more, understand his argument.

The introduction via a kind of co-narrator works especially well when the character themselves tells an anecdote or gives an example. At that moment, the character takes the lead in the narrative. Let's look at an example from a short documentary for German public radio station WDR 2 about the term 'telegram.' After an introductory example (singer-songwriter Wolf Biermann explains why he received telegrams from his mother living in the GDR), the actual central figure of the piece appears. With only one sentence, I try to build the bridge from Biermann to her:

> *Author*: Telegrams. They were very popular and necessary, especially in the GDR.
>
> *Tape*: (Heidi Thoms, studio) Yes, of course. We didn't have a phone. We used telegrams: 'My train arrives then and then.' Or just congratulatory telegrams. All important messages that had to get there quickly were sent by telegram.
>
> *Author*: Within a few minutes or at most hours, the message was supposed to reach the recipient. Payment was based on the number of words. The art of saving money was thus to formulate briefly. Even names.
>
> *Tape*: (Heidi Thoms, studio) It's Heidi, actually my name is Adelheid, but I think that's terrible, so call me Heidi please.

In this case, the central figure also introduces herself, a technique that the podcast *Radiolab*, for example, uses regularly. The idea behind it is that the way someone introduces themselves reveals something about this person, their self-image, their relationship with themselves and their role. This kind of sound bite is very easy to get, just ask for it at the beginning of each interview, something along the following lines: "If you briefly introduce yourself, with your full name, title and function - then I'll definitely have it all correct." Whether or not you actually use the tape is something you can decide afterwards.

Of course, a combination of these four variants is also conceivable. The key message here is: The introduction of the characters is determined by the flow of the story.

4.5   Working with Characters: The Story Interview

How do you prepare for an interview? By this, I don't mean an interview that is broadcast live or recorded, but an interview for original sound or tape that you can use later in a report, documentary or anything else. I cannot emphasise this enough: Storytelling and interview techniques are very closely related. In my experience, there are more or less three types of interview preparers: the spontaneously open ones, the detailed ones and the structured ones. Of course, this is a bit exaggerated, but there is some truth in it.

The spontaneously open ones usually feel at home in a busy, current affairs newsroom. Pragmatism reigns here; otherwise, no daily show would ever get finished. Often enough the reporter is happy to get hold of any sound bite at all. Questions are prepared on the way to the interview or during the interview itself. Preparation is considered extensive if there has been enough time to jot down three or four key points on a piece of paper. Many reporters, who work mainly in current affairs journalism, find it difficult to change this way of working when they are dealing with a longer piece. Why should they change their approach? Experience has shown that something that can be broadcast always comes out in the end. Unfortunately, this is the way the longer pieces often sound—just like longer, current affairs reports.

The detailed ones usually go to interviews very well prepared, often with many fully-formulated questions. So, you don't forget anything. There is nothing wrong with this, but it does cause two problems. Firstly, the line between background interviews (for research) and recorded interviews becomes blurred. Often the factual questions (who, when, where, how, how many) dictate the interview, but the answers are not likely to make it into the final piece. Why is this a problem? It generates more audio material than necessary. So as a reporter I have to listen to more, transcribe more, sort more (the upside is, of course, everything is on tape). This is a factor that should not be underestimated, especially with long stories. The work is a battle with your material anyway. And secondly, in my opinion, this kind of interview reinforces the interviewee's role as a functionary or spokesperson. When people are primarily asked for facts, names and dates, they quickly adopt a certain habitus. That's what makes it difficult to make them recognisable as characters. They are then often unable to switch to another mode during the conversation. The tone of the conversation is fixed and attempts to get the interviewee to give some authentic answers often lead nowhere.

This is why the structured approach is probably the most effective. A good idea is to subdivide questions into clusters, i.e. different, rougher sections. For each of these clusters, there can be an interview goal or a leading question, which is then discussed with the interviewee. However, one big mistake often happens during a structured interview, too. The interview is prepared purely thematically—the clusters used are the classic categories for topics: current developments, genesis/prehistory/background, advantages and disadvantages, problems, solutions, assessments, outlook, done. The problem here is that the recorded answer is all more or less thematic. That is not necessarily a bad thing, of course. And the answers may even convey emotions, for example a passionate argument. But they ignore a large part of what is elementary for the narrative: scenes, examples, motivation and the bigger idea. Of course, it may be that the interviewee provides them of their own accord anyway— lucky you! But experience shows that once a certain tone of voice has been established in the interview, it is difficult to change.

Therefore, audio narratives need different interviews and consequently different interview preparation and techniques. Otherwise, as a reporter, I simply won't get the tape necessary to tell the story. The following four steps are a good guide to preparing a story interview:

1. Set interview target or goal. The basis for the story interview is the narrative sentence. This acts as a guideline and helps to identify the role my

interview partner should play in the story and what I 'need' from them. Checking the story principles has also provided a bigger idea for the story and thus for the interview as well. I can prepare myself accordingly. Or in the words of Ira Glass: "It's best to try to figure out the potential Big Ideas in any story before you go out interviewing people" (2017, 71).

2. Form interview clusters. Based on the narrative sentence and goal, the interview clusters are determined. The clusters are not related to the topic, as they were in the past, but to the story. This does not mean that topics and facts do not appear in the interview, as well, but they serve the story. The clusters result logically from the meta-structure of the narrative. If, for example, I, as a reporter, interview the protagonist and have chosen a purely scenic or scenic-reflective narrative structure, the following clusters can make sense: ignition point, bigger idea (this includes both social relevance and lessons learned from the experience), special events (this may include surprises for the plot points, obstacles, crises and climaxes) and reactions from friends and family.

These interviews are interviews that search for and explore scenes. The associated facts, lessons learned and meanings are of course debated nevertheless (for the reflective part of the narrative). These clusters are supplemented by the character cluster, which is all about the personal stuff (including, for example, motivation and beliefs). Of course, the clusters do not have to be worked through in strict succession in the interview. Go with the flow. Having said that, some order makes sense anyway. The question about the lessons learned from the experience is probably more appropriate towards the end of the interview. The clusters help me to lead the interview and guide it towards the story (see also Fig. 4.1).

In order not to confuse or even discourage interviewees with these terms, they can be translated into more appropriate terms depending on the situation and interviewee. For example, 'ignition point' or 'triggering event' can become 'origin' or 'first idea.' The 'climax' can become 'special event' or possibly also 'target.' The aim of this type of interview is to keep steering the interviewee back into the experience or into the interplay of experiencing and reflecting.

3. Briefing. I can also provide the interviewee with this type of information as preparation for the interview, along the lines of "I would like to talk to you about the following aspects...!" And then I refer to the clusters, possibly supplemented by two or three keywords, which prove that I have already have experience of reporting on the topic. This increases my credibility immensely and thus the chance that my interview partner will engage with me and my interview management. Moreover, the preparation alone ensures that there are no diverging ideas about what the interview is about. In most situations, it is unproblematic and appropriate to inform people in advance about the planned story and their role in it

STORY INTERVIEW: SEVEN MASTER CLUSTERS

CLUSTER "START" (Triggering Event)
→ When did everything start?
→ When did you decide to pursue your plan?
→ How did that happen?
→ What was your goal?

CLUSTER "RELEVANCE & REFLECTION" (Bigger Idea)
→ What does your story show?
→ Which problem or phenomenon does it illustrate?
→ What do you think about that?
→ What did you learn (about yourself) during that period?

CLUSTER "RELEVANCE & REFLECTION"
→ Which problems did you have to solve? How?
→ When did something change? How?
→ When did your plan seem likely to fail?
→ Are there any milestones, special events or defining moments?
   Which?
→ When did you know you would succeed?

Cluster "Personal matters"
→ What motivates you? Why?
→ What helps you solve problems?
→ How do you take care of yourself?

Cluster "Reactions" (Friends & Foes)
→ How did your friends and family react?
→ What is the relationship like to them today?
→ Did you get any help or support?

Cluster "X"
→ Did we forget something important?
→ Is there anything else you want to mention?
→ What are the prospects?

CLUSTER "META-LEVEL" (observe during interview)
→ Manner of speaking and communication?
→ Manner of personal contact?
   Address if necessary.

Fig. 4.1 Story Interview

(there are of course exceptions!). Important: Please do not send interviewees any of your questions in advance. People prepare their answers, learn them by heart, read them out prepared or feel compelled to stick to something. In any case, it is to the detriment of the interview!

4. Create situations. If that's possible. The goal of narratives is to make stories tangible. This naturally also has an effect on the interview. Whenever possible and meaningful, situations should therefore be created for the interview. Meaningful means: something actually happens in these situations and they play a role in the story (on the serious danger of false reporting, see Sect. 6.7) or they help the interview partners to remember a certain event from the past better. Together with hitchhiker Heinrich, Stephan Beuting and I, for example, meet for lunch with another former child and youth psychiatry patient. The conversation brings back memories on both sides.

Of course, these four points only help if I then conduct the interview in a goal-oriented, respectful and confident manner—in other words, if I really lead the interview. Accompanying people through events or steering them into memories is a very sensitive matter that always demands a mixture of closeness, distance, emotional endurance and reflection. And you don't need to do "the full Schwartz" to capture a moment. This particular interview technique was developed by Stephen Schwartz for the Danish Broadcasting Corporation. It is designed to help people remember events in the past by (amongst other things) relaxing, closing their eyes and lying down on the floor (e.g. in a studio, where a mic is positioned right above their mouth to capture what they are saying) (Nuzum 2019, 99ff.). Interviews and settings of this kind are fascinating but place a big burden of responsibility on the reporter (what do you do if this kind of setting triggers something in your interview-partner you do not want it to—what do you do then?), and it is often not realistic to conduct them (and I haven't even started on false memories yet, cf. Shaw 2016).

To make the interview situation less complicated and intimidating for the interviewee (depending on whom I am interviewing of course), I personally try not to bring more than one or at most two pages of preparation to an interview. This makes a confident impression and allows me to handle the interview sensibly. Pen in one hand to take notes. Other hand on the leveller of the recording device (of course, this is only possible if the microphone is on a tripod). In the field, I have the notebook in my pocket—then I can at least make sure that I look at it again before I leave the recording location (important for scenic narratives is above all to record true to scene, see also Sect. 6.4). The following master clusters can help you prepare for a story interview. All you need then is the right attitude for the interview. US presenter Ira Glass recommends trying to revert to a state of ignorance once again, if this is possible, somehow: "I don't want to sound dumb on the air, but I'm willing to sound dumb during an interview" (2017, 75).

Depending on the role of the interview partner, I can adapt the story interview. If the interview partner only plays a role at certain points in the story (e.g. in an explanatory narrative), then I limit the interview to that role. In doing so, I try to cover the character clusters anyway and lead the interview partner into situations. In my experience, even outright expert interviews change significantly through this approach. The important thing is that I, the reporter, always have the situation as much under control as possible. The more nervousness, insecurity and anxiety I radiate, the more this is transferred to my counterpart. PR professionals will even use it against me and influence the situation in their favour. It is also important to check during the interview how someone is communicating with me as a reporter: Are they aggressive, defensive, reticent? If necessary, I can talk about it (see also the cluster 'Meta-level' in the story interview) and thus possibly break through deadlocked interview structures or simply surprise interview partners. And thus, produce new and authentic answers.

The story interview is therefore an interview that produces original sound bites for the planned narrative. Like the story, it also changes levels: between experiences and their reflection.

This also means that you, the reporter, must have done your journalistic homework to ensure that you don't misrepresent your interview partner or assign them an inappropriate role in the story and thus in the interview. Of course, reporters also pay attention to the usual standards of the recording situation (acoustic quality, crosstalk effects, etc.). But the person interviewed does not need to notice any of this. Atmospherically, a good story interview feels like a normal conversation. If you feel comfortable, you like to talk. Or at least more than someone who feels uncomfortable. A good atmosphere significantly increases the chance of authentic original sound material. The central goal of the story interview is to make events and experiences tangible. It is therefore a completely different form of interview from a confrontative interview with a politician. But what do I do as a reporter if the events are my own experiences?

4.6   ME: THE REPORTER AS PROTAGONIST

Just to get things clear: Just because someone says 'I' does not mean they are automatically a protagonist! The protagonist ego and the narrator ego are two different narrative techniques (on the narrator ego, see Sect. 7.4). Both techniques can appear in a story, but do not have to. They are often confused or lumped together. The protagonist ego is easier to explain: All the criteria for narrative sentence, protagonist design and plot apply in exactly the same way, with the one difference that the main character, the protagonist of the story, is the reporter himself or herself. This is the case, for example, in the first season of *Serial*. The protagonist is not Adnan Syed, but Sarah Koenig: She investigates, she experiences situations, and she goes through crises. In the second season, this is no longer the case—and the makers of *Serial* made a conscious decision to change, as producer Julie Snyder explains: "So I think the story itself dictated that we needed Sarah to play that role. And in the story for season 2, we didn't. The structure of the story didn't necessitate it, so Sarah is not as much of a character" (Koenig and Snyder 2017, 82).

Those who work with the protagonist ego will have to answer several questions that are important for the sound design of the story: Can I be heard in the on and off? How do I design this? Do I have to be interviewed for sound bites? If so, by whom? What role does this person then play in the story, etc.? Most of these problems can be solved if I follow the principle that the reporter ego is treated just like any other protagonist.

The most difficult thing is to present one's own personal character development in a credible way. A reporter who tells his own story usually tells it in retrospect—that is, from a more mature position. The developmental steps of the story have already been taken. And here comes the challenge: This should not be allowed to influence the way the development process is described; otherwise, the story will become unbelievable which means the reporter must deal with their own shortcomings transparently and honestly—and adopt the former state of ignorance. But this is doubly at odds with our journalistic self-image. Firstly, we are used to reporting results in any case. And secondly, in journalism, the 'I' is often an expression of wisdom and self-staging—for example in a commentary or to show what great things have been experienced. Neither of these is exactly helpful for a narrative. After all, the narrative attitude is a decisive factor in determining how credible the story is. The protagonist ego in narratives is therefore not a platform for grandstanding.

4.7   CHECKLIST: CHARACTER DEVELOPMENT

Besides the plot, the protagonist and the other characters are the decisive elements in shaping the narrative. They carry the plot and drive the story forward. Real people, however, are not fictional characters. They cannot be arranged arbitrarily and subordinated to a story. And that's a good thing. After all, one of the most important goals is to create an appropriate representation of reality and thus also of the people in the story (which of course can still lead to dissatisfaction, because the people depicted may have a different self-image of themselves). The following checklist can help to stage real people appropriately in a narrative:

Checklist Character Development

- The protagonist is active, focused and flawed (at least not perfect).
- Other characters have a clear place in the story.

- Goal and need are two different things and are staged as such (want vs. need)
- Real people are staged as characters: They emerge very strongly, act at their maximum capacity if possible, are recognisable (use status details and voice!) and reveal their character in actions (especially when overcoming obstacles and in conflicts).
- Create 3D relationships between listeners and characters: build empathy.
- Use the story interview to get tape and sound bites.
- Check continuously: Is the narrative still an appropriate representation of reality?

Two questions I am often asked in this context: Firstly, what about buildings, animals or objects—can't they be protagonists as well? Answer: Try to make all the aspects we have been talking about in this chapter fit for animals or objects (with the help of the checklist above) and be honest about it. There is your answer. And secondly, can't two or three or more people be protagonists at the same time? This one is more difficult. As we know from fictional storytelling, there are novels, movies or series with more than one protagonist: Harry Potter is accompanied by Ron and Hermione. Or workplace dramas (*The West Wing* is a great example). Or coming of age stories like various high-school dramas (*Élite* or *Sex Education*). All of them make great stories, all different, but they have at least two things in common: one, the various characters embody different character traits (Harry is brave, Hermione is a genius and Ron is Ron, the most loyal friend). And two, every single character or protagonist has a goal, a need and therefore experiences development.

Not all the points on the checklist will always be fulfilled. But they help to sharpen the perspective for the story and to shape the way protagonists and characters are treated. Those who have collected good material can then concentrate on making the best out of the material when writing. The story tools and tension techniques in the following chapter will help you do this.

NOTES

1. To get a good idea of *Invisibilia* cf. Spiegel (2017).
2. For the whole manuscript, have a look here: https://genius.com/Serial-podcast-episode-1-the-alibi-annotated.

BIBLIOGRAPHY

Field, Syd. 1979. *Screenplay. The Foundations of Screenwriting*. New York: Dell Publishing.

Frey, James N. 1987. *How to Write a Damn Good Novel*. New York: St. Martin's Press.

Glass, Ira. 2017. Harnessing Luck as an Industrial Product. In *Reality Radio*, ed. John Biewen and Alexa Dilworth, 2nd ed., 64–76. Durham: The University of North Carolina Press.

Iglesias, Karl. 2005. *Writing for Emotional Impact*. Livermore: Wing Span Press.

Invisibilia. 2015. The Culture Inside. Accessed 17 April 2020. https://www.npr.org/programs/invisibilia/382451600/entanglement.

Koenig, Sarah, and Julie Snyder. 2017. One Story, Week by Week. An Interview with Sarah Koenig and Julie Snyder by John Biewen. In *Reality Radio*, ed. John Biewen and Alexa Dilworth, 2nd ed., 77–89. Durham: The University of North Carolina Press.

Maslow, Abraham H. 1987. *Motivation and Personality*, 3rd ed. New York: Harper & Brothers.

Nuzum, Eric. 2019. *Make Noise. A Creator's Guide to Podcasting and Great Audio Storytelling*. New York: Workman Publishing Co.

Radiolab. 2016. On the Edge. Accessed 17 April 2020. http://www.radiolab.org/story/edge/.

Shaw, Julia. 2016. *The Memory Illusion*. London: Random House Books.

Sorkin, Aaron. 2016. Masterclass 'Screenwriting' (online-course comes with charge). Accessed 20 December 2020. https://www.masterclass.com/classes/aaron-sorkin-teaches-screenwriting.

Spiegel, Alix. 2017. Variations in Tape Use and the Position of the Narrator. In: *Reality Radio*, ed. John Biewen and Alexa Dilworth, 2nd ed., 42–53. Durham: The University of North Carolina Press.

WDR ZeitZeichen. 2015. Jakob Bernoulli, Mathematiker. Accessed 17 April 2020. http://www1.wdr.de/mediathek/audio/zeitzeichen/audio-jakob-bernoulli-mathematiker-todestag—100.html.

Wolfe, Tom. 1975. *The New Journalism*. London: Picador.

Yorke, John. 2014. *Into the Woods. How Stories Work and Why We Tell Them*. London: Penguin Books.

CHAPTER 5

Dynamic Storytelling: How to Build Suspense

5.1   BINDING LISTENERS TO THE STORY

The following questions are listeners' constant companions during the first season of *Serial*: Did Adnan Syed kill his high school love Hae Min Lee or not? Has he been wrongfully convicted? What role does Adnan's friend Jay play? And: What else will Sarah Koenig find out? The documentary series *The Hitchhiker* also thrives on these kinds of questions: Is Heinrich still alive? Was he really abused as a child? And are all his stories true? Features like *Papa, we are in Syria* by Christian Lerch work specifically with these kinds of questions (the feature tells the story of a father whose sons went to Syria to join Islamic State): Where exactly are his two sons? Are they still alive? Will the father find them? All three productions work—as banal as it may sound—with open questions, which listeners ask themselves and therefore stick with the story.

Suspense is nothing more than an open question: What is the next step? How does the story end? It is a feeling that is directed towards the continuation of the story. Those who only report results will not create tension.

Dynamic storytelling techniques ensure that listeners want to know how the story continues and finally ends. They tie listeners into the story. Suspense can occur in different ways, either directed more towards the end of the story (How does the story end? Will the hero achieve his goal?) or its progression (What happens next?). This distinction already highlights a problem of many crime stories: We, as viewers, readers or listeners, already have an idea of how the story will end. Most of the time, the perpetrators are caught, after all, and the order of the world is restored. This type of crime thriller is in danger of becoming boring. The tension of these stories must therefore often be fed by the course the story takes: How do the investigators manage to

© The Author(s), under exclusive license to Springer Nature
Switzerland AG 2021
S. Preger, *Storytelling in Radio and Podcasts*,
https://doi.org/10.1007/978-3-030-73130-4_5

catch the culprit? What happens to them on their way to the final confrontation (that's why the personal sub-plots and personality development are so crucial)? Do things get dangerous? Furthermore, it is important that the case as such arouses curiosity: What in heaven's name happened? So ideally, tension runs through the whole story and every scene. If this is achieved, then we as an audience will have the feeling of a 'dense' narrative. One big advantage is that on an exciting path through a documentary story, people also accept all the information that may be particularly important to us as journalistic reporters. Provided that this information is cleverly woven into the story. There are various means that help to tell a story in this exciting and appropriate way.

The American author Karl Iglesias once developed the following formula: "Character-empathy + Likelihood of threat + Uncertainty of outcome = SUSPENSE" (2005, 94). In other words, the more empathy we feel for someone, the greater the likelihood of the threat as well as the threat itself (one could perhaps also say: the greater the resistance and the more that is at stake—these are also elements of threat) and the more uncertain the outcome of the story, the greater the tension. The formula is especially helpful when designing the plot. If the elements are fulfilled, then there is a good chance that people will find the story exciting and join in with the guessing.

Keep in mind: Open questions are like an itch; we find it very difficult to ignore them. That's why they're so important. We also use them to bind listeners to a story for a longer period of time. There may be some listeners who like to listen to long explanatory paragraphs for minutes on end, but most will probably get bored at some point. Maybe as journalists, we would like listeners to want to be informed quickly and comprehensibly. And there are certainly many situations in which this is the case (otherwise many morning shows and information programmes would not be so successful), but in order to follow a longer story, simply lecturing and presenting facts understandably is not enough. On the contrary: It is even counterproductive. Also, shorter forms like a presenter piece or a two-ways can benefit from suspense techniques (see also Sect. 3.9). John Yorke summarises it like this: "Audiences *like* to work; it's the working that glues them to the narrative" (2014, 117).

An effective means of engaging listeners is an unequal distribution of knowledge, working with anticipation or curiosity and compassion. After all, narrator, protagonist and listener do not always have to share the same level of knowledge. "*Curiosity* and *Concern* create three possible ways to connect the audience to the story: *Mystery*, *Suspense*, and *Dramatic Irony*. These terms are not to be mistaken for genres; they story/audience relationships that vary according to how we hold interest" (McKee 1997, 349). According to the American author Robert McKee, mystery means the audience knows less than the characters, which is often the case at the beginning of stories. Listeners have to find and think their way into the story and connect information in order to follow the plot. Stories in which the protagonist keeps a secret for a long time and doesn't reveal it thrive on this kind of dramaturgy.

If listeners know more than the protagonist, McKee calls it dramatic irony. For example, if the narrator has already reported that the protagonist has failed a test, but this information has not yet reached the protagonist, the listener will experience anticipation: Maybe the listener will actually want to protect the protagonist from getting the bad news. The sympathy increases.

If listener and protagonist are at the same level of knowledge (Robert McKee classically calls this suspense), a great closeness between listener and protagonist will develop—they will go through the story together. The conscious distribution of knowledge is thus a central means of working with anticipation, curiosity and compassion—and thus binding the listener to the story.

The narrator is in a sense the mediator, the master of knowledge. She/he can create a balance or an imbalance—and must consider their own role. Because there is often an unspoken agreement: Of course, the narrator knows more than the audience; otherwise, they couldn't tell the story. If the narrator artificially withholds information, the listener may feel that they are being manipulated. The danger of this is particularly great if the narrator appears omniscient from the beginning. If, on the other hand, the narrator credibly adopts an accompanying, exploratory attitude, this danger will be considerably reduced. A particularly good example of dealing with the question of who knows what when is the aforementioned feature *After the Celebration* by Lisbeth Jessen (originally produced for the Danish Broadcasting Corporation in 2002 and adapted for the German market by WDR in 2004).[1] In it, Jessen makes the central figure admit to a web of lies. The story is about Allan who told a radio programme in the mid-1990s that he revealed abuse within his family at a family celebration. This story was the inspiration for the first Dogme95 film *Festen* (English title: *The Celebration*). As listeners, we accompany Jessen in her research and conversations with Allan until the revelation finally comes. In doing so, Jessen lets us share these special moments and does not reveal the result of her research early in the feature - this creates a special listening experience.

The decisive factor here is the narrative mindset and attitude (see also Chapter 7). Only then will the list of revelations and the make-them-wait principle really work. As long as information and revelations arise logically from the story, they are accepted. Things get difficult when possible surprises are held back just for the sake of effect. They then usually cannot be logically integrated into the story and cause bemusement.

Conversely, if listeners know more than the narrator (or the author), this usually leads to feedback after the story is published: short notes on possible mistakes, discreet comments on information not presented in sufficient detail and all kinds of additional facts, which are of course also important and should have been mentioned.

Again: Listeners want to actively participate in the story. They want to be part of the thinking process and develop hypotheses about why a story continues as it does and how it ends. This is illustrated, for example, by the countless responses and debates during the broadcast of the first *Serial* season. The crucial question for authors, producers and reporters is therefore: How can open questions be generated in a documentary acoustic narrative that binds listeners to the story? We have already learned some techniques in plot design. Now it's time for the detailed work, while writing the script. As usual, there are some very helpful techniques and some totally useless procedures. Let's first take a look at suspense killers.

5.2   SUSPENSE KILLER

Some topics just never go away. Every year in May (at the latest!) you should do something about the asparagus harvest (at least in western continental Europe), at the end of August review the summer weather (at least in the northern hemisphere), in September start getting upset about the Christmas cakes and biscuits that are already appearing on shop shelves (whereby 'appearing' is actually a misnomer, a lot of them are available all year round—they are probably only placed more prominently from September onwards). To cut a long story short: There are certain topics and events that recur time and again. And many editorial offices are bored stiff of them by now, which doesn't stop them from resurrecting the topic yet again (but this time with a totally creative twist, namely a report about a person who is thrilled about the reappearance …). And all in the knowledge that listeners don't really want to hear about these topics anymore either. These examples illustrate one of the three suspense killers: telling familiar stories—over and over and over again.

If listeners get the heard-it-all-before feeling, they will be gone sooner rather or later. Probably sooner. Especially when they realise that the progress bar in the player shows that there are still 15, 30 or 45 minutes left to run. That's why no story should start with too much familiar stuff. Listeners make their decision quickly and are unlikely to come back, there are simply too many alternatives. Listeners want to be drawn in and at the same time get enough guidance to understand what it is all about. A fine line. That's why many podcast productions work with a kind of 'value proposition' at the beginning (as a part of the opener), along the lines of "In today's episode you will learn how to build up suspense in your story!" Here too, the more precise this promise is, the better ("In today's episode you will learn how to reel in listeners right from the start, how to bind them to your story over a longer period and how minor revelations work!"). Please do not confuse this with a thematic teaser, which we know from classic radio programmes, often from the beginning of the show ("In the next hour we will look at Berlin, London and Herne").

However, listeners are not supposed to get completely confused. Slight bemusement is allowed, of course, but if there is too much 'eh, what's going on?' most listeners will disappear. The benchmark for an exciting story is to keep them thinking, yes, unreasonable expectations, no. This also means that as an author I have to walk the fine line between new, exciting content on the one hand and guidance on the other. To do this, I have to know my target audience as well as possible. Otherwise, I can hardly assess what listeners know and what they don't. Telling people things they already know quickly smacks of condescension (often in the form of mansplaining!). If I leave too much unexplained, confusion soon sets in. In order to be able to walk this fine line between thinking and confusion, Jad Abumrad from *Radiolab* recommends the technique of signposting: "My own philosophy on storytelling is that people don't want to be told how to feel but they do want to be told what to pay attention to" (Abel 2015, 128). Listeners should not be lectured from above but be made aware that something important is now coming. This can be introduced directly or indirectly. A more direct way would be something like "And then we discovered the decisive fact, namely…"; a more indirect way: "And that confused me so much that I had to think about it again. And then I…" Which variation you choose (or anything in between) certainly depends on you as the narrator and the story. Abumrad recommends something along the lines of "and that's the moment when everything changed" or "and that's when things got interesting" (ibid.). Signposting should not be used too often; otherwise, it loses traction. But especially in *Radiolab* stories, which are often told very quickly and with many people involved, a little explicit guidance is not a bad idea now and then. "Those phrases are like little arrows that tell the listeners: Pay attention to what's about to happen, because it's important" (ibid.).

By the way, there seems to be a big misunderstanding about the target audience. In recent years, many radio programmes have created target figures or target listeners. In principle a good idea: You want to know to whom you are broadcasting. But this has often led to the exclusion of entire subject areas that are supposedly of no interest to these target listeners. The result is that the range of topics in many programmes is felt to be—let's say—unchallenging. World views are consolidated rather than reviewed or expanded. This is not really the way it is supposed to be. The tool of target listeners should help to identify interfaces with certain topics and thus to estimate previous knowledge and hit the fine line mentioned above (to be fair, there are also stations that use the tool in exactly this way). Precisely the principles of storytelling also show that if the craft is right, there is at least a chance of interesting everyone in any topic, but I do have to pay attention to important aspects like narrative sentence, suspense, empathy, protagonists, etc. Nevertheless, there are of course always listeners who reject certain topics either temporarily or as a matter of principle. If you have just had a baby, you will understandably have a hard time with a true-crime story about a child murderer.

And then there's the third tension killer that journalists in particular frequently trigger: the 'that's it then' feeling. This feeling arises in listeners when all results are anticipated. It is deeply etched into journalists' DNA. News is structured like this, reports, even background analyses: the most important things first, then the details, and you should be able to shorten the whole piece from back to front. But if I, as a listener, find out at the beginning of a report how the election turned out, why should I continue listening? Maybe I'm still interested in a few details. But soon it will become clear that this kind of content transfer only holds the attention for a certain length of time—or not. This is also a reason why many journalists find it very difficult to tell longer stories when they have spent a long time working on current affairs programmes. In current affairs programmes, the logic of the news, contribution or discussion often has the following structure: current event, in-depth details, reactions (from all possible and available parties, irrespective of whether they have anything substantial to contribute), possible consequences, outlook. With this meta-scheme almost all lengths between 20 seconds and—let's say— four minutes can be filled without difficulty. But if I as a reporter adapt this form to longer pieces, say, seven to ten minutes or even longer, then the structure stops working. What often happens is that many authors just lengthen the various topic blocks with more information, more details, more reactions and more possible consequences (which then often become pure speculation). The blocks are simply extended (even deepened), but the basic structure does not change. No suspense can arise. In addition, there is the problem that journalists often use loner pieces to demonstrate their knowledge. They answer questions that they consider important in the respective context (How did the conflict arise? Who was not involved? Why have previous attempts at a solution failed? How can things continue now?). But these are often questions that have not yet occurred to the listeners. Thus, longer contributions quickly seem boring and condescending—listeners feel they are being lectured to (see also Sect. 7.1).

When the 'that's it then' feeling sets in, listeners are gone just as quickly as they are with the 'heard it all before' and 'eh, what's going on?' feeling. As authors, we should avoid all three feelings in our stories as far as possible—and this can be done using the following techniques of dynamic storytelling.

5.3   DELIVER AN EXPERIENCE: CREATING A LIVE-FEELING

At the end of the second episode of *The Hitchhiker*, Stephan and I visit the archives together with hitchhiker Heinrich. If there is any proof that Heinrich really was in the child and adolescent psychiatry department in Marsberg (a small town in rural western Germany) decades ago, we will find it here. But we quickly come to the conclusion that there are no medical records for Heinrich, only the hospital registration book from the time. At least this contains the most important meta-data such as admission date. The episode ends like this:

> *Tape*: (Heinrich Kurzrock, archive office) Can you make me a copy to take with me?

Tape: (Archivist Hans-Jürgen Höötmann, archive office) No problem. We'll do it straight away.

Tape: (Heinrich Kurzrock, archive office) Because now I'm running on adrenalin.

Tape: (Hans-Jürgen Höötmann, archive office) You want to look at it in peace, of course.

Sven: And so Heinrich gets a copy. It seems as if this proof is even more important to him than to us.

Tape: (Heinrich Kurzrock, archive office) Well, if you just describe all this today, nobody can understand it, nobody'll believe me either.

Tape: *(Everyone contradicts vehemently and at once.)*

Sven: Perhaps no-one can understand it, but we actually believe Heinrich. He always said that he came to Marsberg as a baby. And the registration book is the formal evidence.

Tape: (Hans-Jürgen Höötmann, archive office) I think...may I just...ah, no. It says day of registration 26.9.57 and then it is chronological...

Sven: Hang on, '57? Heinrich was born in 1949. Then he couldn't have been a baby when he came to Marsberg but was 7 or 8 years old. Something's not quite right here. Next time. (End Credits)

We could also have simply summarised the result in an information paragraph. It would have sounded something like this: "Hitchhiker Heinrich always told us that he had been admitted to the child and adolescent psychiatry department as a baby. But the admission book in the hospital archives shows that Heinrich was only admitted in 1957. A big surprise. We have to follow up on that. Next time."

The founder of the BBC Writer's Academy John Yorke highlights the difference: "Bad writing explains, good writing shows" (2014, 117). It's the classic show, don't tell. The reason is relatively simple: If you really show, you make the event or process, experienceable. A mere summary of the results does not do this. So, it's about creating a kind of live feeling in listeners. To take the listener into the scene and let them participate. It is the feeling that many people know from radio, not just from live football coverage (very famous in Germany especially on a Saturday afternoon when most of the league games take place), but from any radio show. There's someone sitting in the studio right now telling me something. Of course, everyone knows that most podcasts, for example, are not live, but the feeling that listeners have associated with the medium for decades is a live feeling. That is what we have to keep in mind and use. And that's exactly what happens when the action unfolds in front of the listeners' ears.

Action drives the plot and thus the narrative forward. If nothing happens, it gets boring very quickly. Hardly anyone sticks with information passages lasting several minutes. Even short explanatory passages need a justification: They must have something to do with the story; they must either drive the story forward or explain an absolutely necessary fact that the listener cannot understand at this stage but needs to. This is the rationale behind programmes like *This American Life* choosing the ladder of abstraction as a possible meta-structure: because the ladder provides constant interplay between experiencing (on the specific, lower level) and reflecting (on the abstract, upper level). The reporters, editors and producers know that they must always return to the action level in order not to lose their listeners. The scenes are the backbone of the story. Well-chosen action generates suspense at the same time: What's going to happen next? Here are a few techniques that help to create and maintain this suspense.

5.4   INTRIGUING OPENING: REEL LISTENERS IN

You have probably often heard the rule that the first sentence is supposed to reel listeners into the story. But what exactly does that mean? When does a sentence really build this degree of tension? The answer is straightforward: When the first sentence throws up questions listeners really would like to know the answers to, as in the following example, the introduction to the documentary about the Austrian physician Johannes Bischko: "Some ideas really do sound crazy: An operation without classic anaesthesia." What kind of operation is this? Why is there no anaesthetic? And who had this idea? Regardless of whether the sentence appeals to the reporter's personal taste, the point is to show that the first sentence should deliver questions rather than answers. Often the first sentences still form what is called the 'establishing shot' in film: place, time, people, patterned on: "February 1st, 2003, Houston Control Center of the American Space Agency NASA. NASA stands for National Aeronautics and Space Administration. It was officially founded in 1958. And today, on this Saturday, the space shuttle Columbia is scheduled to complete its 28th mission. The mission was …" This kind of introduction doesn't exactly grab me and draw me into the story. The only question I ask myself as a listener is why should I go on listening? Why should I care?

To avoid these questions (not the questions we are aiming for!) arising in the first place, it is often a good idea to leap straight into the first scene, as in the documentary about Stephen Hawking: "Listening to Stephen Hawking, you get the feeling that time passes very slowly." No long speeches. In this case, there is also a thematic allusion—after all, Hawking's research is about space and time.

Of course, sound bites can also do the job of delivering a dynamic, direct opening. Beware, however, of the classic collage, which is said to always draw us so elegantly into the cosmos of a piece. Small and beautifully mounted, the collage is, of course, dynamic, but it rarely draws us into the story. As a listener, I'm not yet familiar with the story cosmos and hardly have a chance to really immerse myself in the story because different sound bites offer too many alternatives at once. So, the fireworks of sounds at the beginning are not necessarily helpful at all. The collage as an introduction is often the result of doer logic and tends to indicate that a strong introductory scene is missing. If you want to start with original sounds, you should make sure that they are integrated into a situation—like the beginning of the documentary about the last flight of the space shuttle 'Columbia':

> *Tape*: (George W. Bush, press conference) This day has brought terrible news. At 9 am this morning, Mission Control in Houston lost contact with our Space Shuttle Columbia.

If you absolutely want to have the collage at the beginning, you could think about a commented or leading collage with the reporter intervening from time to time. This has the great advantage that the short, inserted comments help to use the collage directly to develop a kind of argument. This brings me to one of my—quite subjectively—favourite ways of getting started, which works on the pattern of bigger idea + scene. *Radiolab* often does this, and I love it. Let's take a look at the beginning of the documentary about Bertrand Piccard's first intercontinental flight in a solar plane[2]:

> *Author*: If we are not careful, the genus 'adventurer' will soon die out.
> *Tape*: (Bertrand Piccard, office) You know, if there are no great adventures in the future, it will not be for want of ideas.
> *Author*: There are plenty of ideas...
> *Tape*: (Bertrand Piccard, office) It is because there will be too much bureaucracy and administration.
> *Author*: And this is very difficult for Bertrand Piccard to bear.
> *Tape*: (Bertrand Piccard, office) This is really terrible in our world.
>
> Music change. Plus sfx: Strong wind.
>
> *Author*: The Swiss pioneer has never let himself be daunted by this.
> *Tape*: (Bertrand Piccard, office) When I made the first non-stop flight around the world in a balloon in 1999 - I was totally dependent on fossil energies.

The first sentence is a prelude to the great idea behind the story that will unfold. This idea is explored concisely in just a few sentences. Afterwards, the story immediately continues with the first scene. This opening already indicates where the greater relevance of the story will lie—without completely differentiating this 'bigger idea.' This happens later. This idea to begin in this way derives from the world of fables, in which a lesson or moral is formulated either at the beginning—technically known as the promythion—or at the end, the epimythion. I first got the idea to use this method for audio from the dramaturgy trainer Uwe Walter.[3] In his 'Masterclass Storytelling' we saw, amongst other things, the short film *Raising an Olympian*.[4] The almost six-minute long video tells the story of Gabrielle Douglas, who competed for the US gymnastics team at the 2012 Olympic Games in London. The film begins with a close-up of her mother saying this single sentence: "It's true what they say: it takes a village to raise a child." It is a promythion for the story that will now follow, that is, a prefixed mnemotechnic verse or theorem, the moral of the fable. The film is also a very good example of the hero's journey—just put the twelve steps next to it. By the way, it is only in the credits that it becomes clear that the video is an image film for Procter & Gamble (slogan: Proud Sponsor of Moms). Modern marketing also uses dramaturgic means.

What is important is that if you work with a promythion, you should make a point of surprising the listener and arousing curiosity. Promythions that make generalisations ("Life has some surprises in store.") are often boring, and assumed beliefs ("We all know there is no such thing as true love.") may be true for the author, but not necessarily for the audience. They can therefore elicit a reluctant response. Even the sentiment expressed by Gabrielle Douglas' mother seems like a commonplace at first glance: It takes a village to raise a child. But two elements make this sentence special. Firstly, as a viewer, I see the name super (via aston 'Natalie Hawkins, Mom of Olympian Gabrielle Douglas') and know that this is a mother talking about her own child. And the short introductory remark, "It's true," initially sounds like a cliché but conveys a piece of wisdom to the viewer. The subtext here says: I, as a mother, have experienced this myself and therefore know that this saying is true—which arouses curiosity: What exactly has this mom gone through? The example also illustrates the point that when you use a promythion, every detail, every word and the context really matter. But if it works, it's a powerful intro!

If you can't find a strong, dynamic scene to get into the story and make a good starting point, there's still a very effective tool that sounds quite similar to the promythion in name, but is something else: the prolepsis. The prolepsis gives you an inkling of what will happen later. It works like this: A dynamic scene with strong action is taken out of the story and placed at the beginning. Usually, the scene is found again later at a crucial point: as the deepest crisis (if the scene is supposed to produce dynamics), a plot point or just before the climax. What is important here is that the prolepsis does not reveal the whole scene. Questions must remain open, which will be answered when the whole scene finally appears. Or—if the whole scene is at the beginning—it appears later in the narrative in a different context, so that it takes on a different or additional meaning. This may be because, in the meantime, we as listeners have learned something that changes our perspective. The 'Radiolab' story about Surya Bonaly is an example of this. The story opens with the Olympic Free Skating in Nagano in 1998 and returns to this scene at the climax of the story. The story begins quickly and dramatically. That's one of the reasons why it's true that if you start with a strong prolepsis you will have gained permission to unfold the story rather more slowly at first.

The design of the announcement or the opening credits is also a special feature of long audio stories. The same rules apply to the embedding of the opening credits as for the introduction without them. In *The Hitchhiker* we actually use a mixture of promython ("When someone asks for your help, you have to help") and dynamic scene (Heinrich's begging, especially conveyed by his haunting tone). Formally, we built it as what I call a commented or more guiding collage:

> *Stephan*: When someone stands in front of you, in total despair...
> *Tape*: (Heinrich Kurzrock, Gas Station) I want to scream. Yes, I want scream.
> *Stephan*: ...who wants to end his life...
> *Tape*: (Heinrich Kurzrock, Gas Station) ...if I knew that this was my last day, I would shout hallelujah.
> *Stephan*: ... and who asks you for a last favour, for his last journey....
> *Tape*: (Heinrich Kurzrock, Gas Station) I don't have anything more to hope for. The path to Zurich is clear. Now I only need a few little grains of sand, little stones, by which I mean money, to survive until I get to Zurich and the end. I don't need anything else.
> *Stephan*: Then you have to help, don't you?

The decisive factor in this construction is that the introduction raises questions—in this case, amongst others, the direct question at the end (which merely puts into explicit words what the listeners are probably asking themselves anyway: Would I have helped?). The scene should now draw the listener through the following opening credits, i.e. be so exciting that the listener stays tuned. The opening credits should not be underestimated. Just as in movies or TV series, the announcement is a kind of introduction that fulfils several functions. It forms a bridge between the world outside and the world of the story. It is a miniature of the overall story in terms of genre, mood, soundtrack and tempo. It is thus also a means of anticipation; it contains a narrative promise of what awaits the listener. Good opening credits lead into the world of the story. The legendary opening credits of James Bond films, *Money Heist* or *Game of Thrones* are just a few prominent examples. In the world of audio narratives, the *Serial* opening credits with the piano and tape recording do just that. The announcement also creates an immense recognition effect here. One of the best opening credits (and soundtracks) of the past few years is certainly the one from the podcast *S-Town* (for information on how to get started with series that often briefly summarise what has happened so far at the beginning of a new episode, see Sect. 3.10).

No matter which entry you choose, ask yourself: Do the first sentences of the story draw me in so strongly that I want to know how it continues? Be strict!

5.5   Dramaturgical Expectation Management: Different from What You Thought

Although it is an example from a fictional television series, it illustrates in a wonderfully romantic way how playing with expectations can work. In the HBO series *The Newsroom* (written by Aaron Sorkin) there are the two characters, Maggie and Jim. And, of course, in the end the two have to get together. And that's exactly what happens. However, just when the relationship seems to be growing, Maggie gets offered a job in Washington (but the editorial office, for which both of them work, is located in New York). A job that Jim recommended her for. Maggie wants this job. In one of the last scenes, Jim and Maggie face each other in the newsroom:

Jim: I will take the last plane every Friday night after the show. And the first plane back on Mondays.
Maggie: Or sometimes I could come to New York....
Jim: ...or meet in the middle of New Jersey.
Maggie: That's right.
Jim: Yeah.
Maggie: Have you had a lot of long-distance relationships?
Jim: Yes.
Maggie: Have any of them worked?
Jim: No (goes away towards the door).
Maggie: (calls after him) Why is this gonna be different?
Jim: I wasn't in love with them.

This scene is an example of 'it happens, but not as we thought.' Yes, Maggie and Jim are together. Yes, he declares his love. But the situation is different from what we expected. The declaration of love is not made by candlelight dinner, but in the newsroom—as a confession that slips out more or less accidentally. Appropriate for both characters and the show.

When dealing with true stories, we as reporters naturally cannot simply write ourselves into such situations. But we can consciously look for surprises: When do we encounter a situation or find information that we did not expect? In the fifth episode of *The Hitchhiker* we visit the religious order, together with Heinrich, which was one of the institutions responsible for the abuse in the child and adolescent psychiatry department Heinrich was in. The Mother Superior is available for a conversation and we are even allowed to record our meeting. We are positively surprised by this. We even think the conversation may involve some kind of apology. In fact, this is exactly what happens, but absolutely not as we had thought. The Mother Superior not only expresses genuine regret but offers Heinrich financial help: 3000 euros. It is a moment that unfolds special power.

In order to depict such moments and their meaning appropriately, it is important to build up expectations in the narrative beforehand. This is achieved by using one of the strongest tension techniques of all: anticipation. If you ask yourself how something will continue, you usually end up with an assumption. It's like a second storyline which enfolds in the minds of listeners. It's a matter of building up expectations and then shattering them—or fulfilling them a little differently from what had been expected. This technique is also called misleading.

The idea of a two-step process (sow expectations, reap emotions) is also reflected in another idea we have spoken about before in connection with the unity of plot and action (see Sect. 3.2). Once again, it is about Chekhov's gun on stage. This is both a symbol for incorporating only what is necessary into the plot as well as for the duality of hint and reap or prepare and redeem. This technique normally comprises two steps: setup (hint or sow) and payoffs (cash in or harvest). The rifle can also be understood as a hint. It engenders the expectation that it will be used at some point. This anticipation can then be shattered, for example, by not using the rifle to shoot someone, but to beat them unconscious. The big challenge here is usually not so much the actual resolution, the payoff, writes Robert McKee, but rather the setups: "Setups must be handled with great care. They must be planted in such a way that when the audience first sees them, they have one meaning, but with a rush of insight, they take on a second, more important meaning" (1997, 240). This applies not only to objects, but also to people's behaviour. In *The Hitchhiker*, it gradually becomes obvious that Heinrich's begging trick is designed, above all, to generate maximum pity in the shortest possible time. His constant scrounging is a way for him to create closeness. But listeners only gradually come to this realisation. If as the narrator, I already indicate (indirectly or directly) that something bad is going to happen later, then one also speaks of 'foreshadowing.' The audience already suspects something! Another kind of expectation management.

In order to completely mislead expectations, the 'red herring' is often used in fictional stories. This is an object that makes an important impression, but then doesn't play a role in the story, along the lines of sometimes a briefcase simply contains files. It should not be confused with the 'MacGuffin'[5] which is also an object that doesn't as such play a role in the story, but its importance has great implications. This sounds like a contradiction, but it is not. Whether the 'Holy Grail' is, for example, a cup, a grail or something else entirely is not important. What is paramount for the narrative is the effect of this object on the story—that is, the fact that everyone wants to possess the Grail. Often this technique is also used in spy stories. The goal behind all these techniques is always the same: to build up expectations and then use them to stage surprises. In this way, the audience is emotionally bound to the story. For true audio stories, such possibilities are mainly discovered during research: When are my own assumptions or expectations disappointed or shattered? And why? Those who develop a feeling for such moments lay the foundation for using them in narratives. Again, the same applies here. These techniques can only be used if the story is made tangible. If you merely describe the results you will not be able to create surprises. That is why I personally note the biggest surprises during my research in a special place: on the list of revelations.

5.6   THE LIST OF REVELATIONS: WOW-MOMENTS FOR LISTENERS

It is another of those moments with hitchhiker Heinrich. He has commissioned us to research his family history: who his parents were and why he was committed to the psychiatric ward. We have spent months researching and now we have some answers which we would like to present to him (after all, we are proud to have found something). We don't know yet that the coming minutes will be amongst the most frustrating we will ever experience with Heinrich. We are sitting in his room (barely enough space for the three of us) and want to tell him. But suddenly Heinrich doesn't want to hear about it anymore. We make several attempts, once, twice—we throw in little pieces of information to see if they trigger anything in Heinrich, maybe a memory or his curiosity. But finally, we have to accept that he really doesn't want to know. And, of course, he has every right not to know. As authors, that really gets to us:

Sven: Fuming, we make our way home. We are speechless. Flat out. Emotionally in turmoil. Why should we bother investigating all this if Heinrich doesn't want to know about it now?! But he just gave us the answer himself. The mail. Our packages. Maybe he is interested in his family history...

The following tape-sounds in memory reverb.

Tape: (Sven Preger, Heinrich's room) We also have an address...
Tape: (Heinrich Kurzrock, Heinrich's room) Shamrockstrasse...
Sven: ...or maybe not.
Tape: (Sven Preger, Heinrich's room) And then I think in the Kronen......
Tape: (Heinrich Kurzrock, Heinrich's room) I don't know...
Sven: It's just a little thing, but something's wrong here. Heinrich cannot know this address for his parents - Shamrockstrasse - if he really believes that they died in '49. We have to talk about that. Next time.

And that's what we do at the beginning of the next episode:

Tape: (Sven Preger, office) Bochumer Strasse in Herne is very close to your parents' last address.

Tape: (Heinrich Kurzrock, on phone) (Pause) They were dead.

Tape: (Sven Preger, office) Yes, they were dead in the early seventies.

Sven: We are talking about time. About 1972, to be exact. After Heinrich was released from the psychiatric hospital. He then moved to Herne, to Bochumer Strasse. It's very near to Shamrockstrasse, which is his parent's last known address.

  And this is what puzzled me. How does Heinrich know this address? We found it in his parents' death certificates. And so, I suspect that Heinrich knows exactly when his parents died. Certainly not in 1949, as Heinrich always says.

Tape: (Heinrich Kurzrock, on the phone) According to the information I have, my father died on 10.6.65.

Sven: Just as I said. (Title Music sets in.)

There are two types of revelations: understanding and experiencing. Understanding is the result of reflection—as in the first example, the reflection on the conversation we had with Heinrich. This reflection makes us notice a contradiction. Experiencing, on the other hand, is the result of an action—as in the second example, the conversation I had with Heinrich on the phone. Both moments were on our list of revelations. Both moments allow listeners to share in how the story is evolving. It is the interplay on the ladder of abstraction, already described, between specific experiences and reflecting on them, which in turn leads to a new action. As a narrator of true stories, it is important to register these moments while doing the research. Otherwise, there is a danger that I will not be able to remember them later or that they will have become part of my general knowledge on the topic. As a result, I will no longer associate any special feeling with them. Furthermore, as a reporter I should, if possible, make sure to get the corresponding audio recordings from the real scene. Otherwise, I have to reconstruct the scene afterwards (see Sect. 6.1). That's also possible, but not quite as nice.

These special moments thus get a place on the list of revelations during the research phase. And depending on the narrative sentence, i.e. the story, these moments later become plot points, deepest crises or a climax. And some of these moments do not make it into the story at all. But without the list, I might miss one of the most important passages when writing later. John Truby points out: "Good writers know that revelations are the key to plot. That's why it's so important that you take some time to separate the reveals from the rest of the plot and look at them as one unit" (2007, 305). All the revelations together give a great overview of the essential elements of the story: character development, plot and even suspense arc. And that thrives, amongst other things, on the pace and rhythm of the story, as the next section shows.

5.7   CREATING RHYTHM: ENJOYING THE SPECIAL MOMENT

The most important clue is coming now! But before that, I'll just quickly get a cup of tea, so I can concentrate better on the next paragraph. There we are: Now, just call to mind that quotation from Charles Dickens and William Goldman: Make them wait! One of the most important ways of maintaining the suspense is indeed to introduce delays or interruptions. If, in any story, someone is trying to escape from another person and has to use a car, for example, you can assume that the person fleeing will firstly not find the keys in the rush, then the battery of the electronic door opener will be flat, then they will drop the keys when trying to unlock the car door and, finally, will stall the engine before narrowly escaping with screeching tyres—only to crash into a lorry at the next corner. So, the getaway continues on foot... you get the idea. Key message: There are always obstacles along the way. Just as the crucial conversation, the confession or the wedding proposal is about to begin, the phone rings. These are all delaying tactics to heighten the suspense. As a rule of thumb: If nothing happens, tell it quickly and summarise more. If something exciting happens, slow down the pace of the story. Enjoy the moment. That's how you give your story its own rhythm.

Caution: Especially with true stories, this can quickly seem artificial or exaggerated. But on a small scale, it's useful, particularly for incorporating information into a scene that is important to me as a writer, as in this example from the documentary about Stephen Hawking:

> *Author*: Hawking impressed people early on. His classmates, for example. They made a bet. He was only 12 years old at the time. Stephen Hawking talks about this in his book: *My Brief History*. It is one of the few texts in which he speaks personally. He was living with his family in St Albans, north of London, in the late 1950s. His parents had moved away from the capital when the bombs started falling during WW II. To Oxford, where Stephen William Hawking was born.
>
> *Tape*: (Stephen Hawking, archive) On the 8th of January 1942. Exactly 300 years after the death of Galileo.
>
> *Author*: The famous astronomer.
>
> *Tape*: (Stephen Hawking, archive) However, I estimate that about 200,000 other babies were also born that day.
>
> *Author*: The family is considered to be intelligent and a little eccentric, cranky. At dinner, all the Hawkings like to sit at table with a book. Maybe that's why Stephen's classmates nicknamed him Einstein. Hawking was not a good student. And yet they bet a bag of sweets - that Hawking would one day become something important.

What kind of bet the classmates had thought up is only revealed at the end of the paragraph—biographical information is embedded in between. It is nothing less than an example of "make them wait." We are looking at two sides of the same coin: Interruptions help to delay crucial information or events and thus keep the tension high. At the same time, they are an opportunity to convey facts and figures.

Those who have waited so long and survived the delays may now be properly rewarded. Which means that if it is an important part of the story it should not be over too quickly. This technique is executed well by the authors of the *Radiolab* story about Surya Bonaly. When the figure skater finally goes out on the ice in the 1998 Olympic final in Nagano (at minute 34, introduced by the same sound we already know from the beginning, a prolepsis was used here), the reporters repeatedly throw in short comments and explanations on the actual scene. They explain, ask questions or let Surya Bonaly speak, commenting on and classifying the scene herself (the atmosphere of the scene is largely retained so as not to destroy the illusion). As a result, the whole moment, the climax of the story, is longer, more exciting and more experienceable. The *Radiolab* team never exaggerates. The moment is not artificially extended. All in all, the scene lasts about three minutes until the all-decisive moment of the story (and indeed, there is that moment!): Surya Bonaly lands a backflip that no one has ever executed in a competition before. Two more minutes are dedicated to this special move (to give you an actual idea of what she was doing) and the rest of her freestyle programme. In total, this makes five wonderfully exciting, dynamic minutes of acoustic narrative. These minutes take listeners right back to that moment in Nagano. Slowing down the narrative tempo is an essential means here. The result is that this scene can be experienced in a special way. Surya Bonaly's freestyle programme seems like one of those moments that are larger than life. Condensed reality. It is these condensed moments that often unfold power in narratives. They point far beyond themselves and thus also form a connection to the 'bigger idea' of the narrative. For great stories, look for moments when the 'bigger idea' of your story can be experienced!

There is no space for boredom to arise in this scene either, because the *Radiolab* team uses a different strategy at the same time: The scene consists of a lot of different sound elements; it's fast, lively and assembled like a collage. In this way, the authors make use of the great strength of collage: dynamism! The number of voices to be heard (presenters, reporters, Surya Bonaly and the original tape) is near the upper end of the comprehensibility scale. But this does not diminish the listening pleasure!

In general, a collage also offers at least two other ways of influencing the pace of a narrative: Firstly, the collage can shorten a longer period of time to just a few original sounds ('fast forward' effect). Secondly, it can build up suspense by mounting two parts of the plot, which are cut against each other, in parallel: For example, if one strand of a story depicts a person drowning in a lake, the other strand shows the possible rescuer's path to this person. Interweaving these elements creates tension: Will the rescuer arrive in time? In true stories, the parallel montage also helps to establish relationships between events: "It compares two lines of action, two pieces of content, and makes them equal" (Truby 2007, 329). The collage can be both a tool for suspense and for analysis, as in the following excerpt from a documentary about Stanley Milgram and his famous experiment, which tested the willingness of people to obey orders that were incompatible with their conscience. In the experiment, the test subjects were persuaded to give other people electric shocks when instructed to do so. Therefore, they later argued that they were only following orders. In reality, no electricity flowed, the victims were impersonated by actors who simulated pain.

Author: And then it started.

Tape: (Milgram experiment, Germany 1970, experiment manager) Ready? Begin.

Music starts: We do what we are told. Collage of original sounds from the Milgram experiment in Germany are blended with original sounds from the Eichmann trial.

Collage: (Milgram experiment, Germany 1970) Teacher: Sad - music. Sad - Clown. Sad - girl. (Click) The answer was wrong. I'll punish you with 90 volts. /Student: Ah /Teacher: Cool – Day. Cool – Shadow. Cool – Water. Cool - Cave. (Click) Wrong. 195. (click) /Student: Ow. I'll stop now. /Experimenter: Continue. /Eichmann: I had to obey. /Teacher: The correct word would have been 'Slow – Dance'. /Experimenter: Time is up. /Teacher: That's 255. /Eichmann: I had only one thing to do: I had to obey. Because I couldn't change anything. /Teacher: You get 345. (loud screams). I'll punish you with 390 volts (clack) (Silence) He's not saying anything more (to Experimenter).

Author: Silence. All cries from the next room are muted. And there are no more answers: to the teacher's questions.

Collage: Teacher: If something has happened to him now. /Experimenter: The experiment requires that you continue - that's quite clear. /Eichmann: I had to obey. I was just taking orders. /Experimenter: If he doesn't answer, tell him: He has ten seconds to answer. If he doesn't reply, it's considered a false reply. /Teacher: You have ten seconds to answer. If you do not answer, the answer is considered wrong. /Eichmann: When my superiors ordered me to obey, I had to obey. I was famous for it. /Teacher: You will receive 450 volts. /Teacher: A shock of 450 volts. /Teacher: A punishment of 450 volts follows. /Teacher: 450 volts...

Music takes over: We do what we are told. Fades out slowly.

Author: The first Milgram experiment at Yale and the Eichmann trial in Jerusalem took place in the same year: 1961. The terrifying result of the experiment was that almost two thirds of the participants gave the student the highest electric shock, 450 volts.

The collage (which in written form can be a bit more confusing than listening to the actual voices) builds a connection between the Milgram experiment and Adolf Eichmann's defence strategy—and thus unmasks it. The collage thus also creates a revealing moment of understanding - and possibly a strong emotional reaction on the part of the listener (after all, this type of montage also contains a clear value judgement). This brings us to the next tension-building technique that many journalists still seem cautious about or are even a bit afraid to use: working responsibly with emotions.

5.8   EMOTIONS: NOT IMITATING AND PRETENDING, BUT SHOWING AND CREATING

The American Pulitzer Prize winner Jon Franklin puts it in a nutshell: "Finally, and most important, climactic narrative never, never, never, never tells us how the characters feel. It doesn't describe emotion, it *evokes* it" (1994, 154). It's not about describing emotions, but about showing them and inducing them in listeners. For example, why are you sad, angry or happy? There are probably different events that trigger these emotions in each of us. But one thing tends to be the same for most of us: We react emotionally when things are important to us. Emotions are important. Conversely, this means that if no emotions are provoked, then we couldn't care less about something. That is the great dilemma of journalism. Emotions are still suspected of being frivolous, somehow dirty and the opposite of facts. This misunderstanding is largely our own fault—a perception that is partly due to the way we as journalists deal with emotions.

Narratives are not about the artificial or inappropriate manufacturing of emotions (which, by the way, is not what other forms of journalism should be about either). The danger of doing just this is related to a major misunderstanding in journalism: In order to evoke emotions, journalists are supposed to feel and demonstrate them, too. An example: If a reporter or presenter wants to make listeners feel concerned, they make their voice sound particularly sad, concerned or shocked (without really feeling it). The result is that the voice often sounds over the top, not authentic, but artificial. And more than anything else, that merely causes alienation and rejection, more or less the exact opposite of what is actually supposed to be achieved. To simulate emotions does not help. Karl Iglesias relates this line of thinking to stories: "Whether your character cries is not as important as whether the reader cries" (2005, 17). Or in our case, listener. Of course, emotions are important: Without emotional ties, listeners will not follow stories for long. Emotions ensure that people engage with stories and want to know what happens next. Stories are not a load of information, but an experience. This includes emotions. Here are a few tips on how to create appropriate emotions.

One of the most important emotions, especially for the beginning of a story, is empathy. In one of my storytelling workshops a participant once spoke up and said that he had a big problem with that. He asked how one could feel empathy with Adolf Hitler. A very good question. The answer: Empathy does not mean justifying or supporting actions. Empathy only makes it possible to understand and experience why someone acts as they do. In terms of craft, empathy can often be triggered by a character's motivation. If I as a listener comprehend why someone acts in a certain way, I can feel understanding or even closeness. Behaviour thus becomes explainable, which means we can learn from it—this also applies to the actions of a dictator.

Sometimes, as a writer, I don't want to disclose my characters' motivation too early. There is a moment of surprise in motivation, which creates much more emotional power and depth at a later point in the story (not at the beginning). Hitchhiker Heinrich, for example, tells his story about his planned suicide not only to scrounge money, but also because he generates the greatest compassion with this story in the shortest time. It is his way of achieving emotional proximity. We only reveal this connection very late in *The Hitchhiker*. After all, it took us a long time to understand it ourselves.

A good way to quickly establish a connection to a character is to present a flaw. We've discussed this before when developing characters (see also Sect. 4.2). Let's take a quick look at the first season of *Serial* again. Reporter Sarah Koenig acts as the protagonist. With the opening passage, quoted above, she introduces herself as a non-perfect person ("undignified on my part"). She is not the omniscient top journalist, but someone who finds it difficult to ask young people certain questions. That's something we as listeners can quickly identify with. A clever, emotional start. We experience a similar strategy at the beginning of *The Hitchhiker*. Stephan Beuting meets a needy man at a petrol station who allegedly wants to commit suicide. Above all, Stephan is overwhelmed (as I am later, too) by this situation (what else?), which is exactly what becomes audible.

This example points to another technique: emotional alignment. Listeners often ask themselves: What would I have done in a situation? Would I have simply rejected this strange man? Helped him perhaps, but in a different way? Or would I have seen through his stories immediately? This emotional alignment glues listeners to the story. But the comparison can only work if two factors come together: connection (here to Stephan, who realistically presents himself as imperfect) and action (what would I have done in this situation?). Once a bond to the story and its characters has been established, listeners will react more directly to the characters' emotions. If someone suffers, we as listeners will feel pity. If someone dies, we will mourn for them. If someone is in danger, we will fear for them, and so on. Sometimes the characters' emotions are actually instilled in listeners. What emotion we feel as listeners is related to the situation in which we experience the characters. That's another reason why it's important to narrate scenically. In this context, it is especially satisfying for listeners if they experience different emotions in the course of the story.

The American author Karl Iglesias introduces a very helpful technique for this: the palette of emotions, "which came to me when I considered the analogy of the writer being a painter on the page, using words instead of colors" (2005, 131). When writing a scene, Iglesias asks himself above all: What emotion should my character feel here? When he knows this, he can also control which emotions are transmitted to readers, listeners or viewers. Iglesias is talking about fictional stories, which allow more creative freedom, but the instrument can also be transferred to non-fictional material: Which emotion do I want to show in the story of my character and which emotions can I thus evoke in listeners? During proofreading, these questions can help to check which emotions actually occur in the story and which are possibly missing. To make the palette of emotions a bit more practical, I have designed a quick emotion checklist. It demonstrates the questions or elements that help to represent certain emotions in a character and evoke them in listeners.

Curiosity and excitement arise when listeners have an open question. This can be one of the following: What is the next step? Does the hero reach their goal? Why is she/he doing this at all? Right up to the very end, there should be at least one open question.

Empathy and identification arise when we recognise ourselves in others. This will differ from person to person. Therefore, it is good to offer several facets of a character. Empathy is often generated when characters are portrayed with a failing and/or a touch of self-irony because it often induces the impression that the character is neither perfect nor takes themselves too seriously. This encourages the listener's willingness to get involved with the character. Helpful questions in developing this emotion include: What can the character not do? What is their flaw? Is she/he self-deprecating? How can I make this clear?

Anger often arises as a defensive reaction to a perceived transgression. Once the character is anchored with the listener, an emotion can also transfer to the listener directly. Many people also have a keen sense of injustice. If a character is treated unfairly, this can generate anger in the listener. But be careful: If listeners get too angry for too long, they will hardly be able to continue listening to the story. The next level of anger can be hate—if boundaries are crossed too often or too ferociously. Helpful questions in developing the emotion of anger or hatred include: What constitutes a transgression of boundaries for the character? Do listeners possibly share this feeling? But as an author, I must also ask myself: Do I really want to create this feeling in listeners?

Surprise or even shock arise when unforeseen things happen. Important for real stories: unforeseen does not mean illogical. This is a common misunderstanding. The surprising event must evolve logically from the story but still surprise listeners, nonetheless. It is not sufficient for the event to be possible; it needs to be probable. An unforeseen accident is always an option, but usually does not arise logically from the story, unless someone defies the risk again and again.[6] If the unforeseen accident is a genuine part of the story, then of course it remains so. The fact that hitchhiker Heinrich refuses to listen to his family's story is a good example of a surprise. Helpful questions to create surprises or shock listeners include: How can I plausibly steer the listeners' anticipation in a different direction so that an important event will come as a surprise?

Fear is a special case of anticipation. Listeners are concerned that a certain event might occur. Fear is always a feeling directed towards the future. Helpful questions to generate fear in the character or in listeners include: What is the character most afraid of? What could happen if s/he doesn't achieve their goal? What are many people afraid of? Why?

Grief is a human's response to loss. Here, too, the feelings of the character can be transferred to listeners. Or the death of a character can trigger mourning. Anyone who remembers the end of the second episode of *S-Town* knows what I mean. John takes his own life. Helpful questions to induce grief include: What is important to the character? For whom do the listeners feel empathy? Why?

Relief usually comes when something has been accomplished or finally occurs. Those who have endured a dreaded visit to the dentist usually feel relieved. Once an anxiety-filled situation is over, character and listener can take a deep breath. Therefore, the same questions apply as they do for fear.

Joy or happiness arises when something finds our approval or surprises us in a positive way. This kind of lightness is something that I still miss in many audio stories. Since the topics and people are important to us as reporters, our stories often seem profoundly serious. In the fifth episode ('Route Talk') of the first *Serial* season, there is this wonderful interaction between Sarah and Dana in the car. Sarah is just thinking about the case and wants to talk to Dana about it. But Dana seems to have other things on her mind. In the middle of Sarah's very smart, intense and reflective thoughts, she suddenly bursts in: "There is a shrimp sale at the Crab Crib!" Hunger comes first (as demonstrated by Maslow's hierarchy of needs!). Helpful questions to integrate some lightness, humour and joy into the story include: When did I myself laugh during my research? Why? Can I put this moment in the story?

Depending on the gradation and intensity, other emotions are also conceivable. Of course, the principle applies here as well: All emotions must represent an appropriate reflection of reality. It is not a matter of artificially emotionalising. But reporters or producers who do not sharpen their perception will not notice or overlook emotions during research or will not incorporate them into the story for other reasons. For me personally, thinking about emotions helps at two points in the working process: Firstly, in creating the story. I try not to leave it to chance which emotions occur. Secondly, when reworking the manuscript: The darker and more serious a story is, the more I try to include some bright moments and emotions. However, deep emotions like real joy or sadness need some time to unfold their power. These emotions won't help much at the beginning of the story. Only when a character is really dear to my heart, will I feel stronger emotions as a listener. In my opinion, this is also one of the reasons why current journalism tends to focus on the 'fast' emotions like excitement, anger or horror. Deep sadness, understanding or relief only arise after a longer process of consideration.

Emotions are the pulling force that draws listeners into the story and keeps them in it. Ideally, a narrative addresses both systems: cognition and emotion. Stories are better remembered that way. And that's what we want as reporters. That's why it's important not to be afraid of emotions.

5.9   CLICHÉ PLUS X

The cliché is one of the biggest problems when it comes to portraying people in stories. On the one hand, the cliché helps. There is usually a grain of truth in it: the hyper-careful helicopter parents (who drive their children everywhere they go in an SUV), the totally alternative hipsters (who prefer to drink flat white rather to latte macchiato, the latter is so 2015, after all) or the somewhat nerdy colleague from IT (with the check shirt that is never tucked neatly into his trousers). On the other hand, the cliché obstructs the view of the differentiated world. We know the cliché, so we already know how the world works. The cliché trap. American radio journalist Celeste Headlee puts it in a nutshell in her TED talk "10 ways to have a better conversation." She has hosted various radio shows for years. She is an experienced interviewer and conversation partner. When she reaches the sixth point, she says "Don't equate your experience with theirs. (…) It is not the same. It is never the same. All experiences are individual." Every experience is unique and individual. For narratives, this idea is central, because it helps us to get out of the cliché trap. 'Cliché plus X' means exactly that: to break or develop the cliché. For one thing, it makes use of the cliché, providing a starting point for many listeners. For another, it ensures that the description becomes unique and not superficial. A personal note: again and again, I am surprised (no, not positively) by the cynicism of editorial debates. In order to tell stories, people often still look for a cliché case: the poor beggar, the needy wheelchair user, the oppressed citizen, the victim of justice, the struggling parents etc. These people do of course exist. But the way they are presented is often very clichéd. Journalists can write these kinds of pseudo-stories almost 'cold'—i.e. always following the same pattern and without really establishing contact with these people. It is remarkable that it is often precisely the journalists who produce such clichéd contributions that complain about storytelling and narration—because this kind of storytelling is supposedly far too formatted and would distort the view of reality. A fine example of irony. End of personal note.

Whereby clichés can be quite useful. They have developed as a kind of super-category because they summarise the experiences of many people in specific terms and thus make them concrete. The task of a reporter, however, is now to break away from this categorisation and make uniqueness tangible. One way of approaching this is to consciously shatter the cliché, but to do so, you first have to recognise that it is a cliché, which a reporter can only do by getting close to people: Perhaps I should not pity the beggar (perhaps he doesn't want pity)? Perhaps I also understand the beggar's motivation. Reasons and motives always help to discover the people behind the clichés and make individuals tangible. We have already seen how important motivation is when considering the narrative sentence. And here again it plays a decisive role.

The cliché can be a starting point, but it is never sufficient for a narrative. Those who stick with the cliché will not create depth. The good news is that no one is just a cliché. Everyone is always more than that. Of course, you have to be interested in this kind of differentiation.

5.10   Flashback: More Than a Leap into the Past

Flashback (also called analepsis) is one of the most dangerous and often misunderstood narrative techniques. Just going back in time (according to the motto: "The story began 20 years ago...") is not a flashback, but only a regression. It is often used, for example after a tender, dynamic introduction to a play. Over the reverb music (after, say, 90 to 120 seconds), the narrator says something like: "It all began..." What follows is, depending on the format and broadcasting space, a rather long description of the background and development of the central theme or event, often as a sequence of numbers, dates and facts. The idea behind this regression is that the listener should know how everything came about. After all, this information is important for understanding later events—and besides, as a reporter, I hopefully haven't researched everything in vain.

The big problem is that it slows the story down and doesn't drive it forward. There is a regression and, so to speak, a second beginning (but now from the outset and more reasonable). The transition is, however, a break, often acoustically, and listeners notice this. The story loses pace even before it has really started. Dramaturgically speaking, regressing the story is often useless. And formally, it is not a flashback. It doesn't jump back to the main narrative time from a later point. This kind of regression at the beginning of a story only makes sense after a prolepsis or other dynamic scene at the very beginning of the story. The narrative then drops back in time to the outset—but ideally by introducing another scene and not a couple of minutes of facts and figures.

Key message: The flashback must serve the story and change the now. Only then can the flashback imbue story with power and help to drive it forward.

An example: The episode *Gun Show* of the American podcast series *More Perfect* (a spin-off of *Radiolab*) from October 2017 deals with the meaning of the Second Amendment to the US Constitution, which regulates the extent to which a government may restrict the right to bear arms. The extent to which this right applies and whether restrictions are possible is a matter of ongoing debate amongst legal experts. This is the dispute at the heart of the *More Perfect* episode. The story also deals with the history of the National Rifle Association (NRA), the most important weapons lobby in the US. Amongst other things, it is about a general meeting in Cincinnati, Ohio, in 1977. It is a crucial meeting for the course of the NRA. As listeners, we have reached the middle of the story, almost half an hour has passed (the whole piece takes about 70 minutes). The original sound opening the event is played and fades out. Then the reporter says: "Prior to this big meeting…" It is therefore an immediately recognisable flashback: In short sentences and sound bites we learn how a small group of members had previously held secret meetings. This group calls itself 'Federation for NRA.' Their goal is to take over the NRA. The flashback ends with the reporter's phrase, "And this tiny group was planning a coup…" The sound bite of the opening of the annual meeting then resumes. We are back in the here and now, after about 45 seconds of flashback. As a listener, I now know about the tension in the hall—perhaps even more than some people did back then. Now I ask myself: What exactly is this group planning? And how does it intend to achieve its goal? The flashback has been used to build suspense. It serves the story that is being told. This is excellent craftsmanship!

5.11 THE FINAL SENTENCE: ALL THINGS CONSIDERED

Stephen Hawking is dead. He died in Cambridge on 14 March 2018. When the above-mentioned documentary about him was broadcast in January 2017, he had just turned 75. It ends with the following paragraph: "All his life Stephen Hawking explored the universe, space and time. He is often asked whether he thinks time travel is possible. Hawking once wrote that he wouldn't bet on it because the other person might have the advantage of knowing the future." This anecdote connects the two central elements of the story, Stephen Hawking as a person and his research. In doing so, it reveals the humour that was characteristic of Stephen Hawking. It may take a moment to understand the punch line. That's why the anecdote comes at the end—it may resonate. If the listener thinks about it now, he or she will not miss anything. Music reverb and end credits also give a little space to think and follow up.

The last sentence or paragraph of a piece can fulfil several functions. It does not matter whether it consists of a reporter sentence, a quotation, some tape or any other element. The following aspects offer some ideas:

1. An appropriate ending. The last paragraph should reflect the character of the story in tone and thought. The story is over, the heroes return home and appreciate their own home even more than before. This is one of the reasons why Samwise Gamgee's last sentence in *Lord of the Rings* is "Well, I'm back!" (Tolkien 1991, 1069)
2. An image of the story. The last paragraph delivers the maxim or moral of the story or finally lays out the bigger idea. The documentary about the Milgram experiment ends with the following paragraph:

> *Original sound*: (Eichmann trial, 13.12.1961, closing words Adolf Eichmann) My fault is my obedience. The ruling class, to which I did not belong, gave the orders. In my opinion, it deserved punishment. For the atrocities perpetrated on the victims on their orders. But those under their command are now victims, too. I am such a victim.
>
> *Author*: The judges did not concur with the defendant's arguments: Adolf Eichmann was executed in 1962. Was he convinced of his own claims? The Milgram experiment showed obedience is a part of us. But that is no excuse.

3. Final answers. Be it the central challenge of the story or the hero's unanswered questions. It is again worth taking a look at the end of the first season of *Serial*. Sarah Koenig allows herself a relatively long last paragraph, which given the length of the season is perfectly justified. She raises the main questions of the whole season once more.

Firstly: Can she prove that Adnan really is the culprit? This is the question that has preoccupied listeners: Did he or did he not kill Hae? "But let's put another file next to that one, side by side. In that second file let's put all the other evidence we have linking Adnan to the actual crime, the actual killing. What do we have? What do we know? Not what do we think we know, what do we know? If the call log does not back up Jay's story, if the Nisha call is no longer set in stone, then think about it. What have we got for that file? All we're left with is, Jay knew where the car was. That's it. That all by itself, that is not a story. It's a beginning, but it's not a story. It's not enough, to me, to send anyone to prison for life, never mind a seventeen-year-old kid. Because you, me, the State of Maryland, based on the information we have before us, I don't believe any of us can say what really happened to Hae" (Koenig 2014).

Secondly: Should the verdict against Adnan be overturned? It's a legal question: Was he wrongfully convicted? "As a juror I vote to acquit Adnan Syed. I have to acquit. Even if in my heart of hearts I think Adnan killed Hae, I still have to acquit. That's what the law requires of jurors."

Thirdly: Does Sarah believe Adnan did it? As listeners we really like Sarah, she is the protagonist and has grown close to our hearts. So, what does she think? "But I'm not a juror, so just as a human being walking down the street next week, what do I think? If you ask me to swear that Adnan Syed is innocent, I couldn't do it. I nurse doubt. I don't like that I do, but I do. I mean most of the time I think he didn't do it. For big reasons, like the utter lack of evidence but also small reasons, things he said to me just off the cuff or moments when he's cried on the phone and tried to stifle it so I wouldn't hear. Just the bare fact of why on earth would a guilty man agree to let me do this story, unless he was cocky to the point of delusion. I used to think that when Adnan's friends told me 'I can't say for sure if he's innocent, but the guy I knew, there's no way he could have done this.' I used to think that was a cop out, a way to avoid asking yourself uncomfortable, disloyal, disheartening questions. But I think I'm there now too. Not for lack of asking myself those hard questions, but because as much as I want to be sure, I am not."

Fourthly: What has this immense research taught us? At the very end, Sarah Koenig reopens the debate, giving it broader context and some sense of closure (as far as possible with this story): "When Rabia first told me about Adnan's case, certainty, one way or the other seemed so attainable. We just needed to get the right documents, spend enough time, talk to the right people, find his alibi. Then I did find Asia, and she was real and she remembered and we all thought, 'how hard could this possibly be? We just have to keep going.' Now, more than a year later, I feel like shaking everyone by the shoulders like an aggravated cop. Don't tell me Adnan's a nice guy, don't tell me Jay was scared, don't tell me who might have made some five second phone call. Just tell me the facts ma'am, because we didn't have them fifteen years ago and we still don't have them now."[7] And so it comes about (as we perhaps expected or were fearing): an open end! Life is rarely black and white. We have to live with that. What a lesson!

4. A punch line or anecdote, which has not occurred in the piece so far. It exemplifies once again what makes the story and the protagonist stand out. Like the end of the documentary about Stephen Hawking.
5. And then there's the big bang at the end. The final information or scene, which makes the whole thing appear in a slightly different light, shifts the story a bit. A relevant piece of information—a last open question that is still to be answered. The first season of *The Hitchhiker* ended this way and thus provides the answer to one of the last big questions: Does Heinrich still have a family today? The final punch line is woven into the credits:

Sven: Not completely. Because there is someone else, Heinrich, who would like to meet you.
Announcer: Editor: Leslie Rosin.
Sven: Who we found in Herne.
Tape: (Petra, apartment) Hello Heinrich. This is your niece Petra. If you are interested, I would like to write to you sometimes or we could even meet each other if you want to get to know me.
Announcer: A *Hörweiten* production for WDR 2016.

Which last paragraph or sentence you chose depends on the material, tone of the story and you. The last paragraph and especially the very last sentence do not need to be stylistically particularly elaborate or complex. The conclusion develops its power from the content, hardly from the form. As an author, it helps to think beyond the actual story in the last paragraph. Which bigger idea should the piece demonstrate, prove, explain? If you present these thoughts at the end and elaborate them, you almost always achieve a good, accentuated ending and can be sure that the story will not break off abruptly. We often love stories that resonate in us for a moment. This way a story creates emotional depth. For example, the fourth season of *The Bridge* (the Scandinavian production with Sofia Helin as Saga Norén in the leading role) ends with a sentence, which in a brilliant way brings the series to a nearly perfect close. It leaves the viewer with a feeling of empathy for this great character. Moreover, it is a sentence that consists of only two words and only makes sense in the cosmos of the series. Thus, it unfolds a special power. If you want to experience this effect at the end of the series, just watch all four seasons first—it's worth it!

5.12   THE POWER OF AUDIO: EMBRACE INTIMACY

At the end of the first season of *Serial*, I wanted to be friends with Sarah Koenig. No, that's not quite true: While I was still in the middle of the story, I already wanted to be friends with Sarah Koenig. With this humorous, self-reflective, attentive reporter who does sensitive, fair, meticulous and sometimes relentless research. And I know I am not alone in feeling like this. And not only journalists feel that way, I am sure. Koenig uses, amongst many other techniques, three major strengths of the medium audio, in particular:

1. Intimacy. If the word is too intimate for you, you can replace it with closeness. If closeness is too close, perhaps you should try another medium. Intimacy occurs on at least three levels. Firstly, production related. Recording devices are nowadays so small that, when handled properly, they hardly interfere with the recording situation. The chance that people will open up, feel unobserved and allow deep insights is thus rather greater than with video or photo cameras, for example.

   Secondly: Inside relationships. What I mean by this is that audio is especially powerful when it comes to small groups of people. Two or three people in a situation or debate can be well portrayed. Where the medium has its weaknesses is in dealing with mass scenes or a complex ensemble piece. Imagine the Netflix documentary *Making a murderer* as audio. Without pictures, we as listeners would have to concentrate excessively. Where are we exactly? Who was that again? And what is his or her relationship to the others? The pictures simply help in this situation. In addition, an acoustic narration with too many places and people always needs a lot of explanations, transitions etc. That robs the story of pace. Audio is good when it's about the relationship between a few people—and they can then be particularly intense.

Thirdly: Outside relationships. This is classic: the voice of the narrative goes directly into the listener's ear, and often enough via headphones. All the noise and other people around us, for example on the tram on the way to work, become unimportant. Media closeness like this is rare. And it directly illustrates another strength.

2. The narrator's personality. Reporters who reveal at least one authentic part of their personality carry the story. That's also one of the reasons why *Serial* has inspired so many people. Sarah Koenig becomes recognisable as a person. She lets us participate in her thoughts and reflections. That binds the listener to her. In these passages, she not only tells us the result of her reflections, but also lets us participate in her process of awareness, always remaining transparent and credible. Here another problem becomes obvious: In a reporter, it is a great art to tell a story, not to read from a written manuscript, not to over-emphasise every single word, but to really narrate (we will talk about tracking for a narrative later, cf. Chapter 7). It is an art that, certainly in Germany, is hardly trained and practised. Neither insecure reading nor the over-emphasising-everything-continuous-under-pressure correspondent speech helps here. The two British authors Claire Grove and Stephen Wyatt summarise this in their textbook: "There is no need to shout or lecture" (Grove & Wyatt 2013, 28). Finding your narrative voice and professionalising it is hard work, but the trick is not to let on about it.

3. Detachment from time and space. Also a classic. Sarah Koenig takes us everywhere: To past trials, to the visit at Jay's, to the place where Hae's body was found in Leakin Park, and into the world of her own thoughts. This engages listeners because they use their own imagination to build an image of all these different locations. In audio stories, we the listeners can follow the thoughts of the narrator or the characters anywhere, there are no limits. Within a few moments, we can switch between thoughts, places and different times. We are sucked into the story's stream of consciousness. This technique can be found again and again, for example, in novels such as James Joyce's *Ulysses* where we follow the inner monologue of a character's seemingly random thoughts. Given its flexibility, audio is very well suited to that kind of narrative.

In order to tell a good story, it helps to keep the acoustic strengths of the medium in mind. They can show us the way: to the story, to the core of a scene and to the innermost part of a person.

5.13   CHECKLIST: SUSPENSE TECHNIQUES

Dynamic storytelling asks how I, as an author, can make sure that listeners absolutely want to know what happens next. How do I create suspense? Very simple: start out brilliantly and then slowly increase it! The various suspense techniques are intended to help. As always with true stories, not all techniques will be usable or appropriate. The story should deliver a true reflection of reality or part of it. But the following questions can help to identify and craft elements of suspense:

Checklist of suspense techniques

- Which questions can be anchored in listeners without providing an immediate answer?
    Technique: Involve and engage listeners. Avoid suspense killers.
- Which strong scenes can be used in the narrative?
    Technique: Deliver an experience (show, not tell!).
- Which scene radiates action? Is it suitable for an introduction?
    Technique: Intriguing opening.
- When did something surprise me, the author, during research? Was it a strong surprise? Did it change my view of the story?
    Techniques: List of revelations/expectation management.
- Is there a special moment? Where can I use it? How can I make it experienceable?
    Technique: Creating rhythm.
- While working on the piece, am I touched, sad, amused or angry? Why? Can I create these emotions in listeners? Does this serve my story?
    Technique: Creating emotions.
- How can I make characters more vivid? Do they have a special facet?
    Technique: Cliché + X.
- Does an event in the past explain the behaviour of a person now?
    Technique: Flashback.
- Which scene or anecdote is pars pro toto? Is that a possible ending?
    Technique: The final sentence or paragraph.

The questions are designed to help identify options for creating tension during research, writing and revision. Only then can an author use them. Every technique must serve the story. Not all techniques are equally important. What is always central is the feeling that should be generated in the listener: being immersed in an exciting story. A story is an experience. Central to this experience are the individual scenes. And because they are so important, they are given their own chapter, the next.

NOTES

1. You can listen to the feature here: https://www.radioatlas.org/after-the-celebration/.
2. Bertrand Piccard kindly agreed to conduct the interview in German, even if it is not his native language.
3. If you want to know more about him just visit his webpage: http://www.waltermedia.de/.
4. https://www.youtube.com/watch?v=x17YxZiplxc.
5. Both techniques, 'red herring' and 'MacGuffin', have been widely used and popularized by Alfred Hitchcock, among others.
6. In fictional stories, for example, screenwriter Aaron Sorkin distinguishes between 'improbable possibilities' and 'probable impossibilities'. The former should always be avoided. They seem too arbitrary. The latter are more likely to be accepted by the audience. Especially once they are immersed in the logic of the story-cosmos. That E.T. would ride through the air on a bicycle is indeed an impossibility, but in the logic of the movie it is probable. So it is accepted.
7. The whole manuscript of episode 12: https://genius.com/Serial-podcast-episode-12-what-we-know-annotated.

BIBLIOGRAPHY

Abel, Jessica. 2015. *Out on the Wire*. New York: Broadway Books.

Biewen, John, and Alexa Dilworth (eds.). 2017. *Reality Radio*, 2nd ed. Durham: University of North Carolina Press.

Franklin, Jon. 1994. *Writing for Story*. New York: Plume.

Grove, Claire, and Stephen Wyatt. 2013. *So You Want to Write Radio Drama?*. London: Nock Hern Books.

Headlee, Celeste. 2015. 10 Ways to Have a Better Conversation. Filmed at TEDxCreativeCoast in May 2015. Accessed 20 December 2020. https://www.ted.com/talks/celeste_headlee_10_ways_to_have_a_better_conversation#t-29784.

Iglesias, Karl. 2005. *Writing for Emotional Impact*. Livermore: Wing Span Press.

Jessen, Lisbeth. 2002. *After the Celebration*. Accessed 20 December 2020. https://www.radioatlas.org/after-the-celebration/.

Lerch, Christian. 2016. *Papa, We're in Syria*. Accessed 20 December 2020. https://www.radioatlas.org/papa-were-in-syria/.

McKee, Robert. 1997. *Story. Substance, Structure, Style, and the Principles of Screenwriting*. New York: Harper-Collins.

More Perfect. 2018. The Gun Show. Accessed 20 December 2020. https://www.wnycstudios.org/podcasts/radiolab/articles/radiolab-presents-more-perfect-gun-show.

Preger, Sven. 2013. ‚Raumfähre „Columbia", letzter Start'. Accessed 20 December 2020. https://www1.wdr.de/mediathek/audio/zeitzeichen/audio-raumfaehre-columbia-letzter-start-am–100.html.

Preger, Sven. 2017a. ‚Stephen Hawking, englischer Physiker'. Accessed 20 December 2020. https://www1.wdr.de/radio/wdr5/sendungen/zeitzeichen/stephen-hawking-physiker-100.html.

Preger, Sven. 2017b. ‚Johannes Bischko, Pionier der Akupunktur'. Accessed 20 December 2020. https://www1.wdr.de/mediathek/audio/zeitzeichen/audio-johannes-bischko-pionier-der-akupunktur-geburtstag–102.html.

Radiolab. 2016. On the Edge. Accessed 20 December 2020. http://www.radiolab. org/story/edge/.

Shaw, Julia. 2016. *The Memory Illusion*. London: Random House.

S-Town. 2017. Accessed 20 December 2020. https://stownpodcast.org/.

Truby, John. 2007. *The Anatomy of Story*. New York: Farrar, Straus and Giroux.

Yorke, John. 2014. *Into the Woods. How Stories Work and Why We Tell Them*. London: Penguin Books.

Youtube. ,Raising an Olympian Gabby Douglas'. Accessed 20 December 2020. https://www.youtube.com/watch?v=x17YxZiplxc.

CHAPTER 6

Scenic Narratives

6.1 SCENES: EXPERIENCE REALITY

At the very end, Heinrich can no longer defend himself. The moment of truth has come. It is the fifth and last part of our documentary series *The Hitchhiker*.

Tape: (Sven Preger, meeting room Erlacher Höhe[1]) That means you advised him to tell the truth?

Tape: (Wilfried Karrer, meeting room EH) Yes, come on, out with it. Don't hold anything back.

Sven: After the piano session, we sit with Heinrich and Mr Karrer over coffee. What else? Heinrich just went for a smoke. What else?

Tape: (Stephan Beuting, meeting room EH) Heinrich, while you were out for a minute, we were just talking about the topic of illness.

Tape: (Sven Preger, meeting room EH) And there was the thing about how we actually met you. The same thing happened to both of us at the Cologne motorway junction, one year apart. You approached us and took us both in. We've compared what you said, and you spun us both the same yarn about a brain tumour. That would also be a reason to go to Zurich. Because of the brain tumour. And that really got to me, I know: Oh, my God, how bad is it?

Tape: (Stephan Beuting, meeting room EH) A man on his last journey. Can't I help him somehow?

Tape: (Sven Preger, meeting room EH) Am I going to deny him this chance? At home I started thinking: a brain tumour? But surely there's the skull in between. I don't know if it really is a brain tumour. And so, I casually asked my dermatologist…

S. Preger, *Storytelling in Radio and Podcasts*, https://doi.org/10.1007/978-3-030-73130-4_6

> *Tape*: (Heinrich Kurzrock, meeting room EH) A wen.
> *Tape*: (Sven Preger, meeting room EH) What's that?
> *Tape*: (Heinrich Kurzrock and Wilfried Karrer together, meeting room EH) A wen.
> *Tape*: (Sven Preger, meeting room EH) And you know it!
> *Tape*: (Wilfried Karrer, meeting room EH) Of course he knows.
> *Tape*: (Heinrich Kurzrock, meeting room EH) Wait, wait.
> *Tape*: (Wilfried Karrer, meeting room EH) We had a massive argument about it.
> *Tape*: (Heinrich Kurzrock, meeting room EH) (Laughs) The fact that I used the word brain tumour has another... If I said it's a wen, many people would ask: What's a wen? I'd stand there and not know what to say. So, many years ago it started with this cancer thing: stomach cancer, bone cancer. Then once I just simply said 'bone cancer, brain tumour' and they swallowed it, and that was that. The end. With one or two words (knocks on the table). But if I say: a wen, and don't know what it is, how it got there, then I don't know anything.
> *Tape*: (Wilfried Karrer, meeting room EH) This is the Kurzrock-cunning. He knows exactly.
> *Tape*: (Heinrich Kurzrock, meeting room EH) (Heinrich laughs).
> *Tape*: (Wilfried Karrer, meeting room EH) He knows perfectly well that he just has a skin ailment that can be easily treated. But the market value of a tumour is considerably higher (Heinrich tries to interrupt, and laughs). And it's this system, 'How I can best market myself by deliberately misrepresenting myself' that he has perfected.

It is one of the most powerful scenes in *The Hitchhiker*. Listeners sit right at the table with us, they get all the unfiltered emotions. The scene manages without any text from offstage—except for a short passage at the beginning to establish the setting. Listeners experience the scene very intimately. This works because all four people have clear, but different goals:

- Wilfried Karrer as a social worker at Erlacher Höhe (the social housing facility Heinrich lives) wants Heinrich to finally tell the two journalists, i.e. us, the truth. We can guess his motivation: He believes it is an important step for Heinrich. To face his trust issues and build meaningful connections, based on the truth.
- Heinrich Kurzrock, on the other hand, would prefer not to do anything of the sort. He doesn't want his tall stories uncovered. We can also guess his motivation: He's afraid that the truth will make him lose contact with us. He has never experienced mistakes being forgiven. Moreover, he cannot break out of behaviour patterns he has learned and practised for decades.

- We (here Stephan and I are more like a single unit) want to find out the truth. The scene goes on a while—then the difference between our goals becomes clearer. Stephan wants to understand how Heinrich felt about lying all the time. I, on the other hand, want to know: Did he also lie to me personally?

Sven: Heinrich doesn't have bone cancer. Bone atrophy yes, but he doesn't even need the crutch for that. He can actually still walk quite well when he wants to. But of course, the crutch helps his story. We've experienced that ourselves.

Tape: (Sven Preger, meeting room EH) I gave you a lift to Bonn railway station back then, I bought you a ticket for the next ICE train to Zurich. I told the railway people to put you on the train, and I think I even slipped you 30 or 50 euros.

Tape: (Heinrich Kurzrock, meeting room EH) And I got off the train in Mannheim.

Tape: (Sven Preger, meeting room EH) Where did you get off?

Tape: (Heinrich Kurzrock, meeting room EH) In Mannheim.

Tape: (Sven Preger, meeting room EH) You got off in Mannheim? You remember that?

Tape: (Heinrich Kurzrock, meeting room EH) Yes.

Sven: Glad, we sorted that one. Heinrich gauged us properly right from the start. He had a pretty good idea that we might not just give him a lift but might also be able to fulfil one of his greatest wishes: to tell his story, if somewhat closer to the truth than he had imagined.

Music: A friendly guitar.

Sven: Sister Cäcilie keeps her word. The money comes a few weeks later. And Heinrich invests in a CD player, a few classical CDs and of course coffee and tobacco. When we phone a few weeks later, he only has a few euros left.

Heinrich is coughing.

Sven: He says.

Music echoes.

Tape: (Stephan Beuting, meeting room EH) Have you ever felt at any point something like, let's call it, a guilty conscience?

Tape: (Heinrich Kurzrock, meeting room EH) I think, if at all, then only at the very beginning. So, in the seventies sometime. But not since (laughs his head off).

What this brief analysis shows is that the goals of the central characters (Heinrich and us) are diametrically opposed. This leads to a number of questions: Who will prevail? Which strategies will be used? And what is the relationship between the characters at the end of the scene like? The suspense of the scene is generated by all these questions. On a more abstract level, it is therefore possible to define scenes as situations in which someone wants something, but encounters resistance.

This may sound familiar. Yes, indeed, the definition of scene and narrative is similar. Three essential elements of the narrative sentence can be found in the definition of a scene: a person acting, a goal and obstacles. Only motivation is missing. This does not mean that it is not there. There are also enough scenes in which motivation plays a major role or is revealed. Sometimes the listener's question ("Why is he or she acting like that?") is exactly the element of tension. It's helpful to remember that the mere description of reality ("There's someone sitting there who looks like this and that...") may be a situation but is not a scene.

By analogy with the narrative sentence for the whole story, a scene sentence can be formed for all scenes in a story. In the above case, this could be something like this: The reporters (they are the protagonists here) want to finally know the truth about Heinrich's state of health (their goal). But Heinrich fends them off with various strategies such as distraction, evasion (the obstacles). Social worker Wilfried Karrer supports the reporters, but at the same time makes sure that Heinrich is treated fairly. In an amendment to the narrative sentence, it often helps me personally not to speak of the protagonist's goal in a scene as an intention, but as a description of what actually happens in the scene. In this way I force myself to express the action of the scene in an active way which, in turn, means I myself can check whether the scene really contains action - and what it is. Taking the above example, the scene sentence then reads: The reporters urge Heinrich to finally tell them the truth about his state of health. But Heinrich refuses (at first).

With regard to the people acting in the above example, however, something else is decisive: All of them act at maximum capacity (cf. Section 4.2). The four figures do not just act in any old way, but to the best of their abilities. This applies to Heinrich's distraction and defence strategies as well as to our efforts to find out the truth and Wilfried Karrer's mediation work. In this case, it is a stroke of luck for reporters and listeners alike. The scene unfolds at the very moment the reporters are present. Listeners get the feeling of sitting at the same table with them. This is of course not always feasible. With events that lie in the past, no one can act in the present. But it is still possible to create this feeling for listeners.

For non-fictional narratives, I therefore distinguish between two types of scenes:

- Real scenes (first-hand): These are scenes in which the reporter is present, can make recordings and get a first-hand impression. Ideally, we as reporters work exclusively with this kind of scene. However, it presents us with the challenge of always being present. And being present should not change the situation as a whole, at least not too much. But without a lot of advance trust building, this is rarely likely to happen. How much we as reporters alter the situation and how far we are transparent about that in the narrative is an important ethical question (see also Sect. 9.4 on the debate about proximity and distance and Sect. 9.5 on the debate about the journalistic gonzo ego).

- Reconstructed scenes (second-hand): These are scenes that reporters have to assemble from other sources which applies to all events in the past. These are most likely to be memories and eyewitness accounts, but also books or documents. The big problem with this is that it is not always possible to check the truth conclusively, but we have to get as close as possible. How accurate are people's memories? How much do they change their story because they want to be seen in a better light? Are there other, preferably independent sources that allow verification? Does the coverage meet journalistic standards? At the very least, transparency is required here and does not pose much of a challenge for the reporter.

To mention an important distinction: Situations, anecdotes and examples are not the same as a scene. All three are often used, for example, to illustrate an abstract argument. They are significantly shorter than a scene, often only a few sentences long. Whereby a situation or anecdote is usually even longer than an example. It is most likely to be a situation in which someone describes an experience that is not yet a real scene, so to speak ("I was walking across the road when this amazing car caught my eye. I thought to myself: I'd like to drive one of those as well."). As a reporter, I can record ambient sound bites in a situation, for example in the tram or at the edge of a football field. The situation can therefore be assigned a time and place. Situations are often used in reportages (on the dangers of false reportage see Sect. 6.7). They can be situated (like scenes) in the present or the past. But what the situation usually lacks is a clear goal, a challenge or both! If there is one, then the situation can become a scene.

An anecdote deals with an event from the past. Someone just remembers something. But the person who remembers is not completely immersed in the event. The narrative is not particularly detailed, it is quite difficult to relive. And an example is a short illustration ("In Germany, hundreds of thousands of people also work at night. One of them is a baker. His alarm clock rings at 3 a.m."). There is no action or hardly any. Anecdotes and examples are usually not elaborately implemented acoustically, but simply told. The transitions between situation, anecdote and example are fluid. The important thing is: They are not scenes. One big problem is that reporters often work almost exclusively with situations, anecdotes and examples, but believe they are scenes. However, these elements alone will not carry a story. Because the listener doesn't get the feeling of really being there. A scene, however, draws listeners into the story, making them feel they are part of it or reliving it. And that works as follows.

6.2   DESIGNING SCENES: A COSMOS OF THEIR OWN

Martin is twelve years old when he comes home from school and feels sick. He stays at home for a few days, but he does not feel any better. On the contrary: Martin sleeps a lot, has no appetite, until he gradually even loses control over his body. Eventually he can no longer speak, cannot make eye contact and falls into a coma. The American reporter Lulu Miller tells this story in the NPR podcast *Invisibilia* in the episode *Locked-In Man*. The doctors tell his parents, Rodney and Joan, there is no hope for Martin and advise them to take their son home and look after him there as best they can until he dies. And that's what they do. They bring their son home and wait for him to die:

MILLER: But one year passed, and two years passed.

JOAN PISTORIUS: Martin just kept going, just kept going.

MILLER: So Joan, Rodney and their two kids did their best to care for Martin's body.

RODNEY PISTORIUS: I'd get up at 5 o'clock in the morning, get him dressed, load him in the car, take him to the Special Care Center where I'd leave him. Eight hours later, I'd pick him up, bathe him, feed him, put him in bed, set my alarm for two hours so that I'd wake up to turn him so that he didn't get bedsores.

MILLER: All throughout the night?

RODNEY PISTORIUS: Yeah. Every two hours, I'd get up and turn him over and then get a little bit of sleep. And at 5 o'clock the next morning, I'd start the same cycle.

MILLER: That was their lives.

RODNEY PISTORIUS: Load him in the car, drop him off, pick him up.

MILLER: Three years turn to four.

RODNEY PISTORIUS: Bathe him, feed him, put him in bed.

MILLER: Four years turn to five.

RODNEY PISTORIUS: Five o'clock the next morning, I'd start the same cycle.

MILLER: Six years. Seven years.

RODNEY PISTORIUS: Load him in the car, drop him off, pick him up.

MILLER: Eight.

RODNEY PISTORIUS: Load him in the car, drop him off, pick him up.

MILLER: Nine. Ten.

JOAN PISTORIUS: This was so horrific.

MILLER: Joan remembers vividly going up to him one time and saying...

JOAN PISTORIUS: I hope you die. I know that's a horrible thing to say. I just wanted some sort of relief.

MILLER: Eleven years, twelve.

RODNEY PISTORIUS: Load him in the car, drop him off, pick him up.

MILLER: Was there any life inside?[2]

Lulu Miller uses a very simple method to make the passing of time tangible. She does not simply sum up the result by saying: twelve years pass. She enumerates the years so that the listener at least gets an idea of how long these years must have felt. We get an impression of how oppressive and cramped life must have been for the parents. Miller has obviously established such a good relationship with them that they even share intimate details with her, and Miller will revisit the remarkable sentence: "I hope you die." With this scene, right at the beginning of her story (and this is the beginning, immediately after the ignition point, Martin's illness), Lulu Miller fulfils an important requirement: She creates her own world for the story, which feels narrow, hopeless and dark. As listeners, we can already guess that this won't be a feel-good story, but a drama that takes place within our own four walls, maybe even within ourselves. In a place that we don't usually get to visit. John Truby summarises this approach as follows: "…creating a unique world for the story - and organically connecting it to the characters - is as essential to great storytelling as character, plot, theme, and dialogue" (Truby 2007, 145). Stories need their own cosmos. This should be experienced in the scenes of the narrative.

Strictly speaking, the passage quoted here from the *Locked-In Man* story is not technically a scene, but rather a collaged time lapse. Miller uses several small scenes at once, all of which illustrate the parents' goal: to make their son Martin as comfortable as possible until his death. To start the story, the reporter also chooses the obvious perspective: that of the parents. The story is 23 minutes long in total. Right now, as listeners, we may be assuming that Martin's death will mark the end of the story. But would Miller really tell the story in that case? The course and the story would be tragic, but hardly surprising. Perhaps Lulu Miller asked herself an important question during her research: What would be the most unusual perspective to tell this story? That of the parents? Of the caregivers? The friends? Lulu Miller gives us the answer herself a few seconds later, or rather, one of the characters does:

MILLER: Was there any life inside?
RODNEY PISTORIUS: I was not certain.
MILLER: It was impossible to know.
JOAN PISTORIUS: In my mind, I'd decided he'd died.
MARTIN PISTORIUS: Yes, I was there, not from the very beginning, but about two years into my vegetative state, I began to wake up.
MILLER: This is Martin.
MARTIN PISTORIUS: Yes, using the grid to speak.
MILLER: The grid is just a computer keyboard that allows him to quickly choose words and then have the computer read them out loud.
MARTIN PISTORIUS: Yeah.[3]

Wow, this is a big surprise. Martin is not only alive, but also still able to tell his story, with the help of a voice computer. Lulu Miller chooses the most convincing and intimate perspective, that of the locked-in person himself. In doing so, she immediately changes the focus of the entire story as well, from 'How do parents deal with their dying son?' to 'How did Martin manage to survive?', which is the question listeners ask themselves at this point. Of course, not every story can always be told from the best, most unusual and intimate perspective. But the very beginning of the story illustrates something else: namely, how the listener is drawn right into the story because it is not clear from the outset that Martin will survive. This information is deliberately withheld (list of revelations!) in order to finally introduce this surprise (in a completely logical way) and with it the special perspective of the story (plot point!).

There are other characteristics that make scenes into good scenes, as well. They can all be found in the above-quoted example:

- Enter as late as possible: Jump right into the scene, just before something important is going to happen. This way listeners are forced to orientate themselves. In film, this is even easier than in audio narratives because images can often provide more information (location, people present, time of day, mood) than sound alone—which is why audio can afford a slightly longer run-up. But audio can deliver a large part of the setting, too, which makes it essential that scenes are acoustically well implemented (see Chapter 8). If a scene starts late, this creates dynamics. Nothing is more boring than a long start-up before the crucial point in the scene is reached. Try to start in the middle of a conversation. The third sentence at the beginning of *The Hitchhiker* reveals that Heinrich wants to kill himself. Where Stephan and Heinrich met, what time it was, where they both came from, etc. is not important at this stage. Listeners are also drawn into the scene because they have to work out the meaning and logic themselves (it just mustn't get too confusing), they are forced to catch up.

- Exit as early as possible: The opposite. When the climax of the scene is reached—or sometimes even before it is reached—get out of the scene. Again, this approach creates tempo and dynamics. Also, an early exit from the scene can serve as a cliffhanger. The first scene of *The Hitchhiker* only lasts about 45 seconds and ends with Stephan asking: "Then you have to help, don't you?" Whether Stephan really has helped Heinrich is not revealed just yet. Those who consistently use the two techniques 'enter late' and 'exit early' effectively will give listeners the feeling of experiencing a very dense story. Caution: do not overdo it. The story must not get short of breath. And dramaturgically important scenes need air to breathe. Deliberate slowing down—as in the climax of the Radiolab story about Surya Bonaly, *On the Edge*, creates the deeper emotional effect.

- Reverse the mood. This idea has something to do with defining a scene. As a reminder, the scene is a miniature of the overall story, an intermediate step on the way to the big goal. Someone is pursuing a goal, but encounters obstacles. If this is the case, then at the end of each scene something must have changed during the scene. And we can often recognise this by the mood. Imagine, for example, someone wants to buy chocolate ice cream for their child. The mood at the beginning of this scene is good, it is the first day of spring and chocolate is little Marvin's favourite. But the ice cream vendor doesn't have any chocolate ice cream! There are no other ice cream sellers in sight. And Marvin was so excited. Oh, what a drama?!

The last scene in the third part of *The Hitchhiker* serves as another example. Stephan and I are proud to have found out so much about Heinrich's family history and we finally want to tell him all about it. But he does not want to hear it. The mood changes. Whereby the mood does not always have to change from good to bad. It can also go from bad to good. An exception is the development from bad to catastrophic. A mood development from good to very good, on the other hand, offers very little dramaturgical material, it is too cheesy.

Ideally, the change of mood will result in a new question or task. The ice cream vendor for example says, 'I don't have any chocolate'. Cut. The open question remains: What happens next? Will Marvin change his mind? Will he cry? Little cliffhangers maintain suspense throughout the story. Especially in American audio stories, these cliffhangers are essential because of the commercial breaks which should not lose listeners. Here, too, the rule of thumb is not to overdo it. Listeners quickly get frustrated by artificial cliffhangers. One possible consequence is that they feel they are not being taken seriously and give up.

It's hard to say in general terms how long a scene usually takes. It depends on the total length of the story, the material and the development in the scene. Roughly speaking, between two and five minutes is a good benchmark. But what is more important than the length is that the plot in the scenes is bound to the characters, as it is in the story as a whole. Characters should therefore fit logically into the scene.

6.3 INTRODUCING CHARACTERS SCENICALLY

This is what a normal passage in a script could look like, let's say on the subject of the 'financial crisis':

Author: Many people have suffered as a result of the financial crisis. Cliff Smith is one of them. He lost everything back then.
Tape: (Cliff Smith, living room) I had nothing left. Nothing. My savings were simply gone.
Author: Smith didn't know what to do back then.

> *Tape*: (Cliff Smith, living room) I didn't know how to handle the situation.
> We had never experienced anything like it.

This example is of course purely fictitious. And, as reporters, we would never write so predictably and say the same thing in our text as is said on the tape anyway. We never have, we never will! Because dealing with characters like this makes it impossible to build up suspense. Instead, we should get answers to a few important dramaturgical questions: What situation are we in? What is Cliff Smith's current intention? For example, when did Cliff Smith find out that he had lost everything? Yes, perhaps all these exciting aspects will come later, although experience shows that this often does not happen. But you can improve almost any story with a few simple steps—for example by appropriately designing the way you introduce your characters. In the example already quoted, Lulu Miller introduces her protagonist, Martin Pistorius, accordingly. Namely organically and scenically:

> *MILLER*: Was there any life inside?
> *RODNEY PISTORIUS*: I was not certain.
> *MILLER*: It was impossible to know.
> *JOAN PISTORIUS*: In my mind, I'd decided he'd died.
> *MARTIN PISTORIUS*: Yes, I was there, not from the very beginning, but
>   about two years into my vegetative state, I began to wake up.
> *MILLER*: This is Martin.
> *MARTIN PISTORIUS*: Yes, using the grid to speak.
> *MILLER*: The grid is just a computer keyboard that allows him to quickly
>   choose words and then have the computer read them out loud.
> *MARTIN PISTORIUS*: Yeah.[4]

The passage begins with a question that has already arisen logically from what has been heard before. And the one who provides the answer is Martin! His appearance thus arises logically from the narrative, without any bridge or transition. This is what I mean by an 'organic' appearance or introduction. Miller also achieves a neat surprise by not immediately revealing that the person speaking in fact is Martin. She keeps that piece of information for after we have heard him the first time (even if we, as listeners, already suspect it is Martin). She then explains why Martin's voice sounds like a computer voice, which gives us listeners some time to digest the big surprise we have just heard. This short sequence would have been much less powerful if Miller had written a text to that effect: 'But it is hard to believe. Martin was there the whole time. Today, he can communicate again - with the help of a voice computer.' Martin's appearance invites numerous questions. Lulu Miller takes up these questions and then leads us back to the familiar scene in Martin's room, but this time told from Martin's perspective:

> *MILLER*: Now, I will get to how he regained consciousness and developed the ability to operate a keyboard and the wheelchair that he uses to get around. But what you need to know is that for about eight years, while all the world thought that Martin was gone, he was wide awake.
> *MARTIN PISTORIUS*: I was aware of everything, just like any normal person.
> *MILLER*: He thinks he woke up about four years after he first fell ill, so when he was about 16 years old.[5]

And so we have already arrived at the moment when Martin wakes up again, without anybody noticing. Even if the exact moment of time is not quite clear—whether it was after four years (as in the last excerpt) or after two years (as in the previous excerpt). Miller thus manages to introduce her protagonist organically and scenically. She never diverges from the story, but keeps us listeners bound into the story, sometimes even into the situation. A few sentences later we also get to know what Martin's goal is from now on: "I am sitting in my bed. My heart is beating as my father undresses me. I want him to know, to understand that I've returned to him."[6] Now, the goal of the story has been revealed.

Key message here: Characters should be introduced organically and scenically. This means they should appear as a direct, logical result of the story, possibly even of a certain scene. Within the scene, the characters have a specific intention.

This way of thinking also helps to develop the story further. Characters should be shown in scenes as often as possible and have a purpose or goal in them. That goal should itself be a sub-goal on the way to the big overall goal. Ideally, each new scene will uncover a new character trait. The beginning of the second episode ('Closed Institution') of the *The Hitchhiker* series begins with Heinrich telling us reporters about his experiences in child and youth psychiatry. It is the first time we experience Heinrich since the beginning of the series. We got to know him as a very demanding person, who obviously didn't take the truth too seriously. In the meantime, we have been warned about him and his stories. That's why we (and therefore the listeners) are now introduced to another facet. Heinrich is touched and vulnerable when he tells us about his memories: "Nuns came from the neighbouring department and held us each by a leg and an arm and pulled us across our beds. And the fifth nun tore our pyjama trousers down and hit us on our naked arses with a cane. And these beatings on our bodies were the only physical contact; there was no human touch – apart from shaking someone's hand: 'Hello Heinrich' or 'Good Morning Mr Kurzrock' – that was it."

After these memories, we change the scenery. We emerge with the listeners from the story of the past and sit with Heinrich in the studio where we recorded it. And already another facet shows up (which we encountered at the beginning, but which we can experience here intensively once again). Heinrich begs us for money - and his tone is suddenly much more demanding: "Could you think about it, if you somehow could scrape together 150 or 200 (meaning euros, note: Sven Preger) or whatever – no way more. Then when I'm down there (meaning the social institution Erlacher Höhe, note: Sven Preger) I'd buy tobacco and coffee in the shop with the money and would be covered for a month or two. That's exactly how I imagined it."

In both scenes, Heinrich has a very specific goal. In the reconstructed scene from the past, he wants to avoid pain and arbitrariness (but fails), in the real scene in the Now he wants to scrounge money from us (here he has more success). The scenes show different facets of his character. For the work as a reporter, one of the biggest challenges becomes clear from these examples: The way in which original sound bites and tape are handled changes fundamentally in this type of story compared to other journalistic products.

6.4   Tape: True-to-Scene Original Sounds

We have had the debate about money and scrounging with Heinrich countless times. Sometimes the microphone was on, sometimes not. If someone had asked us, "Do you have enough tape and original sounds to illustrate how Heinrich tried to scrounge?" then we could have answered, "We discussed this with him in various situations, sometimes we made recordings. There is certainly something in it. We'll put something together from it." And that would have been a problem because it would not really have helped us with the story. We might have recorded one or two sound bites of Heinrich in his room, another sound bite while we were with him in the car, then another on some car park and finally, a last sound bite on the phone. Together, the four or five situations would have clearly reflected the most important aspects of scrounging from Heinrich's point of view. However, we would still have had to decide on one, maybe two quotations. Why? Because there's a big problem here: The quotations wouldn't have been recorded true-to-scene.

What I mean by that is that when sound bites on one subject are created in different shooting situations, they cannot be combined into one scene afterwards. The reason is that the sounds simply do not fit together. The sound clip from the car park will sound quite different from the tape of the telephone call or the original sound from Heinrich's room—in many different ways: On the one hand, there are the characteristics of the spoken word (i.e. posture, volume, mood) and of course the acoustics of the recording. Despite all the technology and post-production, sounds recorded indoors and outdoors cannot usually be mixed in one scene. Not even if you create a completely new ambience and sound-world in post-production. The sounds will always be different and cannot be organically combined into a scene. Hence, they should not be used together. If you work with sounds from different situations, you will probably choose the best sound from the various recording situations and not use the rest. Sometimes, you strike lucky and recordings from different situations sound similar or can be edited to sound similar (for example, if the recordings were made indoors in similar sounding offices). However, this does not usually solve the problem that you can hear the differences between situations, pitch, and speaking posture.

But sound bites that have been recorded on a topic in different locations and situations cause dramaturgical problems, too. Because there is obviously no real scene. Dramatically speaking, the sound bites are in an empty space. The origin of this dramaturgical error, which has such serious consequences, often lies in the planning: What a character should say was planned thematically, not scenically. That's why the same holds for sound recordings: It's better to work true-to-scene.[7] This also applies to reconstructed situations, for example when people tell us about events in the past. If this requires several interviews, I should make sure that the acoustic situation is always the same (or as close as possible). The old principle applies here: the cleaner the recordings (i.e. with little background noise and good presence), the better I can deal with that tape in post-production and create a special kind of atmosphere if I want to (i.e. work with ambient sounds, music or effects to match the memory). Key message: Ideally, sound bites are recorded true-to-scene, i.e. they derive from **one** acoustic situation.

This places special demands on reporters. They have to plan or see situations coming and then record constantly. I am making such a point of this because non-true-to-scene sound bites are one of the most common and, above all, difficult problems to solve. Many reporters deal with this later (i.e. during the writing process) in a very pragmatic way: They take the sound bites from different situations anyway, write a few sentences of reporter text in between and do not even bother to acoustically link the sounds to a situation or scene. And that's what it often sounds like. The result is that listeners find it difficult to immerse themselves in the story.

In order to quickly assign the recordings to the corresponding scenes, it helps, for example, to structure your own manuscript like a radio play—i.e. according to scenes. At the beginning of the scene, you should note whether a scene takes place indoors or outdoors, whether by day or night, and where (all important information for creating atmosphere, sound, music, etc.). In addition—and this is even more important for true stories—the original sound clips in the script should not only show who says something, but also where the recordings were made (see also the examples from *The Hitchhiker* in this book). In this way, I stop myself from putting original sounds from two different recording situations into the same scene. Otherwise, this can happen quickly with long pieces and extensive recordings. It's also a good way of managing your material.

In one particular scene in *The Hitchhiker*, we had the debate with Heinrich about scrounging. The situation was also quite typical for him. He had just talked to us about his past. It was a very intense conversation (see excerpt above). From his perspective, he had probably done us a favour—now it was our turn. It was a true scene that really happened like that and in which Heinrich had two specific goals: first, to beg for money and second, to convince us to keep this whole debate about money out of our story. This example shows something else, as well: If you work true-to-scene, you have a good chance of getting sound bites of dialogue rather than isolated, free-standing sound bites—which brings us to our next aspect. For a narrative, a new or different classification of sound bites/original sounds may be in order.

6.5   SCENIC ORIGINAL SOUNDS: DIALOGICAL, DIRTY, DENSE AND INDIRECT

Which original sound or piece of tape from a report or story can you still remember? And by that I don't mean sound bites that you've heard quite often and that have entered the collective memory, such as the words of the first man on the moon, Neil Armstrong ("That's one small step for man, one giant leap for mankind."), or those of the American President John F. Kennedy during his visit to Germany ("Ich bin ein Berliner!") or Martin Luther King's "I have a dream" speech. The rest is history! What I am searching for are quotations you remember that are not the great statements of contemporary history. Either because you heard a sound clip and it impressed you as a listener, so to speak, or because you used a sound clip as an author in one of your stories. None of us will find it easy to answer this question. Most sound bites are not remembered. You could argue that it doesn't matter, after all, there are so many recordings and sound bites out there. But perhaps we are not looking at sound bites properly and could make them more memorable. Maybe we as reporters are not choosing the sound clips we and our listeners will remember. If you summarise the criteria used by reporters to select sound bites, then roughly the following categories emerge, which also overlap from time to time in everyday life:

- Expert tape. A person who is particularly versed in a subject states their opinion. They will tell you whether the issue presented is a major or minor problem, what solutions might be possible and how it all started. The expert tape is one of the most frequently used sound bites. Interview partners are selected according to 'expert criteria' (knows at least a little about the topic, can and wants to say something about it, speaks fairly straightforwardly)—both for sound bites and for whole interviews. Ideally, the original sound bites deliver context and opinion, not only explanation. As a rule, the journalist can explain better—provided he or she has really understood the problem. That an expert can explain better still tends to be the exception (at least in Germany, a lot of experts struggle with comprehendible answers and explanations). If they can, that is great. These sound bites can also make it into the report. A notable exception are the frequently broadcast sound bites from police, fire brigade or court spokespersons, who often resort to the descriptive level or facts alone. They say what happened in the accident or fire or what the verdict was. The big advantage of this (or at least this aspect is often emphasised) is that the police, fire brigade or court expert really knows the facts of the case. If the police describe what happened, it might garner greater credibility, or at least have a more official touch, than if the reporter says everything themselves (of course this also says something about the credibility of journalists).

There are two major problems with expert voices: First, the speakers are only recognisable as functionaries and that's the way they behave and speak. They probably think that using convoluted language and officialese is more appropriate. Press spokespersons apparently imitate other press spokespersons and thus make the problem even worse. And second, expert voices are often detached and isolated, so they are not integrated in any situation or scene. We journalists also reproduce these types of sound bites every day. But they do not generate distinctiveness and memorability.

- Victim or eyewitness testimony. Someone has experienced something and relates it. Only they have that first-hand knowledge. It's a kind of expert's commentary on their own case. Reporters have to be aware that people don't always remember correctly. But if a person is injured in an accident, they will be the best person to tell you how they experienced the accident. This category includes all first-hand sound bites. The big advantage is that they often describe an event in an emotional way that would otherwise be difficult to reproduce. The big problem is credibility. Are the perceptions they describe correct? Is the memory perhaps distorted, false or sugar-coated? Quotations like this must always be checked for credibility, inherent contradictions and plausibility. That these are subjective statements usually becomes transparent anyway.

- Reaction tape. Some random people react to events without playing a direct part in them. Well, maybe that's a little too arbitrary a statement. Ideally, important people react to important and meaningful events with meaningful reactions. This kind of sound bite is often the first thing journalists ask for when a newsworthy event has happened—and the event has already been portrayed as such. We are talking about reactions to winning the World Cup or to the first exit polls at a general election. The more people who are interested in the event, the greater the chances of obtaining meaningful sound bites; after all, there are plenty of people available to react. Whilst the tape with the eyewitness or victim helps to depict the event, reaction tape moves the story forward (or at least that's what we journalists believe). For many events, there are now preformulated punchlines and phrases that are reeled off just as lifelessly ("We will now wait for the result and then analyse it in detail." or "Our thoughts and prayers are with the families of the victims."). Reaction tape helps to depict an event and make it experienceable. It is therefore especially useful in news journalism. The big danger is, the more clichéd the language, the less credible it is. And yet we still broadcast these sound bites. Every day.

- Vox pop. The street polls. The voice of the people. Quickly done, frequently banal and not very meaningful. Often suits the programme well and fills airtime. No disrespect to the people who comment. But how meaningful, original or well-founded can an opinion be on a subject that a reporter throws at me in two sentences before I spontaneously say something into the microphone (Reporter: "What do you think about the rising right wing parties in… [fill in any country in Europe]?" Answer: "Yes, that is strange, right?!"). Often the polls are ready in the reporter's head before asking people in the streets. The answers are predictable anyway. There is hardly any room for differentiation. The individual sound bites should be no more than 10 to 15 seconds long (preferably shorter, the entire vox pop should be 40 seconds long and reflect real diversity of opinion) and should be coherent. Oh yes, and if you could drop your voice at the end that would be great. Make it easier to cut!

  In terms of content, these are either original sound bites featuring people who are involved ("Have you ever experienced cold and slippery weather in winter?") or some kind of reaction ("Football player xy has changed to that and that club for the unbelievable sum of so and so many millions of euros, what do you think?") or opinions. The opinion tape is a special form of the expert tape, i.e. an opinion, but often without any knowledge or expertise ("What do you think about the current development of the Syrian conflict?").

  In many cases, the original sound bites in a street poll are also chosen for their scurrility value. This does not serve the debate about a topic but is rather amusing. The juicier the sound bite, the better. It is often selected for broadcast.

Many of these quotations make most sense in current affairs reporting and are also justified there, at least partly. As a result, these sound bites are often detached statements between ten and 25 seconds in length (the tendency is clearly towards ten seconds or less), which are hardly integrated into the piece dramaturgically at all. Many reporters transfer this way of thinking and approach to longer stories. And that is where the trouble starts. They work with the same types of original sound bites and tape. The result: boredom, little originality and precisely no scenes.

Exciting stories therefore require other types of sound bites which are characterised by one or more of the following four features:

- Dialogical. If you want to work with scenes, you will usually need dialogues and have to record them. There is a simple dramaturgical reason for this: Language is one of the most important means of overcoming obstacles and of solving and resolving conflicts. Dialogue is thus an important means of generating action—and thus speed, tension and density in a story. It is important to remember: Dialogue delivers scenes delivers dynamics! Robert McKee puts it like this: "To say something is to do something, and for that reason, I have expanded my redefinition of dialogue to name any and all words said by a character to herself, to others, or to the reader/audience as an action taken to satisfy a need or desire" (McKee 2016, 4).

  Two aspects are particularly noteworthy in this definition and helpful for true narratives. Firstly, McKee points out that language always has the goal or intent of satisfying a desire or need. Both can be the goal of a scene or story. McKee emphasises the special dramaturgical link between dialogue and plot. And secondly, he includes two situations in his definition that are important for non-fictional stories: monologue or dialogue with oneself and dialogue with the audience. Both forms are used, for example, in the feature *Squirrel's Ongoing Revolt* (a 2010 production by the German broadcaster Deutschlandfunk). The feature is about the environmental activist Cécile Lecomte, who repeatedly climbs trees (hence her nickname 'squirrel') and stays there. It's her way of fighting against the expansion of airports or motorways. Reporter Nadine Dietrich could not always climb up with her so, she gave the 'squirrel' a recording device. On several occasions, Cécile Lecomte reflects on the day for herself (like in a diary entry). Or she sometimes explains to listeners what happened that day. This also gives the explanatory passages a personal touch. These are very intimate and moving moments.

  When it comes to explanations, the following rule applies: The more comprehensible the explanations are, the better. And that's just as well. This principle only becomes a big problem if you as a reporter try to pack explanations into dialogues. Unfortunately, it does not usually work: One of the worst misdemeanours that you can commit in a story is on the nose dialogue. These are sentences or tape that no one would ever say in a real conversation. They only occur in the story because they transport information that the reporter cannot otherwise convey. Or at least that's what some authors think. This kind of dialogue often occurs when reporters ask their interview partners or even protagonists for facts (What is that building over there? Where are we?). The very character of such questions means that no real dialogue can develop. It gets even worse when fictional elements are written into a story. Dialogues then often look like this:

> *Character 1*: Wow, what is that over there, that big church with all
> those people in front of it?
> *Character 2*: That's Cologne Cathedral.
> *Character 1*: Wow, is it a Catholic church?
> *Character 2*: Yes, exactly. Construction of the Cathedral Church of
> Saint Peter, as the church is officially called, began right back in the
> 13th century...

I think you get the point. On the nose dialogue is the ultimate hallmark of bad dialogue.

- Indirect. It's one of the first rules reporters learn. Original sound recordings must not only be technically ok, but also comprehensible in terms of content. If it's not crystal clear what someone is saying, it is not a good sound bite. Original tones must be unambiguous, explicit and direct. These rules often make sense in current affairs reporting. But when every reporter tries to produce sound bites like this, they all sound the same. There is no individual style of writing or speaking. Nothing that is recognisable. Moreover, once again, when everything is already clear, no suspense can arise. Of course, this insight also applies to sound bites. Therefore, savour the subtext of a sound, i.e. what lies beneath what is said. What does a person in a specific situation want to achieve? Why does he or she say something? And why do they say it like this? These questions create suspense or can help create suspense. Let's look again at the final scene in the fifth part of *The Hitchhiker*: Heinrich is squirming, he somehow wants to explain why he has lied to us, but just admitting it, that's not for him. And that is exactly what is transported by the way he talks in this scene. According to the classic criteria for good and useful tape, the following recording should have been thrown out: It's too cluttered, too long, too unspecific. But the tape conveys Heinrich's inner conflict: "The fact that I used the word brain tumour has another... If I said it's a wen, many people would ask: What's a wen? I'd stand there and not know what to say. So, many years ago it started with this cancer thing: stomach cancer, bone cancer. Then once I just simply said 'bone cancer, brain tumour' and they swallowed it, and that was that. The end. With one or two words (knocks on the table). But if I say: a wen, and don't know what it is, how it got there, then I don't know anything."

Usually, we humans only very rarely speak directly and without subtext: For example, when a conflict escalates and we really say what we mean, unvarnished. Or when characters accidentally let something slip and we as listeners finally learn the truth. Then original sound bites or dialogues are also very short—like at the end of the final scene in *The Hitchhiker*, when Heinrich finally tells the truth (as far as we know):

Tape: (Heinrich Kurzrock, meeting room EH) And I got off the train in Mannheim.
Tape: (Sven Preger, meeting room EH) Where did you get off?
Tape: (Heinrich Kurzrock, meeting room EH) In Mannheim.
Tape: (Sven Preger, meeting room EH) You got off in Mannheim? You remember that?
Tape: (Heinrich Kurzrock, meeting room EH) Yes.

All the sentences above are concise, precise, unambiguous. Don't worry, even in narratives, more classic original sounds are justified (we'll look at that in a moment). But if scenes are the backbone of a story, then indirect sound bites with lots of subtext should be part of it. Only then can tension arise and characters become recognisable.

Screenwriter and director Aaron Sorkin goes yet one step further. He sometimes writes dialogues that the audience doesn't understand. And he does it on purpose. This goes against all journalistic principles that have ever been learned and internalised. Original sounds that nobody understands frighten the listener off immediately! As an example, in his 'Masterclass Screenwriting' Sorkin cites a situation from the movie *Steve Jobs* for which he wrote the script. At the beginning there is a scene that takes place shortly before the first presentation of the Apple computer. The problem of the scene ('Fix the Voice Demo'): The computer can't introduce itself, something has obviously gone wrong with the voice demonstration. In the scene, Steve Jobs has an argument with software developer Andy Hertzfeld. The dialogue between these two experts is incomprehensible for a layperson. And this is exactly what Aaron Sorkin wants: He wants the audience to feel that they are watching experts at work. These guys obviously really know what they're doing, and we can watch them. An idea that can also be transferred to true dialogues (the control centre of a space mission or a coach giving his basketball team instructions on tactics in a short time out). These dialogues nevertheless fulfil two functions: They convey the speaker's attitude and create authenticity.

- Dirty. Another word that does not stand for clarity and unambiguity but for true and revealing moments in which something unforeseen happens. These moments are often more meaningful than any others. They are the moments when someone struggles for words or is overwhelmed, such as when we have an appointment with hitchhiker Heinrich to meet Thomas Profazi, deputy hospital director and head of the 'Psychiatric Treatment & Rehabilitation Services and Marketing' department to talk about possible compensation. At the end of the meeting, we talk about home and belonging, which is understandably not an easy topic for Heinrich. Thomas Profazi mentions in passing that he had lived in the Black Forest for 20 years, but that it was no longer his home. What comes next, Stephan and I have already experienced several times: Heinrich's inner navigation system (as he calls it) starts up. He describes the route to the Black Forest (we are in Münster at that moment, so it's a distance of roughly 375 miles), enumerating motorways, main roads, exits, places and rest stops—and he does it fast, very fast. Heinrich knows his way around, after all he has been living on the streets for decades. It's a moment that inevitably overwhelms Thomas Profazi and also sounds a bit insane. Even the recording quality is not very good, because we are already on our way out. But this situation shows exactly what many people experience when they meet Heinrich: You feel totally overwhelmed, which can turn into rejection, because you don't know how else to respond. Heinrich wants to demonstrate his knowledge to prove that he should not have been in the psychiatric ward in Niedermarsberg. Therefore, he ends his list with the comment: "But I was in Niedermarsberg. Do you understand my cynicism?" Profazi can only reply with consternation: "Yes, I get it." It is a deeply tragic and revealing moment. Precisely because it is what it is, uncomfortable, messy, true.

- Dense. An essential thought always helps me to make this aspect clearer. The two-time Pulitzer Prize winner Jon Franklin sums it up as follows: "Your tale represents an extract of reality, not reality itself" (1986, 139). Journalists are of course aware that they are only depicting an extract of reality. But Franklin adds that this extract of reality should be condensed reality. Only then do stories deliver what they are supposed to deliver: "The reader and editor want a story with a minimum of loose ends, a tale that's been simplified and crystallized in such a way that it clarifies and enlarges the mind" (1986, 213). These thoughts help to select the appropriate sound bites, that is, the sounds that advance the scene and are condensed reality. The big question for audio productions that comes with this relates to editing: What do I cut out? How much do I smooth out the voice duct? Is a hesitation or 'um' meaningful or does it hinder comprehension? And do the interventions produce condensed original sounds, but also a distorted image of reality? My very personal experience is that the more I, as an author, have penetrated and clarified the subject and story, the less often these conflicts arise. The clearer it is to me which functions a scene has, the clearer it is which tapes should be created in the first place and which ones should make it into the narrative.

Dialogical, indirect, dirty, dense. In order to achieve sound bites of this kind, planning and the story interview help (see Sect. 4.5). Planning is important because the scenes don't just happen - or at least very rarely. As a reporter, I usually have to plan events (or at least make sure I'm there when they happen). And the story interview ensures that I don't ask everyone everything but have a clear idea of what story and scenes I want to tell and how. But what do I do if I can't witness scenes live as a reporter? Because I can't be there at the time or because they are in the past? There is also a solution to this problem: the reconstruction of scenes. Let's look at that immediately.

Not quite immediately. Before we start with that, a few urgent questions about the original sound bites. I could imagine that the characteristics of original sounds will meet with incomprehension or criticism: Must all sound bites always be dialogical? Will that always work? Don't expert sound bites, for example, still have a right to be heard? The answers: No. No. And yes. In more detail: No, not all sound bites must always be dialogical. No, that won't always work (e.g. if I only have one original sound source and no dialogue partner). And yes: Normal expert sound bites still have a right to be heard, for example in passages that cannot and need not be scenic. Remember: The scenes form the backbone of the story, the actual narrative. Now think again about the ladder of abstraction. The scenes are located on the lowest rung and they are as precise as possible. But a debate or a bigger idea can always emerge from the scenes. This takes place on the upper rungs of the ladder (for example in a scenic-reflective, explanatory or argumentative narrative, see Sect. 3.8). And in these passages, too, acoustic narratives require sound bites, which may include experts explaining or classifying arguments. The other sound bites can also continue to feature: A vox pop may make sense (e.g. to build up anticipation of a concert at which something will happen that is important for the story). The existing sound bites are supplemented by other features that are particularly suitable for telling a story. The most important question remains: Does the tape serve my story? If so, then it will get a place in it. How, for example, an eyewitness report can provide the essential original sound bites to reconstruct a scene. That's next.

6.6   RECONSTRUCTED SCENES: ACCURATE, CREDIBLE AND TRANSPARENT

This is one of the first lessons reporters learn on *This American Life*: "Have the person give you a tour of the key places in the story, on tape, explaining the significance of each place" (Abel 2015, 26). In the graphic novel *Out on the Wire* by Jessica Abel, Ira Glass tells the story of a woman (Jackie, she lives with Kenny) whose home has been hit by a bullet. Ira Glass visits her in her home. Jackie is supposed to show him the places that are important for the story. Granted, this technique may not be exclusive to *This American Life*, but popular with many other shows and programmes, as well. This kind of questioning puts people in the right mood, at best they relive scenes. A good indication that it really happens is when at some point people start telling stories in the present tense. In the example of Ira Glass, he and the woman finally arrive at the place and moment when the bullet hit her home. She retells the scene, including the dialogues she remembers. It is the reconstruction of a scene. Glass says: "All I'm doing is prompting her to tell me the events, in order, and look how vivid everything suddenly gets - (…) and she gives me the actual words Kenny spoke. When you get dialogue, you know you've arrived at the center, at ground zero" (Abel 2015, 26). Dialogue is crucial here, too. Reconstructed scenes occur in two different forms:

- First, as a retelling. Someone remembers an event in the past.
- Second, as a true reconstruction. The scene is relived as realistically as possible and recorded in the process. An example of this is the attempt in the fifth episode of the first *Serial* season (title: Route Talk) to get from the school car park to the shopping centre in a certain time (see Sect. 2.7).

The same dramaturgical rules apply to the reconstruction of scenes as to first-hand scenes. The recording situation of a true reconstruction does not really differ from that of a real scene—something actually happens at the moment of shooting (action and dialogue can be used accordingly). The situation is somewhat different when a person retells a scene. As a reporter, you don't always manage to get to the dialogue bits (not everyone can always remember everything), but as a listener, if a person remembers things during the interview, you get a feeling for it. This is an important mark of quality for reconstructed scenes. In *The Hitchhiker,* Heinrich tells us about the daily routine in child and youth psychiatric unit, the daily struggle for survival that began in the morning: "Quarter past five was wake-up time. We then had to get washed, make the beds, and the whole dormitory had to be cleaned before we were allowed to have breakfast. And anyone who did not have a clean plate had to put his head on his folded arms on the table (Heinrich demonstrates) for an hour, sometimes for two hours. And if anyone dared to look up, then he got punched in the face by a nun." The short note in brackets shows that Heinrich is reminiscing, even if he chooses the past tense. He is reliving and re-enacting the scene. The fact that he briefly hits the recording microphone is a bit unlucky for the acoustic quality of the recording (it's less than a second anyway), but it shows that, Heinrich has obviously forgotten the microphone.

When it comes to re-narrated scenes, the big question for journalists is the following: How do we know that the reports, memories and scenes are true or which part is true? After all, as a reporter you can't simply believe everything you hear and publish it. The risk of inaccuracies, euphemisms or even lies is just too great. And even an explicit reference to subjective memories does not relieve you of this responsibility. Conducting the interview, that is only half the job. The other half is doubting and researching. Doubting means checking the statements for plausibility and (in)consistency. Do all facets fit together? Are there any contradictions? Is something illogical or implausible? Are there permanent gaps? Why? After the necessary proximity, journalistic distance is now required, which as a reporter I now have to rebuild. Doubt, then, involves a critical examination of the tape and the person. Working with hitchhiker Heinrich we always had big questions: When is he telling the truth?

When did he bend reality just slightly? And when is he lying? What we quickly learned was that it's often a mixture of everything. For us this meant that we critically checked all the recordings to see if they were consistent. And it doesn't always have to be intentional. How are people supposed to accurately remember events that happened a long time ago? In Heinrich's case, this re-examination has always brought us very special moments—like the following, which I have already told you about. When Stephan and I want to tell Heinrich about his family background and he doesn't want to know, a minor detail slips out:

> *Stephan*: Ok, a conflict of conscience. We have been researching for more than a year, and at his request. So, it's worth a second try. Something more direct...
> *Tape*: (Sven Preger, Heinrich's room) We know where your parents used to live.
> *Tape*: (Heinrich Kurzrock, Heinrich's room) In Herne.
> *Tape*: (Sven Preger, Heinrich's room) In Herne. We also have an address...
> *Tape*: (Heinrich Kurzrock, Heinrich's room) Shamrockstrasse.
> *Tape*: (Sven Preger, Heinrich's room) First. And then I think in Kronen
> ...

Only later, when critically reflecting on the recordings, do we notice the contradiction in the seemingly trivial commentary. This is why the third episode ends like this:

> *Tape*: (Heinrich Kurzrock, Heinrich's room) You won't take me with you to Bonn?
> *Sven*: Fuming, we make our way home. We are speechless. Flat out. Emotionally in turmoil. Why should we bother investigating all this if Heinrich doesn't want to know about it now?! But he just gave us the answer himself. The mail. Our packages. Maybe he is interested in his family history...
>
> The following tape-sounds in memory reverb.
>
> *Tape*: (Sven Preger, Heinrich's room) We also have an address...
> *Tape*: (Heinrich Kurzrock, Heinrich's room) Shamrockstrasse...
> *Sven*: ...or maybe not.
> *Tape*: (Sven Preger, Heinrich's room) And then I think in Kronen......
> *Tape*: (Heinrich Kurzrock, Heinrich's room) I don't know...
> *Sven*: It's just a little thing, but something's wrong here. Heinrich cannot know this address for his parents - Shamrockstrasse - if he really believes that they died in '49. We have to talk about that. Next time.

We know from our records that Heinrich's parents did not live in Shamrock-strasse until after 1949. So how could he know this address? We'll talk about this at the beginning of the next episode and then learn some more.

This issue of doubt is complemented by classic journalistic craft: research. Are the facts correct? How do other people remember what happened? What other sources can be used? For example, we compared and checked Heinrich's memories about the child and youth psychiatric unit with other sources, including several conversations with former patients, staff and scientists. We also searched for clues through the complete medical file of another patient—hundreds of pages. Only when a consistent, plausible picture emerged did we include Heinrich's reports in the story, such as quotations like the one already mentioned: "Nuns came from the neighbouring department and held us each by a leg and an arm and pulled us across our beds. And the fifth nun tore our pyjama trousers down and hit us on our naked arses with a cane. And these beatings on our bodies were the only physical contact; there was no human touch – apart from shaking someone's hand: 'Hello Heinrich' or 'Good Morning Mr Kurzrock' – that was it."

Doubts therefore have more to do with the plausibility of the figure and the inner logic of the tape. Research refers to their external verification. Reconstructed scenes only have a place in the story if both aspects are satisfactory. The advantage of acoustic narratives is that the listener automatically hears that a person is speaking subjectively. Nevertheless, high standards must be met before this type of scene makes it into a journalistic story. The following applies to every type of scene, first-hand and reconstructed: It must advance the story. Self-evident really. But if it were self-evident, then one of the most common mistakes would not occur so often. I call it: the wrong reportage. It occurs so often and is so irritating that it gets a sub-chapter of its own in this book, the next.

6.7   WRONG REPORTAGE: WHEN A SITUATION HAS NOTHING TO SAY

I'm going to speculate here. Some day in many editorial offices, production companies or author collectives someone will probably say: "Pimp it up with some ambient sound, at least it will sound like a reportage." The sentence may be formulated slightly differently but the results often sound as though that was the advice given at some point. The idea behind it is probably a good one: The piece should be made more tangible, acoustically enhanced. But if the ambience or the whole situation has nothing to do with the actual story, then listeners become more perplexed than anything else. There are two variations on the theme of wrong reportage: 'Use some more ambience' and 'situation without a story.'

'Use some more ambience': I was once at a journalism conference, it must have been a session at the annual conference of 'netzwerk recherche,' if I remember correctly, the German equivalent of 'Investigative Reporters and

Editors' (audio was underrepresented here from the very beginning in 2001, but that's another story). And it was about audio reportage as THE great narrative form. At some point, an editor on the panel says something to the effect: "Our reporters are asked to add ambient sound to all their original recordings. If a sound is recorded in the office, then at least there should be street ambience added to the mix, as if the window were open." That's a hell of a tip. And one that's sure to move the story forward. It should be obvious: Just adding ambient sound to a statement does not create a reportage or scene. On the contrary, it probably rather confuses listeners. It also raises questions: Should the ambient sound continue under the narrative text as well, even if it is a passage on the top rung of the ladder of abstraction? Or do I add ambient sound only to original sound bites? But then there will be a sonic breach in the transition from original sound to narrative text. Even if I smooth over the transition, i.e. use a bit of ambient overhang to make the transitions less obvious, the result is at best disconcerting: Is this a scene or not? Is there something to experience or not? All in all, however, this is the much less painful version that also does less harm to the story. Now, it gets really annoying.

'Situation without a story': Ideas are often born of need as, probably, in the following case. Let's say I am aware as a writer or reporter that I don't actually have any good scenes for my report. Can happen. Nevertheless, I want to include all the information that I have collected. What do I do? I insert a pseudo-scene. I pretend that something important is happening here—but it's not. These sections often start with phrases like "We are on the way" or "I'm standing/going here right now" or "Here is the place where it (possibly) happened" (only unfortunately the protagonist is not with us, but never mind...). You can also recognise such pseudo-scenes by the stilted transitions to the actual story. Because the scene has nothing to do with the story, the transitions always automatically seem artificial, even if they are executed quickly. There are often speculative phrases like "Is this the place where...?" or "Did xy do this and that here, too?" All these formulations indicate that it is probably not a real scene at all, but more or less well-intentioned illustrations. There are countless examples of this variation. Many authors, myself included, have certainly used this rather paltry trick. Whenever the temptation arises, go back to your narrative sentence and examine your situation or scene: How does it drive the story forward? If you don't get a satisfactory answer, then it has no place in the story. Cut it.

6.8   CHECKLIST: SCENIC NARRATIVES

Good scenes are the backbone of any story. They contain what moves us, what we remember and what we tell others. One of my favourite scenes in *The Hitchhiker*, if you can call it such with a topic like this, is in the fourth episode. We meet another former patient, Peter Köhler (we changed the name for the story), for lunch. Eating our soup, the following dialogue between Peter and Heinrich finally emerges:

Tape: (Heinrich Kurzrock, restaurant) But what interests me now is this: you, just like me, have Marsberg behind you, the St Johannes Foundation. And on the other hand, there are always new problems coming up, new setbacks in society. How do you manage? What do you do about it? That's what would interest me.

Tape: (Peter Köhler, restaurant) Yes, well, in my case, it's really all behind me. What's the point? It happened - what can you do about it?

Sven: Peter Köhler has built himself a life. Heinrich only has his tobacco.

Tape: (Heinrich Kurzrock, restaurant) I smoke 70 cigarettes a day. I have two addictions: coffee and tobacco. No alcohol, nothing.

Tape: (Peter Köhler, restaurant) What? Don't you have a wife, at least have that!

Tape: (Heinrich Kurzrock, restaurant) Nah.

Sven: That's one way of looking at it. Köhler is now married to another former patient.

Tape: (Heinrich Kurzrock, restaurant) So, you've managed better than me!

Music: Guitar.

Stephan: Heinrich is disappointed. He sees that it hasn't been easy for him, but he also sees that others have taken different paths. And found a place in society. But even Heinrich has a place - where he feels at home and likes drinking coffee. We're going there because Heinrich wants us to and also because this is our chance to understand how Heinrich has been able to survive on the streets for so long.

Music fades out. Cut to petrol station.

This scene (Heinrich's aim here is to find out how someone has dealt with similar experiences) is archetypical for Heinrich. As narrators, we only add short transitions and the facts that are necessary for understanding or classification. The scene ends with a tragic punch line: Heinrich can't be pleased for Peter, he remains trapped within himself. Stephan immediately picks up this thought in the following transition text and jumps up the ladder of abstraction. He also uses the prevailing feelings of tragedy and pity to introduce the next situation. Quickly, briskly, directly, without getting hectic. Perhaps the scene helps to recall the most important points.

Checklist Scenic Narratives

- Do I have enough scenes (first-hand or reconstructed) for the intended length of my story and not just information to accommodate? Scenes are the backbone of any narrative. If they are not present, there is a danger of setting an encyclopaedia entry to music.
- Are my scenes strong scenes? Can I build a scenic sentence for each of them? Each scene is like a mini story within the story: someone wants to achieve something, but encounters obstacles. The scenes have to push the story forward, step by step.
- Are my characters scenically introduced? Do they pursue specific goals within the scenes? Characters become recognisable and experienceable through actions. Ideally, each scene features a new, additional character trait.
- Are my sound bites recorded true-to-scene? Do I have all the sound bites I need for a scene? If not, major problems usually arise when writing or at the latest during production.
- Do my sound bites fulfil a distinctive function within the story? Are they, for example, scenic sound bites, i.e. dialogical, dirty, dense or indirect? Is the meaning conveyed through the subtext? Then listeners are drawn into the story.
- Have I checked any reconstructed scenes sufficiently? Are the memories of characters logical in themselves and verifiable by other sources?

Scenes cannot be valued highly enough for stories. They provide the experience and ensure that the story is remembered. At the same time, they place immensely high demands on reporters, both in terms of planning, shooting and production. But if they succeed, listeners can immerse themselves completely in the story. In strong scenes, the reporter or narrator almost completely recedes into the background. Yet they are the ones who hold the whole story together and guide the way through it. Not only with their voice, but with their entire personality. This brings us to one of the most exciting chapters for sonic narratives.

NOTES

1. ‚Erlacher Höhe' is the name of the social facility Heinrich lives.
2. You find the manuscript and the audio here: https://www.npr.org/2015/01/09/375928581/locked-man.
3. Ibid.
4. Ibid.
5. Ibid.
6. Ibid.

7. Before confusion or annoyance arises now: There are still sound bites that do not have to be integrated into scenes. Namely in the reflective passages of the story, which take place on the upper rungs of the ladder of abstraction. Cf. Section 3.3. We will also come to sound bites from experts in the next section.

BIBLIOGRAPHY

Abel, Jessica. 2015. *Out on the Wire*. New York: Broadway Books.

Dietrich, Nadine. 2010. 'Eichhörnchens permanente Revolte'. Accessed 20 December 2020. http://www.deutschlandfunk.de/eichhornchens-permanente-revolte-pdf-dok ument.media.bc8724b1da32d9adefae5cf9f64954b4.pdf.

Franklin, Jon. 1986. *Writing for Story*. New York: Plume.

Invisibilia. 2015. 'Locked-in Man'. Accessed 20 December 2020. https://www.npr. org/2015/01/09/375928581/locked-man.

McKee, Robert. 2016. *Dialogue. The Art of Verbal Action for the Page, Stage, and Screen*. New York: Hachette Book Group.

Sorkin, Aaron. 2016. Masterclass 'Screenwriting' (Online-Course Comes with Charge). Accessed 20 December 2020. https://www.masterclass.com/classes/ aaron-sorkin-teaches-screenwriting.

Truby, John. 2007. *The Anatomy of Story*. New York: Farrar, Straus and Giroux.

CHAPTER 7

Who Speaks: Developing and Implementing a Narrative Attitude

7.1 THE NARRATOR: BEYOND THE 'GERMAN NARRATOR'

The narrator only conveys the story; they would never ever actively intervene in the plot or interact with the characters. Like at the beginning of the 9th case of private detective Frank Faust (*The Immortal King Arthur*, Igel Records 2013):

EXT. A DIRT ROAD SOMEWHERE IN CORNWALL. DAY.
Narrator: Private detective Frank Faust had had enough.
Faust: (sniffs)
Narrator: Discontentedly he stomped along a field path at dusk. Like a grey wall of water, the rain obscured his view of the world.
Faust: Camping. In England. IN OCTOBER!
Narrator: The wind whipped the rain into Faust's face. The drops hit him like little bullets that burst open on his head, then slowly crept down his neck in rivulets...
Faust: Yes ... that's enough!
Narrator: Hang on! Who wanted to come here?
Faust: Killanowski!
Narrator: And you wanted to...
Faust: Not now ... Where do I have to go?
Narrator: (sighs) Am I the sat nav around here?!
Faust: Just do it.
Narrator: (sighs) Over there on the right. Into the street.

© The Author(s), under exclusive license to Springer Nature Switzerland AG 2021
S. Preger, *Storytelling in Radio and Podcasts*,
https://doi.org/10.1007/978-3-030-73130-4_7

> Patch.
>
> *Narrator*: The other right.
> *Faust*: Argh…all backwards!

The beginning of the story comes across as a fictional narrative. In fact, the *Faust jr.* audio plays are a mixture of fictional story, real-life experts and tape as well as historically accurate facts. The example shows the extent to which the narrator can be recognised as a character and thus become a formative part of the story: The narrator not only guides us through the story, but also interacts with characters and becomes recognisable as a character himself. Perhaps the first impulse we have as journalists is something like: "This has nothing to do with the stories we tell." Oh, yes it does, because the narrative style here makes us aware, albeit in a rather intense way, of the narrative elements we often do not consciously create. In non-fictional stories, we as reporters and authors often act as if there were no narrator at all, or as if the narrator presented the story in a completely value-free way, as objectively and distanced as possible. It is the claim of being a non-existent narrator and a speciality of my home country: "*The German narrator* is what the western European colleagues rather mockingly called the voice from the clouds, which was a trademark of our ARD feature" (Kopetzky 2013, 146, translation by the author). These are the words of one of the most experienced German feature authors, Helmut Kopetzky. "Until the 1970s (and beyond), the omniscient narrator with the mannered radio voice and the badge of "objectivity" on his cap, who announced *ex cathedra* (ex studio) how the world was supposed to be, still prevailed largely unchallenged in German-language radio" (Kopetzky 2013, 146, translation by the author).

To this day, this kind of narrator still dominates in numerous (not only German) productions (fortunately, there are many other productions as well). The result is the greatest possible distance from the content presented and often an artificially over-articulated narrative attitude (combined with many false accentuations, no, not—every—word—must—be—emphasised). In contrast to this, a story should really be told so that listeners feel someone is actually telling them something at that very moment. Anyone who seriously pursues this goal will soon notice that it has a great impact on the way a manuscript is written and how the voice tracking works. The narrative attitude should not just happen, it has to be created and staged so that it really feels authentic (even if that sounds like a contradiction in terms). The American story coach Eric Nuzum puts it this way: "What most listeners and aspiring podcasters miss is that there is a big difference between being spontaneous and *sounding* spontaneous" (Nuzum 2019, 59). Yep, exactly that! But narrative attitude also means something more, namely an audible attitude towards the story. The narrative attitude provides an answer to the question: What is the narrator's actual attitude towards what he or she is telling? It is more about transparency than about alleged objectivity. To answer this question, the familiar categories such as 'personal' or 'omniscient' narrator are not sufficient because the central element takes place, so to speak, at the subtextual level of narration. John Truby sums it up like this: "The storyteller is one of the most misused of all techniques, because most writers don't know the implications of the storyteller or its true value" (Truby 2007, 310). Truby writes about narrators in film, but once again I think the statement can just as well be applied to audio narratives. So, let's approach the unique selling point 'narrative attitude' in three steps:

- Developing narrative attitude.
- Writing narrative attitude.
- Staging narrative attitude (see Sect. 8.4).

In order to develop a narrative attitude, the tasks of a narrator should be clear. Here they come.

7.2   The Job of the Narrator: Presenting and Commenting

It sounds banal: The narrator tells the story. With audio narratives, we have no choice in this respect. We need some kind of narrator to present our story. A pure collage or purely scenic story, which (almost) works completely without an audible narrator, is feasible, but is the exception when it comes to non-fictional stories (on purely scenic narrations, see Sect. 3.8). It is used, for example, in oral history approaches. This pure form consisting only of tape and original recordings is excellent training for reporters, because all the information necessary to understand the story must be heard on tape. There is no narrator to explain, give context or additional figures or information. Every author who has tried this form for a non-fictional story knows how time-consuming and complicated this can be. So, there will usually be a narrator. But what exactly does it mean to tell a story? The narrator has two core functions:

- The narrator presents the action, debates and scenes in the story. The narrator is the listener's anchor, leading from one scene to the next and providing the facts absolutely necessary for understanding the scene. The more inconspicuously this occurs, the better. Then the listener is not distracted from the scene by the narrator. The narrator thus leads through time and space, but subordinates themselves to the story, disappearing, so to speak, behind the story. This will be especially palpable in non-fictional scenes. If the narrator becomes too much of a character, there is a great danger of distracting from the actual story—unless the narrator is part of the story and plays a role in the scene. In reconstructed scenes, this means that the narrator will clearly adopt the perspective of the character who relates the scene. Thus, in this type of scene, the narrator is very close to the personal narrator in prose (cf. Stanzel 2008, 68ff). This is where restraint is called for—which is the very opposite of what is required for the second function.

- The narrator comments on the action, debates and scenes of the story, classifies them or puts them in context. This can be done in many different ways: humorous, angry, caustic, ironic, short and concise or detailed. In this way, the character of the narrator becomes apparent. The narrator thus makes a clearly perceptible appearance.

The two functions are a bit like the two opposite ends of a scale: on the one hand rather withdrawn, on the other, more classifying and commenting. Depending on the narrative, the narrator can oscillate between the two poles, in accordance with the course of the story. The second, classifying function is the decisive point for audio narratives. This is where the narrator becomes recognisable, a situation which bodes danger in its own right: "Notice, that a storyteller calls attention to himself and, at least initially, can distance the audience from the story" (Truby 2007, 310). Again, Truby is referring to a narrator in a movie who appears as a voice. But the same idea can also be applied to audio narratives and taken one step further: If the narrator's character is revealed, listeners will react to that character. There is a danger that listeners will therefore be distracted or even put off by the story, especially if they don't like the narrator for whatever reason. The rejection of the narrator will be quick, impulsive and probably unthinking. Those who do not like or accept the narrator will find it difficult to follow the story. In order to avoid this problem, many real-life stories follow a devastating strategy: They work with the most distanced narrator possible, who, from an authorial, i.e. omniscient, perspective, presents the story in an apparently journalistic/objective way, and who uses precisely this tone of voice. But this attitude produces exactly what one actually wants to avoid. Listeners are rubbed up the wrong way by this supposedly omniscient narrative attitude, which explains the world from above, and turn away from the story. That is why this narrative attitude is so dangerous and destructive. The supposedly omniscient narrator without personality generates the greatest possible distance between the narrator and the story and this condescending attitude causes the audience to reject it. Thus, a narrator of this kind often does not serve the story. The goal must therefore be to develop a narrator who serves the story and at the same time is accepted or even liked by the audience. First of all, the narrator should be clear about where they actually stand in relation to 'their' story. What exactly is their narrative attitude?

7.3   The Narrator's Mindset: Developing a Narrative Attitude

On radio and podcasts, the narrator will almost always be recognisable as a real person, simply because of their voice. Listeners will immediately engage with the narrator, responding to voice and narrative attitude as well as to the story itself. That is why the narrative attitude is so crucial. I also call it the narrator's mindset. Four questions can help to develop it:

- What does the narrator think about their story (what fascinates them, why are they telling the story in the first place)? The question primarily targets what in psychology is also known as beliefs. (Beck 2013, 223ff) Beliefs express the views people have about themselves, others and the world—for example, how the world should be or what values are important. These basic assumptions are very strongly anchored in our personalities. Therefore, when we put them into words, they usually appear in the indicative, they are subjectively seen as truth. Some of the more common assumptions even become sayings like 'work before pleasure.' This belief expresses the conviction that you must earn leisure time. Normally, we as humans rarely reflect on these deep-seated convictions. But they have a strong influence on how we see the world. They influence our ideology and our behaviour. It is therefore crucial for a narrator to be aware of the beliefs that play a role in the story. As a writer, I do not necessarily have to share these beliefs in real life, but they help me to develop a narrative personality. And probably should correspond to my own real assumptions when I use a first-person narrator in my piece. Otherwise, I will not only find myself on very thin ice in moral terms but will also have problems to authentically convey my attitude during the voice tracking. An example from *The Hitchhiker* illustrates how working with basic beliefs can be successful: In the first scene, Stephan meets Heinrich. Stephan's narrative passages in the first scene read as follows (in the story he is interrupted by short remarks from Heinrich): "When someone stands in front of you, in total despair...who wants to end his life...and who asks you for a last favour, for his last journey...then you have to help him, don't you?" What Stephan expresses here is a belief: You must help people who are desperate and in a hopeless situation. People will probably share this conviction or at least understand it. Thus, Stephan is anchored as a sympathetic and comprehensible narrator.

  Basic assumptions or beliefs are also a good means of developing narrative attitudes because they tell us something about people's motivation and can thus be used as a means of identification for listeners, along the lines of 'If I know why someone does something, then I understand their actions better.' In order to identify convictions or find convictions for the narrator, ask yourself: What does the narrator think about the world they are reporting on (e.g. do they believe that in the business world, money comes before humanity)? And why does this help? Because it gives the narrator an attitude when telling a story. At the beginning of *The Hitchhiker*, for instance, Stephan cannot simply turn round and walk away, although he realises how weird the situation is, how demanding Heinrich can be. And it is precisely this inner struggle that we want to recreate. But for this we have to be aware of the inner struggle within Stephan himself. Beliefs therefore help to get the narrator into the desired and appropriate speaking attitude (for the actual tracking, see Sect. 8.4).

- What is the narrator's attitude towards the characters in the story? What perspective, what place, does the narrator take in relation to the world of his or her characters? At first glance, these questions seem very similar to the first category. But they are not. To stay with the example from *The Hitchhiker*: Stephan's conviction only says that he should help the person. The conviction says nothing about whether he finds the person likeable or irritating. So, the relationship between narrator and character is not (yet) clear. The scene from *Faust jr* at the beginning of the chapter, for example, reveals the relationship between narrator and main character very clearly. Apparently, the two have known each other for quite some time; they are a bit annoyed with each other because they have experienced each other's behaviour many times before, but they can probably rely on each other, at least Faust can rely on the narrator. On the one hand, there is the somewhat unfocused detective who wouldn't be able to cope on his own (played by Ingo Naujoks); on the other, the rather diva-like narrator (played by Bodo Primus) who likes to be specially asked to do his job, namely to tell the story. But something else becomes clear at the same time: The narrator would never seriously endanger his hero. If Faust makes a wrong turn, he is put back on the right track, more or less gently, by the narrator ("The other right..."). This is also the narrator's promise: Nothing bad will really happen (after all, *Faust jr* is a production for children). All these levels become clear in just a few lines of dialogue (which also shows once again how powerful dialogue can be).

   In *The Hitchhiker*, the question of the relationship between the two narrators and the protagonist is one of the most important in the entire story. The relationship develops and changes constantly. It is therefore also the motor of the story. The changes must take place in front of the listeners' ears. That is why it is so important to know the narrative attitude for each scene.

- What is the narrator's attitude towards the audience? To answer this question, the narrator (and thus the author writing the narrative) must have an idea of their audience. This audience imagination will provoke a reaction (Does the narrator like these people? Or are they perhaps even alien to them?) and thus essentially determine the tone of the narrative. For example, if I don't like someone, I will quickly start mansplaining to elevate myself and humiliate the other person. When listening to stories or current radio and podcast productions, ask yourself whether you can guess how the presenter or reporter feels about their audience. Very often you will sense the answer.

There is probably a clear difference between radio productions and podcasts. Podcasters often have a much clearer idea of their community (possibly also because it is less heterogeneous). This means that greater proximity is possible which can be detected in the narrative style. Good examples of this are *Radiolab* and *This American Life* on the US market, whilst the same applies to *Einhundert* by *Deutschlandfunk Nova* in Germany.

- What perspective, what place, does the narrator take in relation to the story? This question concerns the narrator's point of view. In two ways: On the one hand, there is the issue of the external point of view: Is the narrator located inside or outside the story; are they part of the story or an observer? On the other hand, there is the question of the inner point of view: Is the narrator part of the world they report on (i.e. are they familiar with it?), or do they observe a world that is actually alien to them?

  On the external point of view: In documentary narratives, there will probably be a change of perspective depending on where the story is located on the ladder of abstraction. The more specific, the more the narrator will immerse themselves in the story. The more abstract, the more likely they will be to move away from the story to some extent. If the narrator is at the centre of the story or is an active part of it, it will probably end up as a first-person narrative anyway. Then the narrator is central to the story, along with their personality and thoughts.

  On the internal point of view: In non-fictional narratives, the narrator tends to look at the reporting world more from the outside (this applies just as much to stories about homeless people as to those about top managers). There is a very high risk of going to the one extreme or the other: either to present the story in a somewhat condescending manner in the tone of the 'German narrator' who has researched everything, completely understands the world and can now judge it; or to adopt the tone of no-distance-at-all-enthusiasm, because everything is so exciting and fascinating. This is more likely to happen to reporters who are dealing with a topic they know nothing about for the first time. Everything is new and thrilling or particularly repugnant. This attitude, however, often makes a less confident and wise impression, apart from boding the danger of a lack of objectivity. People who know something about the topic will find it naive. It is important to remember that just because it is new to the reporter (because it is the first time they have dealt with it), it is not new to all the listeners.

The four questions help to develop the desired narrative attitude, the mindset of the narrator. In addition, there are a few characteristics that make it easier for storytellers to build a positive relationship with listeners and thus bind them emotionally to the story. Probably, the most important feature is that the narrator should be modest and not brag about the knowledge they have accumulated. Or their experiences. They should not pretend to be omniscient and that the story has nothing to do with them. An authorial (omniscient) attitude of this kind can also hinder the development of the story. Because an all-knowing narrator who boasts about their knowledge will betray far too much too soon. It is better if the narrator is also instrumental in uncovering or revealing the story, the kind of character who learns as they go along.

It is obvious to listeners that the narrator is telling a story in hindsight, sometimes just a few days later, sometimes centuries. But the consciousness always resonates that it is a past event. On occasions, you can consciously make use of this fact. For example, if you specifically point out that a story happened in the past and is finished, this can make it more melancholy or even tragic. A 'what if' feeling or a sense of missed opportunities arises that accompanies the whole story. But even if this is not explicitly pointed out, listeners are aware that the story takes place in the past. This has a direct impact on the narrative attitude and on listeners: "They also feel that the story is complete and that the storyteller, with only the perspective that comes after the end, is about to speak with perhaps a touch more wisdom" (Truby 2007, 311). This wisdom gives listeners the guarantee that the narrator can keep a story together emotionally, no matter how dramatic. It is as though the narrator had made a promise: I will guide you safely through this story; it will not slip through my fingers. In my opinion, the wisdom of the narrator shows itself in two specific behaviours:

- The narrator observes and reflects, is smart without being a wise guy. The argumentation the narrator uses is transparent. So, this kind of wisdom is especially evident at the upper level of the ladder of abstraction. Especially in the first season of *Serial*, Sarah Koenig embodies exactly this type of narrator. She pauses again and again, reflects and develops insightful thoughts, which then finally lead into a new scene. The narrator's wisdom has much more to do with their ability to analyse and reflect than with knowledge. This is often misunderstood—which leads us on directly to the second aspect.
- The narrator doesn't tell you everything they know. They don't need to in order to showcase their ego. The narrator only says what is important for the story. Of course, there is infinitely more that could be said in relation to this or that fact, but the narrator does not do that—they can hold back. And listeners sense that, too. The narrator is so well informed that they can distinguish what is really important for the story and what is not. Sarah Koenig mastered this technique in *Serial* in a very special way, as well. It is more noticeable in the first season than in the second or third, mainly because the narrator's attitude in the seasons is different. Koenig

says 'I' in both the first and second seasons but there is a fundamental difference between these two 'I's'. More on that in a moment.

It is as easy as that. Initially, a modest, ignorant, but discovering and wise narrator is a fundamentally good narrator.

In the end, this also means that the narrator does not take themselves too seriously. They know they can make a mistake or simply behave clumsily – another feature that Sarah Koenig establishes in *Serial* from the very beginning. Already the first, previously quoted survey of the first episode, in which Koenig asks young people if they can remember a day that happened a few weeks ago, reveals her sense of humour: "This search sometimes feels undignified on my part. I've had to ask about teenagers' sex lives, where, how often, with whom, about notes they passed in class, about their drug habits, their relationships with their parents." She reflects on her own behaviour and has to smile at herself. Sarah Koenig manages to tell an emotionally very difficult story easily. And she never acts inappropriately. This is not only good craftsmanship, but absolutely necessary for people to be able to cope with this story. The more difficult a story is, the more it needs lighter moments. Koenig never slips off this tightrope by introducing plenty of transparency, reflection and self-irony in the right places. And probably this approach helps to create a narrator who really serves the story. It is especially important for the narrator to recognise themselves and their own convictions and to abstract from them or use them consciously—especially in the stories in which we as reporters reach for one of the most difficult words: I!

7.4   I, NARRATOR

The narrator is a personality in their own right. This is also true when the story is designed as a first-person narrative. The narrator personality is then part of the reporter personality. If the first-person narrator claims to be something that the reporter does not embody at all, then the story will probably be unbelievable. I think a distinction between two quite different first-person narrators makes sense:

- The active first-person narrator—as protagonist. The reporter is also the protagonist and tells the story from their own perspective. The same standards apply to this protagonist as to all other protagonists, which means the reporter faces a real challenge in the story or wants to achieve a goal, has to overcome obstacles, solve tasks, etc. The reporter, then as the narrator, should make the listener perceive this development. And this is exactly what the first-person narrator often fails to do. The reporter has reached their goal by now (or not), the story may be completed in real life. So, it is obviously tempting to portray oneself as being a little smarter, better and not quite so clumsy and vulnerable from the very beginning. But this is exactly what is needed for the story to develop strength. At this point, one's own ego may get in the way of the story. At the same time, this kind of first-person narration offers a lot of scope for humour, for example when you don't take yourself too seriously: You can comment on yourself in scenes and thus not only look at yourself benevolently from the outside, but also provide information on your motives and views in this situation. Sarah Koenig is a first-person narrator and protagonist in the first season of *Serial*.

- The reflective first-person narrator—as rapporteur. The term may imply a little more distance than this narrator should really keep. It is a first-person narrative, but one in which the first-person narrator is not the protagonist, as in the second season of *Serial*. Again, Sarah Koenig tells the story as a first-person narrator but is far from being as involved in the story or as active and recognisable a protagonist. The *Serial* team chose the type of first-person narrator that best serves the story as the comment, quoted earlier, by *Serial* co-inventor Julie Snyder shows: "So I think the story itself dictated that we needed Sarah to play that role. And in the story for Season 2, we didn't. The structure of the story didn't necessitate it, so Sarah is not as much of a character" (Koenig & Snyder 2017, 82).

   Although the reporter is not the protagonist, there can be very good reasons for telling the story in the first person.

   'I' is honest. It emphasises the fact that the story is told from a subjective perspective. The narrative attitude does not even pretend that there is an objective truth, which is now being presented. Especially with complex stories this seems appropriate. Of course, this is not a justification for neglecting research, along the lines of I am telling the story subjectively, so I do not need to do any homework. Subjectivity refers not so much to the facts that can be researched, but rather to their emotional impact. Cases like that of Bowe Bergdahl (in the second season of *Serial*) may also touch reporters emotionally. And that may also become audible. So the narrator becomes recognisable, not only emotionally, but also in her analysis of the events. Sarah Koenig is particularly good at this. Her personality is especially apparent in they way she cleverly analyses and reflects. Often, for example, she dives into the subtext of a scene or dialogue. She analyses why we just heard something and what it means. Only she can do it this way, no one else. And in doing so, she makes the story her own, not as an active protagonist, but as a narrator.

Both types of first-person narrative thus lead to more transparency and subjectivity. These characteristics must serve the story; otherwise, they are meaningless. Consequently, for non-fictional, i.e. journalistic stories, this means that the journalist's work process becomes more transparent. This is a useful side-effect because it creates more understanding for the way we think, the approach and the limitations of our work—but it is nevertheless a side-effect. Which is why I am pointing this out so explicitly: In many work-shops, format development sessions and discussions, I have encountered the idea that journalists simply reconstruct their research path for their narration, which would then supposedly create suspense, because it would give an insight into this otherwise unknown world. That's what I call the 'misunderstanding of re-narrated research.' This procedure does not usually produce a good or exciting story, but a boring sequence of everyday journalistic activities. It's true that in formats like *Serial* or *The Hitchhiker* we experience again and again how journalists work. These situations or scenes offer good insights, but also, and above all, serve the plot at that moment. In the first part of *The Hitchhiker*, for example, you can hear from time to time how I try to convince authorities or institutions to give me information about Heinrich. You actually only hear my side of the phone call because I am not allowed to record the other side in Germany without consent. It is important to notice that these scenes have two functions. Firstly, they demonstrate our search for Heinrich (the more difficult it is, the greater the satisfaction feels later). This search must serve the actual story which is exactly what happens here. The main task in the first *Hitchhiker* episode is to find Heinrich. And secondly, the scenes reveal character traits. This applies to my attempts on the phone as well as to Stephan's search for Heinrich in other places. These scenes thus strengthen the bond between listeners and narrators, in this case, us. The fact that our research paths are made transparent is therefore a consequence of the scenes, not a primary function. Disclosing the research path must produce scenes that serve the story, then this approach makes sense.

Does this mean that every narrative always and absolutely needs a first-person narrator? No, of course not. Analyses can be carried out and trans-ported without saying 'I' or 'me'. On the other hand, the narrator's person-ality can also be experienced without explicitly mentioning 'I', as well. And sometimes the distance to a topic is necessary and journalistically appropriate.

The great danger of 'I' is that the reporter becomes too great a centre of attention. This can result in listeners turning away from the story because they do not want to listen to an ego show. Conversely, the great danger for the omniscient narrator is the degree of narrative distance and potential for condescension. Listeners also turn away from a story because they do not want to be lectured. There are of course gradations in between. There are first-person narrators who seem extremely distanced and condescending—not so good. And there are narrators who get close to the emotions but don't use the word 'I' even once—rather good. The simple truth is that if you say 'I' you always become part of the story—as an active or reflective narrator, or both.

All in all, the narrator will probably switch between different positions whilst maintaining a basic emotional attitude towards the story. In scenes, they will tend to disappear behind the story because the scenes should speak for themselves. The narrator will only provide facts or information that are essential for understanding what is going on, nothing more—unless, of course, the narrator repeatedly comments on the scenes by interjection, so to speak, offstage. On the one hand, this offers scope for humour and unexpected elements, but on the other, always interrupts the scene and thus emphasises that it is only a narrative. Listeners cannot completely immerse themselves in the story but are regularly pulled out of the scene, which makes re-entry more difficult.

The commentary option is, of course, also possible in reconstructed scenes in which a person retells, for example, an event from the past. However, if a narrator interrupts too often, they not only destroy the narrative situation but may even appear disrespectful towards the person speaking. If, in these reconstructed scenes, the narrator does not comment from their own perspective, but from that of the character speaking, then they can use these comments, by contrast, to deconstruct the subtext of what is being said.

Given all the possibilities, the same applies as usual: be experimental! It is important to consciously shape the narrative attitude and not just let it happen. The earlier the narrative attitude is developed, the easier the further work process will be. Once the narrative attitude has been identified and developed, the author must make sure that it is reflected in the script.

7.5   Writing for Narration

The manuscript is the basis for developing your own voice during the voice tracking (if you speak yourself and do not work with actors). What is not laid out in the script is unlikely to be created in the studio (or wherever you record: at your desk at home, in a cupboard or under a blanket). Complicated sentences, hectic mental leaps, inappropriate style, all this will be reflected in the voice afterwards. This also applies when someone else presents your text (for whatever reason). That person will have to fight their way through the story rather than tell it. Even if you tend to improvise your text you must make sure your line of thinking is more or less straight. There are no secrets about the basics of writing for audio: formulate actively, develop thoughts step by step, use figurative speech and work with metaphors, one thought per sentence, avoid nominal style, redundancy instead of variance, create text flow and so on. You can find all this, for example, in Vincent McInerney's book *Writing for Radio* (McInerney 2001). These are the technical basics. Sometimes, at least that is my impression, you just want to cry out to authors, reporters, correspondents and announcers alike: "Take these basics seriously, really seriously." Then many pieces would sound less stilted and distanced. Or it would be much more difficult to create this distanced attitude in voice recordings. But if the text itself already comes across as distant and omniscient, then the voices usually sound like that, too.

The crucial thing is always to have a clear narrative attitude, in every passage and scene. That means the courage to be subjective. Then it becomes easier to write the appropriate text. If 'writing for listening' is the basis, then we should go one step further with narrations: I call it writing for narration. Writing for narration means having found your own voice, being able to write it down and stage it. But if I don't know how I feel about something, then I won't be able to write it down. Already in the first passages of *Serial*, for example, Sarah Koenig's attitude and thus her personality becomes obvious:

"I first heard about this story more than a year ago when I got an email from a woman named Rabia Chaudry. Rabia knows Adnan pretty well. Her younger brother Saad is Adnan's best friend. And they believe he's innocent.

Rabia was writing to me because, way back when, I used to be a reporter for the Baltimore Sun, and she'd come across some stories I'd written about a well-known defense attorney in Baltimore who'd been disbarred for mishandling client money. That attorney was the same person who defended Adnan, her last major trial, in fact.

Rabia told me she thought the attorney botched the case – not just botched it, actually, but threw the case on purpose so she could get more money for the appeal. The lawyer had died a few years later. She'd been sick.

Rabia asked if I would please just take a look at Adnan's case. I don't get emails like this every day. So I thought, sure, why not?"[1]

Koenig makes us feel how innocent and naïve she was. She doesn't want to seem wiser than she was at the time. And we, as listeners, can sense that. In *The Hitchhiker*, we adopt this technique from the word go, trying to make it clear to listens what we actually thought and felt at the time. We relate our first encounters with Heinrich as a parallel montage (remember we met Heinrich at the same petrol station in Cologne, Stephan talked to Heinrich there, I picked him up and brought him to Bonn main station):

Sven: When I was sitting in the car with Heinrich on the way to Bonn, he suddenly put his hand inside his jacket, then quickly whipped it out again and said, 'I could also draw a gun.' I almost drove into the crash barrier. Of course, his hand is empty. He laughs. Very funny.

Stephan: While Heinrich is talking like this, I am waiting for the right moment to tell him not to throw away his life, to get things into perspective. But the longer he goes on, the more it becomes clear that I am not going to be able to talk him out of the Zurich thing.

Tape: (Heinrich Kurzrock, mobile phone recording, parked car) For me there is now only one goal, one destination, and that is peace, which I am looking for and will find soon. And I will only find peace through death. It's that simple.

Stephan: No-one makes that up.

Sven: I wouldn't have thought so either.

Stephan: Of course, you can never see into people's minds.

Sven: Yes, but this is different. You can't just reject Heinrich. At least, I can't. It touches a very deep conviction in me: there are situations in life when you can't just look away. You have to do something even though you don't quite understand why. And it's like that here. It's one of those situations.

These examples show some of the key features of how writing for narration can work. I have summarised them in six theses that can help you to find your own narrative voice:

- Get to know your own way of speaking. Sarah Koenig sometimes works with short phrases ('actually' or 'sure'). I myself like to use reinforcing sentences ("there are situations in life when you can't just look away. You have to do something even though you don't quite understand why. And it's like that here. It's one of those situations.") If you want to put your own voice and your own style on paper, you have to know them. And there is a simple method to help you practise: Record yourself when you tell people about an experience for the first time. Or tell something you have just experienced to yourself. Then listen to it. The more often you do this, the more you will notice special features. Do you use filler words or reinforcements, or do you perhaps speak elliptically? Of course, your own way of speaking should be based on 'writing for listening' and not be (too) quirky. Why all this? If you write the way you speak, it will be much easier for you to sound natural and authentic when tracking your voice. Because you will be able to develop the thought at that moment and thus really feel it.
- Practice saying 'I'. It sounds banal, but practise talking about yourself, your thoughts and experiences. This will not only help you later when you are recording, but it will also help you find your attitude towards your narrative. Which thought feels natural? What is your real attitude? How can you use it for your narrative? Do you even want to? Here too, a test recording can be a great help in putting this characteristic style on paper.
- Imagine your dramaturgy. What I mean by that is have your narrative sentence and plot always visible when you write, as a reminder. Because you should always know where you are dramaturgically when writing. Are you building up suspense, are you just transitioning from A to B or are you in the middle of one of the most dramatic scenes? What is the mood in the situation? This will change your own tone of voice and thus your choice of words, which will add variety to your narrative. If you don't know exactly where you are in your own narrative, then you'll probably retreat into a distanced, uniform style of writing. Not helpful!
- Test the manuscript, read it out loud to yourself or read through it with others. Check that these sections feel good and natural. One of the most important questions (also later for the work in production) you should ask yourself: Do you feel the thought again when you are expressing it? That is the goal, to tell a written thought as though it had only just occurred to you. If that is the case, it will feel like real narration and will sound much more authentic. The important thing to remember is to try to resolve the contradictions in your head, which many narrators carry with them to the microphone. These contradictions are created when I

want to tell a story on the one hand but am convinced I have to articulate every single syllable extremely clearly on the other (of course, people should be able to understand you). This causes two big problems: First, you will speak unnaturally, because hardly anyone articulates every single syllable clearly when they are speaking normally. And second, you will build up too much pressure in your voice. This usually leads to you emphasising too many things in a sentence, making everything sound incredibly tight and pressurised. It becomes hard to listen to—which is where the next point comes in.

- Find the right pace for your story. We have talked about tempo before (see Sect. 5.7). Try to vary tempo as well. When something dramatic happens that you have been working towards for a long time: slow down. Shape the moment. If you have to get through stretches when not so much is happening: accelerate.
- Trust your own voice. Do you roll your 'rs' a little? Can people hear that you come from a certain region? If so, work on that accent. After all, people be able to understand you. But you still have to feel comfortable, otherwise you won't find your own narrative voice. Of course, if your voice has features that distract from the content then you'll have to work on that first, for better or worse.

All these aids and features are not only useful when you speak yourself, but also when someone else tells your story. Because if you take these tips into account when writing, you will create a narrator whose personality will be recognisable and tangible. This also helps colleagues, speakers or actors (whoever lends their voice to your story) to tell the story better. That's why it also makes sense to involve the director at an early stage, if there is one (if you are not directing yourself or producing everything on your own anyway), see Chapter 8. The big goal for the narrator is what I call creating a live impression (we'll get to an example in a moment)—the feeling that the story is unfolding at that moment. Writing for narration or writing for storytelling is the basis for this. And if you find you can work just with keywords or bullet points to help you develop the thought, that is also fine!

The key message here is this: A good narrator is an authentic narrator. Listeners get the feeling they are developing the narration at the very moment they are telling the story, as if there were no manuscript. Such a narrator never sounds hypercorrect, but natural and authentic: a genuine storyteller.

7.6   Creating a Live Impression

It is one of the great advantages and unique selling points of radio: the feeling that something is happening somewhere right now, and listeners can, well, listen. A connection also develops because listeners know 'there's someone talking to me right now or talking to someone else about something.' We have already considered the live feeling (see Sect. 5.3), that is, what listeners feel while diving into the scene of a story. Now it is a matter of establishing this feeling at the level of the narrator. There is someone who is telling me something right now. There were times in the past when this feeling could become so strong that listeners couldn't always differentiate between fiction and reality. The classic example is the 1938 CBS production *War of the Worlds* (based on the novel by H.G. Wells). Orson Welles produced it as a radio play, which repeatedly contained seemingly genuine reports about Martians allegedly invading the US. The piece is said to have caused major panic in New York, but how great this panic actually was is still disputed today. Nonetheless, the example shows how powerful this live feeling can be. In recordings and pre-productions, this is of course an illusion (which is also often referred to for reasons of journalistic transparency), but the feeling is and remains a very strong one. Many podcast productions also rely on this live feeling (although everyone is aware that a podcast has already been produced). But especially podcast makers know that if you create a live feeling in your stories, you will draw listeners right into the story.

One programme that specialises in this kind of impression is *Radiolab*: "In producing the show, I imagine Improvisation and Composition as two equally matched boxers" writes one of the hosts of the show, Jad Abumrad (Abumrad 2017, 54). "We're not standing at a podium or across the street from the action and holding our nose - we're right in the thick of it, and we don't know the answers" (Abumrad 2017, 58). *Radiolab* adopts an unknowing narrative attitude and tries to make everything as tangible as possible so that listeners get a real experience. To create this live impression, the hosts and authors use two simple tricks:

- Almost everything is in dialogue: "There's a thing I realized about Radiolab. With some exceptions, everything that's said on the show is said to someone else, literally" (Abumrad 2017, 122). Either the two hosts talk to each other, or the reporters talk to the hosts, or experts or other people talk to the reporters and/or hosts. The big advantage: dialogue generates attitude which prevents major distancing.
- Not everything is scripted in advance. This is at least true for the parts involving the (former) hosts, Robert Krulwich and Jad Abumrad: "The scripting part, we don't do. It's a lot of improvisation. Robert and I are there, bantering back and forth, burning hours of tape—which we then cut into the best bits" (ibid). They sit in the studio, try out, improvise, try again and finally cut.

This method particularly suits the special requirements of *Radiolab* and cannot easily be transferred to other productions. But it does raise an interesting question: Is it always necessary to have a completely formulated manuscript? It certainly has many advantages: It makes it much easier to get approval from the editorial staff or have script meetings with colleagues;

everyone involved knows exactly where they are. But if you want to create a real live impression, you have to let the story unfold as it goes along. This is one of the reasons why many presenters work with keyword models, thought-steps, clusters or other techniques. It forces them to re-develop the thought in the present. Many reporters who prepare live talks use a similar technique. And it works. They often actually create a special impression in the studio. Of course, not all productions have to sound like *Radiolab*. In some of their stories, for example, the number of people involved is so large that listeners don't always know exactly who is speaking at any one time. So there is a risk that listener orientation suffers. And there are also good reasons for formulating a script in advance. After all, with some topics every single sentence and word can be important. And yes, if in doubt, you the reporter need an editorial team that is actually prepared to accept a kind of keyword concept in lieu of a manuscript.

Personally, I solve this for myself by prioritising a working step that many reporters probably don't think about until later or not at all (because they don't direct their stories themselves): I start the directing work at the latest whilst writing: ambience, noises, music, effects, I test and assemble all this during the writing process. This approach also means that for productions that use a lot of collages there is no initial manuscript (or it has to be created afterwards). But even for less collaged productions this pre-assembly can help with the writing. Music, for example, can change the choice of words and speech in your text or provide a certain rhythm. A text can often develop much more power if we write 'in time to the music.' For me, it's the only way I can make sure that everything really will fit together later and that a sonic universe will be created. This brings us seamlessly to the third step (staging narrative) and thus to the next chapter which deals with the activity that I still enjoy most to this day: working in the studio or working on the production (which can also happen at home at a desk or laptop). But first, here is the checklist for this chapter.

7.7   CHECKLIST: NARRATIVE ATTITUDE

A thought experiment at the end of the chapter: What actually happens when the distanced narrator becomes an active part of the story? It is the exact opposite of the 'German narrator.' John Truby takes up this idea again: "An all-knowing storyteller has no dramatic interest in the present. He already knows everything that happened, so he becomes a dead frame. Instead, the storyteller should have *a great weakness that will be solved by telling the story*, and thinking back and telling the story should be a struggle for him" (Truby 2007, 313). Truby suggests that the narrator becomes part of the story at some point, about three-quarters of the way through. He is talking about movies and you can imagine the moment in the film when the audience suddenly realises that this character is also the narrator (maybe at another point in his or her life)! But does that also work for audio narratives? Think again about Rainer Kahrs' feature *Urgently seeking Willy* (Radio Bremen 2015) which we talked about in Sect. 4.3 when considering the relationship between listeners and characters. Just to remind you, it is about German farmers who, with the help of Dutchman Willy van B., wanted to invest in large farms in the US. All without European bureaucracy. One of the German farmers appears right at the beginning of the play: Bärbel. At some point, the narrator confesses that this Bärbel is his sister. It's a great moment, because the narrator is part of the story in a very special way, but he doesn't betray it at the beginning. This is one of an infinite number of ways to create a narrative attitude. The crucial thing is that every story needs a narrative attitude. To develop and implement this, the following questions help:

Checklist narrative attitude

- Mindset of the narrator: What does the narrator think about their story, the characters and the listeners? Often basic assumptions or beliefs help to develop the narrator's personality. It is almost always helpful to have a wise, not omniscient, but humble narrator who is able to learn.
- Tasks of the narrator: Does the narrator fulfil their functions? They should provide orientation, lead through the story, drive the action and classify or comment on it. As a rule, the narrator varies the perspective between closeness and distance, depending on where the story is currently located (on the ladder of abstraction).
- First-person narrator: Is a first-person narrator appropriate? Here, the following distinction makes sense: first-person narrator as active protagonist or first-person narrator as reflecting, analysing commentator. It is helpful that if the reporter is the first-person narrator, the narrator represents a part of their personality.
- Writing for storytelling: Is the narrative attitude noticeably reflected in the script? The script should help to develop the thoughts in the narrative and to feel them again. In order to capture this in the manuscript, authors should know their own way of speaking. Feel free to experiment with keyword concepts and improvised speech recordings.
- Live suggestion: Does the narrator help the story unfold in the now? A live performance gives the listener the feeling of being completely immersed in the story. The unknowing narrator, who can learn, helps here, as well.

The three steps described above cannot always be clearly distinguished from one another: developing a narrative attitude, writing and staging. It is a continuous process. But the last step, the staging, always takes place in a location where the whole narrative is created acoustically: in the studio (however big, in a radio station, or small, at home, it may be). Or rather: in the voice tracking. This is usually where the creative process of production begins, before moving on to montage and post-production. And that brings us to the next chapter.

Note

1. You can find the whole manuscript here: https://genius.com/Serial-podcast-epi sode-1-the-alibi-annotated.

Bibliography

Abel, Jessica. 2015. *Out on the Wire*. New York: Broadway Books.
Abumrad, Jad. 2017. No holes were drilled in the heads of animals in the making of this radio show. In *John Biewen and Alexa Dilworth*, 2nd ed, ed. Reality Radio, 54–63. Durham: University of North Carolina Press.
Beck, Judith S. 2013. *Praxis der Kognitiven Verhaltenstherapie*. Weinheim: Beltz Verlag.
Franklin, Jon. 1994. *Writing for Story*. New York: Plume.
Genette, Gérard. 2010. *Die Erzählung*, 3rd ed. Paderborn: Wilhelm Fink.
Genius. n.d. Episode 1: The Alibi. Serial Podcast. Accessed 14 April 2020. https://genius.com/Serial-podcast-episode-1-the-alibi-annotated.
Koenig, Sarah, and Julie Snyder. 2017. One Story, Week by Week. An Interview with Sarah Koenig and Julie Snyder by John Biewen. In *Reality Radio*, ed. John Biewen and Alexa Dilworth, 2nd ed., 77–89. Durham: University of North Carolina Press.
Kopetzky, Helmut. 2013. *Objektive Lügen. Subjektive Wahrheiten. Radio in der ersten Person*. Münster: Edition Octopus.
McInerney, Vincent. 2001. *Writing for Radio*. Manchester and New York: Manchester University Press.
Nuzum, Eric. 2019. *Make Noise. A Creator's Guide to Podcasting and Great Storytelling*. New York: Workman Publishing.
Preger, Sven, and Ralph Erdenberger. 2013. *Der unsterbliche Artus*. Audio Play. Dortmund: Igel Records.
Stanzel, Franz K. 2008. *Theorie des Erzählens*, 8th ed. Göttingen: Vandenhoeck & Ruprecht.
Truby, John. 2007. *The Anatomy of Story*. New York: Farrar, Straus and Giroux.

CHAPTER 8

Staging: From Script to Sound

8.1   GOOD STAGING SERVES THE STORY

How not to work if you want good results: There is an author who works on a subject and writes a manuscript. This manuscript is discussed with an editor and revised until it finally emerges in a version for the production. This final script is then passed on to a director, who stages it together with a sound engineer. All four trades have their place. And if everything goes well, all four contribute to making the production and thus the story better. But that only works if they all talk to one another, the earlier the better. Otherwise, different perspectives will be at work on the piece, which will not support each other but, in the worst case, act against each other. The reporter is interested in the subject, but the editor would rather tell a story than present a subject, the director has some crazy, innovative staging ideas and the sound engineer prefers to work in a minimalist way. Or something like that. As a result, you will hear a story that is not a unified whole, not developed with a central idea. Podcasters, on the other hand, are used to working alone and being responsible for every step of the way: from first idea and recordings to final mix and mastering. No matter whether you work alone or in a team, the basic principle is the same: A good production serves the story and in this sense is hardly noticeable as such. It seems like the only feasible, organic way to tell the story. It does not refer to itself. To find ideas for meaningful staging, the following principles can help:

- Good staging is consistent staging. It tells the story on an additional level. This overall impression is created when all means used pick up and support the central elements of a story or character. Good staging uses the levels that make sense (not all the ones that are possible). These

© The Author(s), under exclusive license to Springer Nature Switzerland AG 2021
S. Preger, *Storytelling in Radio and Podcasts*,
https://doi.org/10.1007/978-3-030-73130-4_8

might include original sounds, voice tracking, ambience, music, Foley sound and other effects. In this sense, a good production is really like a score. Consistent staging also means having a target audience clearly in front of your mind's ear. Only then can cultural allusions and references be understood and classified. Furthermore, the production should take account of the likely listening situation. A surround sound 5.1 production will not always be able to unfold its full power on a smartphone. To put it mildly. On the other hand, intimate listening using headphones can tolerate more dynamics (special productions for headphones are now available), similar to a sound design in a film.

- Create or intensify moods and emotions. That's what sound design is for. Use all reasonable means, be it music, ambiance or the editing of sounds. In order to create emotions or moods in a targeted manner, it should be clear to me as author and director which emotional effects I want to achieve and why.

- Be aware of your genre. *Serial* is an investigative story, *The Hitchhiker* more of a road movie and *S-Town* the psychogram of a person in a small community. If you are clear about this, you will get an idea of what the overall impression of a production should be. *Serial* is allowed to sound minimalistic again and again, like a sober plea laying out its evidence in court. *The Hitchhiker* may sound dirty from time to time, like a dirty toilet at a service station, but sometimes it may also radiate the romance of being on the road. And *S-Town* is allowed to sound like a slightly off-track parallel world. These descriptions may not seem very specific, but they help as an initial approximation. They can deliver terms for it, put them into language and thus make it possible to explain (working in a team!) how something should sound.

- The staging leads me into the story. This is especially true for scenes. In the ideal case, the interplay of the acoustic elements alone creates a picture before the listener's ears. The listener knows where we are, how and when. Or they want to find out. Cliché sounds like a honking tuk-tuk (somewhere in Asia), a muezzin (somewhere in a Muslim country) or simply passing cars (somewhere in nowhere) are not enough for that and merely reproduce stereotypes. Ideally, each scene has a special sound (which the reporter also recorded). Keep in mind, scenes need some time to unfold. That doesn't mean, by the way, that the dialogue starts at an early point in the conversation (remember: get in late, get out early).The production draws the listener into the scene, for example by making a sound audible that I cannot immediately identify. It builds up slowly, the scene is created, only then is it revealed what can be heard or where we are (beware of too clumsy resolutions). In this sense, a good production also gives orientation. In a longer story, recognition elements are also helpful. This thought brings me to the next point.

- Signature elements create settings. What is the special atmosphere or the special sound of a scene? It could a nozzle being replaced in a petrol pump, a cigarette being lit with a match, or a clock ticking. And yes: Sometimes we don't have these signature elements, so we have to work without them. Intimate scenes can also be underlined by the absence of other acoustic elements. An intimate or haunting conversation in a café will hardly ever have loud ambiance, like bar and tableware noises, but will come across more quietly.

- Use psychoacoustics. The question is not: Which sound or which atmosphere is inherent to this situation and in this sense real? The question is: Which atmosphere or which sound creates the desired impression? This of course involves moral and ethical difficulties which you have to address in every new production (on the ethical and moral debate on whether narrations represent reality, see Sect. 9.2). But normal, average applause also sounds like rain. Whining cats and crying babies can also sound very similar. This may not help, even if it is the authentic sound. Or have you ever tried to stage wave sounds on a sandy beach? You will discover that the sound that comes closest to our desired impression is not recorded on a sandy beach, but mostly on a pebble beach.

One of the central questions is always: How and why can the production serve the story? And, ideally, provide its own level of meaning or additional support for the story? The best way to achieve this is perhaps to understand sound design as a concept. Sound design, the sum of all acoustic possibilities, helps you to make your story tangible. In this sense, it is a separate level of the story. Don't ask yourself what kind of noise a microscope makes, ask yourself: What does it feel like to be tiny, to be searching or discovering? Don't ask yourself what kind of noise a marathon runner makes? Ask yourself: What do hard training, perseverance, pain or running rhythm feel like? *Radiolab* host Jad Abumrad explains it using another example: Imagine someone telling you that they were riding a motorcycle. If you do not use the actual sounds of a motorcycle, Abumrad advises: "Instead, think abstractly. For instance, think about speed and what speed feels like. Then find and create sounds that evoke that feeling. Which, of course, prompts the question, "How the heck do you evoke the feeling of speed in sound?" (Abumrad 2017). This is another reason why it is so important to know how to create emotions (see Sect. 5.8).

The earlier you think about it and put the sound design concept and the staging ideas into words, the better. You will be able to take it into account when writing the script. For example, if you want to acoustically translate a person's inner conflict, you might come up with the idea of tearing off original sounds and music. Granted, a troubling but highly effective element. For this type of production, ideally one would not use sound bites where someone drops their voice. In order to emphasise the effect, the author would have to remember—while writing—to choose a sound piece of somebody whose voice goes up at the end, depending on where it is supposed to be broken off. If the voice is already down (like finishing a sentence), a director can still remove the last couple of words and let them break off more abruptly, but the author might not be happy with that because it was precisely the last two words that were so important. And then you are in the middle of the debates that sometimes shape the relationship between authors and directors. That is why good staging begins with writing (or even earlier as we will see in a second).

That means: If I am both the author and director, I should remember to develop staging ideas and keep them in mind. If someone else is staging a production, this director should be involved at an early stage. Only then is it possible to gain a common idea of a production. A good time to involve the director is to discuss the plot, then all those involved (colleagues, authors, editors and directors) can pool their ideas, taking care to show respect and understanding for each other's craft. In order to implement an abstract sound design concept, many aspects have to be considered on the pragmatic level. I have written down those I find most important and helpful in practice. The first thing that becomes clear is that the staging does not actually begin with the writing, but already with the recordings.

8.2   The Clean Original Sound

As reporters, we often pay attention to what our counterpart says. And that's a good thing. In the story interview, we have already seen that content for a narrative changes in comparison with other forms of reporting. But the sound of the recordings is just as important. Of course, recording devices have made a huge leap in quality in recent years, and we can also use audio recordings made with a smartphone these days. But because the technology works so well and is so far developed, there is perhaps a danger that we don't always listen quite as closely as we should because, after all, I can definitely ball back on the recording. But if I want to give listeners a chance to really immerse themselves in the story, then a "this'll do all right" recording is often not enough because it creates big problems during production at the latest (despite spectral cleaning and denoising). Here are a few simple guidelines can help:

- The cleaner the original recording, the more creatively I can handle it during production. Clean means a clear, very present voice recording— check the distance to the microphone. As reporters we tend to be too far away from the microphone. Get as close as possible without discomforting the original sound source too much. This requires high discipline on the author's part. Whether you record in mono or stereo or whichever microphone you use influences the recording but is not as decisive a factor in comparison. A stereo voice recording reproduces the room much better. For some productions, however, a mono voice recording plus embedding in a stereo ambience can also work very well. Then you may have a more present voice recording that is well embedded in an acoustic space. That depends on the respective recording situation. No matter what or who you are recording, be sure to consider the next point.

- Shut up a minute. Preferably together with your conversation partner. In the respective recording situation. Actually, this is a frequently emphasised matter of course. Experience shows, however, that many reporters forget about it. The result is that in the finished production, cuts and tearing transitions can often be heard (because no really suitable ambiance could be found in one's personal archive to lubricate). Separately recorded atmosphere is an absolutely necessary lubricant, for example to make the transitions between the original sound and the narrative text or other original sounds smoother.
- Check when recording. That means wear headphones. Actually, also a matter of course. Nowadays high-quality, closed, in-ear headphones are available. They are therefore not so visible and distracting for the person you are talking to, but they allow you to keep a constant check—passing aircraft, ventilated computers or humming refrigerators are usually better perceived through headphones. As a reporter, I can then still decide whether I should do something about the situation or accept the background noise. In connection with the optical level, you get a good impression of the overall sound quality of the recording.
- Be disciplined in your work. This is especially relevant for scenically recorded sound bites when you accompany people at a real event. Of course, it is not at all bad if the recording reflects the vividness of the situation (it is supposed to be 'dirty'). But dirty does not mean acoustically unclean or incomprehensible. Stay close to it, control continuously, decide what you want to record. Don't record everything at once, then the microphone will be constantly panning or at half-distance to everything and you won't be able to do anything with it afterwards. If a situation is happening before your eyes and ears, go with the speech and the action. You can get ambiance later or re-stage it, if necessary.
- Know the sound of your recordings. What I mean by that is no matter how clean your sound bites are, every sound bite sounds different. A bit thin, a bit echoey, a bit muffled. Why is this important? Because it makes sense to make use of it in the production. Do not stage something against the character of a sound clip (unless you want to make a statement!). If a person needs a moment, maybe speaks slowly or the voice has a certain sound, think about which elements could fit in, maybe some music that exactly reflects this rhythm of speech. In *The Hitchhiker* we often experienced intimate situations with Heinrich in the smallest of spaces, for example in his room (Heinrich would say 'cell'). We also took this into account when writing and staging. The very dense original sound recording could only tolerate a little ambiance or music.
- Know your equipment. Actually, also a matter of course. Confident handling is the basis for producing good sound bites in the first place. Do you know what the recording device and microphone can and cannot do? Test your equipment in different situations and remember what you have learned in certain situations. This is especially important if you are

going to act confidently in decisive situations when you're in an exciting scene (then you will be able to get a good record quality in an authentic situation, perfect!).

If you record clean sound bites, you have a lot more options when writing and producing. That doesn't mean that you have to use them all. And there will still be enough situations where there are acoustic problems. As an author, you should be able to assess what can and cannot be got out of recordings. This applies both to the acoustic processing (To what extent can a noise be reduced? How does the sound sound afterwards?) and the editing (What can be cut, what can't be cut?). If you do everything yourself anyway: Try it out! With every production you get better. If you work with a technician, then please do not work on the assumption that the technician will fix it. And another seemingly minor detail: time and again, authors tend to write the wishful thinking of a sound bite into the script rather than the transcript of the real sound bite. That's fine if the original soundtrack doesn't need to be edited. But it always creates problems if passages cannot be cut out cleanly from the middle or if the voice of the original sound source is always at the top at the end of the original sound. Therefore: be strict! Listen to your quotes before you write them into the script. Don't assume that everything can be corrected in some way. It's true, many things are possible now. But the better the selection you make, the better the production will be.

8.3   EDITORS AND DIRECTORS: MAKING A GOOD STORY BETTER

As an author, have you ever thought "But this is my story! I know best what's right?" If projects or stories are particularly important to you, this thought may come up. Especially if your manuscript has just been criticised, whether by editors or other colleagues. Most of the editors I have met so far are as interested in a good story as I am. They see themselves as supporters, not opponents. If there are major problems in the work on the manuscript, it's likely that something didn't go quite right in the first place. It may also be due to the fact that work processes, even for longer stories, tend to follow the following pattern, at least in the larger public editorial offices: The editorial office commissions the author or the author suggests something to the editorial office (such as "Let's do something about Germans in the UK because of Brexit and so on"), then the author submits travel plans and finally the travel expense report (including a short story about the trip: "I have some great ingredients!") and then at some point a script is presented. Maybe that's a bit exaggerated (but only maybe) and of course great stories can be created this way, but usually this procedure neither serves the story nor the collaboration. At some point (for workflow, see also Sect. 10.2), the editor and author have to commit to one story, including the narrative sentence and plot design. It is the duty of the editor to demand this. To deliver it is the author's obligation. And if I work alone, then I force myself to do it anyway. The big advantage is that if you agree on story and plot, there can be no more unpleasant surprises during the work on the manuscript—on either side. Then a sit-down or read-through with your editor can really be used to make the story shine even brighter.

As a story doctor and editor, I usually pay attention to two different levels when reading and editing manuscripts: story and style.

- Story level: This level assesses whether the story has really been told. The core questions to judge this level are the following: Has the plot design been implemented? Where have there been deviations? Are they useful? Does every scene work? Is the story told appropriately for the intended target audience? What are the ideas for the sound design? Do they fit the story? And of course: Do I understand everything (at least when I reach the end)?

  Of course, you can't judge everything by the amount of paper. You have to hear some of the original sounds (the mood, the tone of voice) to really judge them. When talking to the author, the questions mentioned above are the ones to be answered first. Only when the story level is coherent does the work on the second level begin.

- Style level: This level assesses whether language and style serve the story. The core questions are: Does the story flow? Does it flow quickly into scenes? Do the scenes end on a cliffhanger or punch line? Is the overall language appropriate for the story? Is emphasis placed on active, verbal formulations, especially in the scenes? Are there any author's quirks (insertions, know-it-alls, condescending attitude) that stand in the way of the story? Are there passages that are difficult to speak (sound sequences, etc.)? And of course, once again: Do I understand everything?

  The greater goal of this level is not to impose one's own style on the author. Rather, it is to help the author to use the elements of their style that serve the story.

Experience shows that, very often, attempts are made to process both levels simultaneously while working with manuscripts. At first glance, this seems efficient. The only problem is that often everything gets mixed up. The layers become blurred, no distinction is made between important and less important corrections. The story layer is more of a macro-layer, the style layer more of a micro-layer. If the story layer is not yet correct, so many changes will be made on the style layer anyway that it is not yet worthwhile to edit them in detail. As an editor, you should work through the two levels separately. First story, then style. Not the other way around.

The following applies to both levels: Criticise consciously and constructively! Back up your criticism with an argument, not with a gut feeling or an empty phrase. And if you can't come up with something better, at least in part, don't make the comment. As a rule, all participants should be able to get by with two or at most three run-throughs. If manuscripts go back and forth between author and editor, then there is usually something wrong with the story level. It is clearly the more important level! Listeners will occasionally ignore a weird sentence or bad style in a good story, but great style alone doesn't carry a story. This is one of the biggest misconceptions, "polish is probably the most overemphasized aspect of writing craft" (Franklin 1994, 169). And I'm not the only one who sees it that way, so does two-time Pulitzer Prize winner Jon Franklin, even if he refers to print products: "The brutal fact is that structure is far more fundamental to storytelling than polish" (ibid, 170).

In addition to story and style level, audio productions have a third level, the sound design level. It is an elementary component of every acoustic narration and thus also more of a macro-level. Of course, it features most during production. The earlier you clarify an important, pragmatic question, the better: Is the author also directing or not? Nowadays, it is quite normal for many radio authors, and even more so for podcasters, to do everything themselves anyway. Recordings, scripts, editing, staging, montage, mix, mastering. Author, director and sound engineer in one person. For short formats or uncomplicated productions, there is nothing wrong with that. In current affairs journalism, for example, a production session seldom consists of more than six or seven tracks, i.e. the reporter, one or two original sound sources, perhaps one or two music tracks and one or two sound or ambiance tracks. If that. When it needs to be done quickly, the final acoustic polish is not the decisive quality criterion either. However, it is different when it comes to elaborate and long productions: As an author, am I really able to keep my track management together when there are significantly more tracks? An average documentary for our history programme, for example, can have between 10 and 15 tracks, a production like *The Hitchhiker* more than 30 tracks, and a radio play-like production with mixed elements of reality and fiction can have well over 40 tracks. That means that whoever produces must also be able to manage these tracks. Hardly any sentence is worse than: 'I think a part has shifted...' Anyone who has ever experienced this knows that the production can now get very labour-intensive.

A good writer knows their limitations. This also applies to staging. Anyone who has so far done shorter pieces and is tackling a longer story for the first time will find the staging difficult in my experience. There will probably be a lack of ideas. And there may also be a lack of certainty in making decisions. A director must quickly and confidently assess what is and what is not acoustically possible, and how difficult it is to get there. That's why they will approach the material asking two questions, in particular:

- What does the material offer? It's the old mnemonic frequently repeated by the former head of rbb-Feature Editorial, Wolfgang Bauernfeind, in his workshops: "Trust your material." He's got a point. What he means is that by listening carefully, your material will show you ways and opportunities. The scenery, the sound, the way somebody speaks or a special moment. All this can be a starting point for a staging idea. A director will try to derive a staging concept from the material or set it in relation to it.

- With which acoustic elements can I serve the story or tell the story? All conceivable possibilities are open: from music, sounds and ambiance to montage techniques and effects.

The better a director knows the material and the story, the better he can work around these two questions. That's also one of the reasons why it can make sense to listen to recordings together. Then a coherent production can be created. If this doesn't happen, the author's greatest fear may be realised: that a production of 'her/his' story is created that she or he doesn't like. A good director will always try to serve the story and not to implement their oh-so-creative ideas for better or worse, according to the motto: You have to brush against the grain. Central to constructive cooperation is mutual understanding for each other's roles and jobs. If you work alone, it can sometimes be useful to tell other people about your plans and ideas. This way you also get inspiration from others and initial feedback.

If you are an author who produces and/or directs themselves, you should above all be able to take a step back from your own material and assess the story once again from the point of view of acoustic possibilities. Those who find this difficult or who are short of ideas may pass on this task, if possible. In any case, the author is responsible for presenting a final manuscript for the production, which all those involved can work with. It sounds obvious, but everyday life tells us it's not. In addition to letterhead and contact details (for any queries), a script provides a cleanly formatted text, numbered or systematised original sound bites, as well as sounds and ambiance. If the author directs it themself, the work in the studio has to be just as well prepared: music to listen through has been selected, ambiance provided, sound clips pre-cut or at least well developed (with appropriate time codes!) and all speakers have been provided with scripts and commissioned. Then nothing stands in the way of constructive work in the studio.

8.4   STUDIO WORK I: CHECK AGAINST DELIVERY

You neither pre-cut nor numbered your quotes, but they were there somewhere. Weren't they? In addition, you quickly have to look up ambiance and some other sounds. Unfortunately, there are no original recordings, so you have to search in the archive.[1] And with the music, you had hoped the technician would have an idea, after all, he is also a musician. Anyone who arrives at the studio like this has the advantage that after an hour nobody feels like working anymore. On the other hand, you lose so much time on things that are taken for granted that you have less energy and time for the actual production work. Unfortunately, if you want to work creatively, you first have to be structured and have a plan. One of the most important tasks often has to be done at the beginning of a production.

Normally the production starts with the voice tracking of all participants. If you are staging and speaking yourself, make sure you either work with a very attentive sound engineer or, even better, organise another pair of capable ears to help you sound like yourself. If you do your voice tracking all by yourself, record the first few passages, then stop and check that you really hit the desired pitch. If there are passages that make you feel unsure, do the same. Regardless of how you work, get into the right position immediately before recording, for example by sitting at the microphone and telling the sound engineer, director or whoever what the story will be about. Get yourself into the narrative mood. It should seem more like a meeting with colleagues or a hosting role than a classically presented news broadcast.[2] If you don't practise this in advance you will usually have a hard time getting used to it. The *Radiolab* method is one way to find your own voice at the microphone. The following always applies: If you are narrating, it is difficult to listen carefully to yourself at the same time. This is another reason why it helps if someone else is present. As a narrator, pay particular attention to the following points:

- Have a clear narrative attitude. Experiment a little before each new scene or new paragraph. You will be shooting multiple versions anyway.
- Know how to pronounce everything. What is the pronunciation dictionary and, if available, the pronunciation database there for? Check things before, not during production. It only causes unnecessary stress.
- Don't put too much pressure in your voice. This is tiring in the long run and can cause recordings to drag on, especially with longer stories. And the pressure comes across in the story. Keep it light.
- Don't over-articulate. Nobody pronounces every single syllable when they tell a story. If they do, it engenders a strange feeling in the listener, seeming artificial and distant. And it often causes the speaker to accentuate wrongly (see the next point). Find an accurate narrative style. This requires a bit of practice.
- Don't emphasise too much. This often goes hand in hand with too much pressure in the voice. Usually every sentence has a core of meaning. That is what is emphasised, not every second word—and usually not even the verb alone.
- Feel the text and be yourself. If you actually sense this, then you will come close to your natural narrative style.

If you put all this into practice, you will create a natural narrative attitude. As I said, this requires some practice, but it's worth it! If, in turn, you are directing other speakers, actors or colleagues you will face other challenges. For speech directing, the following guidelines will help:

- Cast sensibly if you have any influence on that. As a director, that is your job. If you give enough thought to the casting process, you will not have the problem of making impossible demands on speakers, actors or colleagues afterwards.
- Rehearse in a read through. Yes, that's pure luxury. But it helps. Actually, it should be standard production preparation. As an author, you should always read your work aloud from time to time while writing to check rhythm and speakability. If you work with a cast of several speakers who react to each other, a run-through before the actual recording can make sense. It gives everyone the chance to tune into each other.
- Be clear what you want to create. If you do not know where you want to go with the recordings, you will not be able to guide anyone else. For this you must have a definite narrative attitude in mind and be able to articulate it. Sometimes it is also helpful to play back original sounds or music to create the appropriate tone of voice. Give it a try.
- Talk to each other. Preferably in advance. Share your ideas, impressions and hear what speakers and actors have to say. It's also good for the atmosphere in the team.
- Sometimes just let things roll. If you interrupt others too quickly, it can seem rude, to put it mildly. Give people room to find their voice. This is especially important at the beginning. Once the common tone of voice has been found, it usually goes faster.
- We're not playing adjectives! It's one of the most important rules. 'A little sadder' is not good direction. Work with attitudes, situations and scenes. Make it clear where you stand in the story, why someone is doing something. Or work with a similar situation. This is a good way to get someone to adopt the right attitude. Method acting at the microphone. (cf. Strasberg 1987)

Take enough time for tracking in the studio. It is difficult to say exactly how long that will be. However, assume that you will be recording several versions of all passages. Most of the time, you will already know during the recordings which version you are likely to use. Note this down in your manuscript. This will facilitate and speed up the editing process later. If you have to listen to the entire versions over and over again, you will not only lose time but also the will to live.

Of course, it is also conceivable not to do the tracking in the studio but outside. With fictional stories or radio plays, this is not so unusual and can be done with non-fictional stories, too. However, this requires much more effort and planning, but it does produce a realistic sound. With recordings in a low-noise room (if available!), you can also produce everything you need. Once you have finished the voice recordings, you can then start having fun with the staging. Now you can really let off steam. Before you start using everything that is possible, ask yourself: Why am I doing this? How does it serve my story? Also, make sure you are in control of organising your material. If you produce your own, you'll have to do it anyway. But even if you work with a technician or sound engineer, it helps to understand a little bit about montage, effects, mixing and mastering. Then it's easier to develop a shared language—not least for one of the most important sound design tools—tada—the music.

8.5   Scoring with Rhythm and Reason

One of the most important means to create moods is music. It has a very strong influence on how the overall acoustic impression of the narrative sounds and works. The very reduced piano for *Serial* sets a tone just like the lovingly composed soundtrack to *S-Town*. People's taste in music is subjective, but whether music fulfils its function in the story can be determined quite well without considering the question of taste. This is linked to the way music affects us in stories. There are at least two ways:

- Emotionally. First of all, we as humans usually react to music with our feelings. Music makes us happy, sad or melancholic. The gradation is individual. But the emotional direction is often similar. To assess this effect, you yourself should have access to this type of emotion. You feel something in order to reproduce it in others. Most people don't hear what key it is in, what the technology behind the music is, but they feel the effect.
- Contextually. Many people associate a certain time and place with music. The idea is often shaped by clichés. But for a lot of people a certain musical idea will conjure words like 'space,' 'western' or 'reunion.' They are also largely related to cultural imprints (depending of course for which cultural context you are producing). That means you can use these associations to create spatial and temporal contexts.

You never know whether you might accidentally choose music that people associate with a very personal story. Then, in the minds of these listeners, a very special film will start, which you can hardly stop. The more familiar a piece is, the greater the chance that this will happen. You therefore need a particularly good reason for using well-known melodies or pieces of music. Also, don't be too flat. Badly used theme music is one of the most annoying ways of devaluing your stories. So, please don't play 'Bicycle Race' by Queen when you talk about cycling or ABBA's 'Money, Money, Money' in a story about finance. Unless there is a very good reason… no, no, just don't do it. From the way we listen to and perceive music, several functions can be derived as to how music can have an effect in narratives:

- Emotionally reinforcing. A chorale accompanying a biblical quotation will tend to enhance the clerical mood, the elevated quality. Or music by Emilíana Torrini the drug trip (as in the feature *K* by Jens Jarisch), a strong musical idea. The big danger of utilising music in this way is that it can seem over-emotionalised, a bit over the top, and therefore empty and melodramatic. So, the range is very wide: very big moments are just as possible as involuntarily funny ones. The more you use emotional reinforcement as a technique, the more confident you have to be: The listener is already immersed in the story and will go along with it emotionally. The music, too, eventually develops beyond the story. It can become more intense. If the music stays the same from the beginning through to the end, there is a danger that you will say musically: 'Not much has really developed in the story.' If you choose to work with music, you can do so from the very beginning. If music is only introduced as a sound medium in the middle of the story, it can often be disturbing and distracting (which may be the desired effect). Try to convey the 'sound' of the overall story from the beginning. A production that does this brilliantly in narration, text and music is *S-Town*. Even the first minutes of this narrative tell me I am being taken into a world I don't know, a world that is a bit remote. This impression is also created very strongly by the music.
- Emotionally decisive. A very nice way to create tension. In the middle of the scene, for example, music sets in that transports a certain mood or attitude (the threat of danger or grief). The music thus announces or decides how listeners should perceive the scene emotionally. Subcutaneously, it is a very powerful vehicle.
- Emotionally contrapuntal. The music shapes a completely different mood or attitude than the scene. We are more familiar with this in film because there is an additional level (sound and images) for the audience to deal with. In audio narratives, it is only acoustic levels that compete with each other. A famous example for contrapuntal music in film is the song 'What a wonderful world' by Louis Armstrong in the film *Good Morning, Vietnam*. The music is combined with images that show the misery of the Vietnam War. This makes the absurdity of the situation and the suffering of the people even more poignant.
- Situational orientation. This also has something to do with the way we listen to music. But it does not only mean that music can give us an idea of place and time, it also helps us to know where we are within the narrative. Music can show listeners what they should pay particular attention to in a certain scene. For example, imagine a scene in an attic. In this attic, there are an infinite number of objects that will be described to us during the scene. There is an old train set, for example, a musical box and a broken guitar. With music, you can now draw attention to the object that plays a role in the continuation of the narrative.

- Narrative orientation. I use this term to indicate that the music in a narration is a kind of soundtrack that uses leitmotifs and variations to hold the story together and create bonds. The piano leitmotif in the first season of *Serial*, for instance, fulfils this function very clearly. It is often used when central points are developed, explained or summarised. It gives the listener orientation: it is musical signposting.

Every music cue can always take several different paths. Option one: the music starts before the scene, as a kind of introduction or lead-in. Option two: The music starts at a certain point in the scene to emphasise that the scene is now developing in a certain direction (something terrible or beautiful is happening). By analogy with film, this could also be called musical prolepsis—the music indicates (keyword: anticipation) that something specific is now happening. This expectation can of course be broken to create a surprise. And option three: The music starts as an accent after the punchline of a scene. Which way you use it is always decided by the interaction between scene, music and desired effect. There are an infinite number of gradations between these three options. Music can stand alone in a scene to create tension. It can drive the scene forward to pick up speed. Or it can be alienated (accelerated, slowed down, distorted, noisy, tearing off, etc.) to create a desired effect, time or mood.

Music can also have a particularly beautiful effect when it changes from 'on' to 'off.' It can first be heard in the scene when someone plays an instrument, sings, or because the song is playing on the radio. Then it fades and can still be heard outside the scene as narration music. This method is also used in films from time to time. Just think of that wonderful scene between Bella and Edward in *Twilight*. The music begins in the 'off,' we see Bella and Edward roaming through the woods together. This scene cuts to the scene where Edward sits at the piano and plays exactly the same song to Bella that we heard while the two of them were climbing trees. So now the song feels as though it is in the 'on' (even if this is not quite true, see below). Isn't that romantic?! In movies we also speak of diegetic (in the scene) music and extra- or non-diegetic (from the 'off,' i.e. music without a visible source) music. When using and changing these types of music, several variations are conceivable. From 'on' to 'off' and vice versa. In the scene with Bella and Edward, there is a visual change, but the quality of the music does not change. We don't hear Edward playing the piano at that moment, but the music remains in the quality of the extra-diegetic dimension. In audio narratives, the change would have to be clearly audible in order for it to develop dramaturgical power. Otherwise, it will not be perceived. Well used, the effect is often very beautiful: It combines the real scenes with the musical dimension of the narrative. This makes the music an even stronger part of the narrative, increasing its authenticity.

No matter which music you use and how, there should always be a reason for it that serves the story. Unmotivated or unfounded use of music can be recognised, for example, when it is only used as a break or pause. That might often not be enough. Music never just fills a pause or break in what is being said. Try out whatever comes to your ears (but don't forget rights issues!). No matter whether you work with production music and the corresponding databases, classical, experimental or whatever kind of music, when it is used well, music enriches your story. And the use of music ties in with our culturally socialised perception of stories. After all, nearly all great stories in film and television (both fictional and non-fictional) have music. We are used to stories with music. And it is such a great, playful, emotional, tragic and romantic dimension!

8.6   Studio-Work II: Collage & Co

If scenes are the backbone of the story, then they must also play a special role in the staging. Listeners should really have the situation in front of their ears. If you have designed your plot well, i.e. if the scene really says something and serves the story, if the sound clips are recorded true to the scene and if both ambiance and signature elements exist, then you have a good chance of bringing the scene to life acoustically. Avoid some of the most common mistakes:

- Acoustic clichés. These include the horn of the tuk-tuk or samba music for Brazil. You are not telling a clichéd story. Find atmospheres and sounds that are unique to your story.
- Staging too fast. By this I mean that the scene does not really unfold acoustically. One sound or a short breath is just not enough. Give the scene room to breathe. Nevertheless, start your dialogues late in the action and get out of them early. Give the scene room to reverberate when it comes to an end. If the scene ends on a punch line or cliffhanger, allow it to sink in for a moment. In films, after something important, there is often a black fade. Also try to set acoustically clear start and end points. These can be accents in ambiance as well as individual noises (pulling and fixing a seatbelt, for example, is a somewhat more unusual noise than starting the engine to indicate driving off). Then chapter cuts or rather chapter transitions are created, which, combined with the appropriate sounds and music, can evoke wonderful moments. These are the moments that resonate in the listener's head and develop depth.
- Comic-like staging. A frequently occurring error. Along the lines of "When Karl opened the door (door opens), loud music hit him (loud music starts)." Even as you read it you realise it is either a case of deliberate exaggeration designed to achieve a certain humour or scurrility, or the intentions are serious, which make it rather difficult. If you have distinctive sounds, you do not need to explain them. A slamming door can be recognised as such. And if you are not quite sure, pick up the sound in the script indirectly, more like: "(door slams) Karl looked

around the room..." Then it is obvious that it was the door to the room. What else? The order of staging: noise/ambiance and then the narrator or original sound often works better than the other way round. This way you avoid the danger of your staging becoming too comic-like.

Personally, I also often differentiate between first-hand scenes and reconstructed scenes in the staging. I stage first-hand scenes so that the image really evolves before the listener's mental ear, live and in colour, so to speak. I often stage reconstructed scenes (e.g. when someone retells something) more discreetly. Less noise, a quieter atmosphere, the whole thing somewhat removed (e.g. by a minimal echo in the music or a slightly distant sounding space). This emphasises the dimension of memory more strongly. But that also depends on the narrative tempo of the original sound source. If somebody tells a story from the past in the present tense, it allows you to stage the scene more like a first-hand scene.

One of the most attractive ways of making scenes seem real is Foley sounds. It's a term that actually comes from the film industry. Foley means the reproduction of everyday sounds or ambiance that are added during post-production. Think, for example, of a person just getting out of bed, still tired. In the film, you might hear the bed covers much more clearly than would normally be the case, which can enhance the impression of how comfortable the bed is. Anyone who has ever been a guest at a live radio play where a noisemaker is active on stage will have an impression of this special art and its tricks. Foley sounds emphasise certain aspects acoustically. If you choose them appropriately, you can significantly reinforce the impression of a realistic scene. The sound of a seat belt being pulled over and finally locking into place can be much more realistic than the car engine starting up. It is more intimate and creates the right perspective (assuming you are supposed to be inside the car). After all, a car starting rarely sounds spectacular inside the car. In the best case, listeners don't even notice Foley sounds because they are organically woven into the story.[3]

I had the opportunity to be involved in one of the acoustically most challenging productions together with Ralph Erdenberger and Timo Ackermann. This was the previously mentioned series *Faust jr*, which deals with nothing less than the great riddles and secrets of mankind. The acoustic concept was to integrate real-life sound sources into a fictional plot. Of course, we were not the first to come up with such an idea and try it. But we did try to implement it as consistently as possible. It meant we always integrated the sound clips into scenes (e.g. we conducted a real medical examination with the space physician for Frank Faust's astronaut training). We recorded this scene at real locations and slipped into the role of Frank Faust; otherwise, no dialogue would have been recorded. Faust was later played by Ingo Naujoks and his voice recordings were then done in the studio. This meant we had original sound recordings (partly indoors, partly outdoors), which we had to combine with studio recordings in an acoustic space to create the illusion of a real scene for the listener. Here we always had to take the original sound material and the corresponding ambiance as our starting points and build an acoustic room from there, that is, Timo, the sound engineer, had to do it. We always used a mixture of ambiance, sounds and effects to create the desired illusion.

It makes work easier if you are aware of the difference between ambiance and sounds. The ambiance or atmospheric sound is more like a general soundscape. This can include wind noise as well as general vocal murmurs. Sounds, on the other hand, are more clearly defined, like the slamming of a door or the screeching of a saw. To achieve the appropriate mood, you usually need a mixture of both: an ambiance as a basis in which significant noises are embedded. You will soon notice that the lovingly recorded original ambiance and sounds are often a good point of departure, but in terms of psychoacoustics they are not sufficient for the perfect illusion. For this purpose, sound databases are available at radio stations, in production studios or on the Internet.

A decisive factor for the overall impression of the story is also how densely you build your montage, i.e. how large the distances are between the individual sound bites, dialogue sections or narrative passages. This depends on the overall impression of your play or individual scenes. Humour and dynamics may be cut and assembled quickly, more complex content or emotionally deep scenes may need some space, even between sentences. However, it should never seem sluggish. But these are only rough guidelines, which can be violated if the reasons for doing so are good enough. Just don't try to gain time through a tight montage. The story will become breathless for no reason and you can feel that when listening to it.

One of the very densest forms of montage is the collage, be it a pure collage (i.e. consisting only of original sound clips) or some kind of annotated collage (i.e. additionally supplemented by a narrator or narrator sentences). The great advantage of collage is that it bridges time, space and content as quickly and dynamically as almost no other technique in audio narratives. It is therefore very suitable, for example, for quick re-entry into the story at the beginning of the next episode of a series, as here in the third episode of *The Hitchhiker*:

Announcer: Previously on *The Hitchhiker*:

Music starts: unsettling strings. Sound: cigarette lighter.

Collage: (Heinrich Kurzrock) Beaten on my naked arse with a cane. And these corporal beatings were the only physical contact. / (Helmut Fahle) So, quite obvious repression that could not be carried out differently. / (Hans-Werner Prahl) Well, I see him as a show-off, as someone who bends the truth. / (Angela Müller) I think a big topic is the exclusion of the mentally ill from society. / (Helmut Fahle) And they were forgotten. No-one wanted to know about them. / (Hans-Jürgen

---

Höötmann) I think…may I just…ah no. This says day of registration 26.9.57.

Sound: lighter produces flame. Music fades over in ambiance: a busy street.

Tape: (Sven Preger, in the Marsberg car park) Want a smoke?
Tape: (Heinrich Kurzrock, in the Marsberg car park) Yes, yes. You don't need to ask. I would have said that anyway. Hello Germany.

The catch-up collage enables listeners to re-enter the story. The quotes are arranged according to two criteria. On the one hand, they should summarise briefly, concisely and precisely the previous conflict lines in the series, which have still not been resolved. On the other, they should indicate the exact situation with which the third episode begins. As a reminder: At the end of episode two, we learned that Heinrich really was in a ward for young children. And we are now standing in the parking area immediately in front of it, today's child and youth psychiatry unit in Marsberg. We also added a special feature to the collage between the different tapes: A lighter that simply won't ignite the flame. It only works at the end of the collage. The music breaks off at the same time and I ask: "Want a smoke?" By the way, the information in parenthesis on the original sound not only shows who is speaking, but also where the recording was made or played. It is therefore also an example of what a manuscript with true-to-scene sound recordings can look like (see also Sect. 6.4). The noise of the lighter prepares for the scene. This creates the impression of a high narrative density—a technique which the listener does not really notice, but which builds up anticipation, because something seems to be coming. We have used this anticipation technique on several re-entries into the series, not always using the noise of a lighter, of course.

One of my own favourite uses for collages is time lapse—involving just a few steps over a longer period of time, especially if something happens during this time. It's especially suitable for the part of a story Blake Snyder refers to as the 'Fun & Games' part, a part that involves action and tempo while radiating a special lightness, as at the beginning of the second act. (Snyder 2005, 80f) We built a sequence like this into the sixth part of *Faust jr* (the episode is called the *The Lonely Astronaut*). Main character Frank Faust wants to sneak into astronaut training under a false name. To do so, he has to undergo a series of medical tests and examinations:

Narrator: And so a real marathon began…

Music. Voices in the foreground. Plus noises.

Tape: (physician Götz Kluge, examination room) We will document your cardiovascular functions. Long-term blood pressure measurement...
Voice: 170 to 130...
Tape: (Götz Kluge, examination room) With the ultrasound we'll take a look at your kidneys, liver and pancreas.
Faust: That is slimy...
Tape: (Götz Kluge, examination room) We check whether you are sufficiently resilient.

A treadmill.

Faust: *hard breathing*
Tape: (Götz Kluge, examination room) We will examine your head, using vascular imaging of the vessels in your head.

MRI.

Faust: The tube is very narrow.
Tape: (Götz Kluge, examination room) You will go to our ophthalmologist.
Voice: Which is clearer now: the green or the red?
Tape: (Götz Kluge, examination room) Rectoscopy.
Faust: Holy sh...
Tape: (Götz Kluge, examination room) The dermatologist will look at your skin, the orthopaedist will look at your extremities and the mobility of your joints, especially the spine...

Crack.

Fist: Ouch!
Tape: (Götz Kluge, examination room) And so on.
Narrator: And only five days later, Faust was admitted for the final test.
Faust: Final test?!
Narrator: In the centrifuge.
Faust: OK?!
Tape: (Götz Kluge, examination room) Well, you just have to keep your head still, then nothing will happen.
Faust: Your word in the narrator's ear.
Narrator: What?
Faust: Man, I'm starving!

The whole sequence transcribed here takes almost exactly **60** seconds, including the cliffhanger for the next scene (centrifuge!) and complication (hunger!). You can guess where this leads to. By the way, we used a little trick here and recorded some typical sentences used by doctors about blood pressure or during an eye test and threw them into the scene as a distant voice.

This brings us to the question about number of speakers or narrators. In *Faust jr* it's relatively simple: there is one narrator. It's the same in *Serial* although Sarah Koenig repeatedly emphasises that she does not work alone at all. Nevertheless, the team has chosen one female narrator. And that makes sense, a second narrator would not have been different enough from Sarah Koenig, the narrative attitude would probably have been very similar. In *The Hitchhiker*, too, we thought long and hard about how to solve this narrative problem. After all, we are two men who are also about the same age. One option would have been: One of us tells the story, but both appear in the original recordings. In the end, we chose two narrators for several reasons. Both of us are protagonists, we each have a relationship to Heinrich which plays a big role: It helps us portray the events realistically. In addition, we take on slightly different roles: Stephan is the more hands-on reporter, I am the more analytical one. This also corresponds to reality and complements a scenic-reflective narration.

Often, at least in German-language productions, you hear the unfounded second or even third voice. And you get the feeling that this was just a way of dividing up the text. After all, there was so much text, you couldn't possibly expect the listener to hear it from one single voice. So, thematic blocks are divided up amongst different narrators. This is not a good idea for directing! Every narrator needs a narrative attitude that is clearly different from that of another speaker.

A radio play production like *Faust jr*, which may appear playful and perhaps a bit silly, can tolerate more alienation and thus effects than documentary material like *The Hitchhiker*. By the way, both productions were the work of the same brilliant sound engineer: Timo Ackermann. He not only gets the best out of the material, contributes his own ideas and masters all the effects, but also knows how to control such huge productions in terms of organisation and track management. Look for people with whom you can work well together. As author and director, you will at least need to familiarise yourself with the most common effects and work steps in a production. The more you know about it, the better you can estimate what works and how complex things are. This includes common effects such as EQ (important for vocal processing), reverb (which can be used, for example, for the end of the music and acoustic space), compressor or, to a greater extent, limiter (for the dynamics) as well as understanding mono/stereo (it can make sense, for example, to record several speakers together in the studio with a stereo microphone) and work with panoramas. And these are only a few of the essential fundamental skills. It also helps to have a basic idea of what happens during recording, montage, mixing and mastering. Podcast productions, for example, can make much better use of the potential dynamics (i.e. really make some parts quieter and others louder). Without a linear broadcast in a radio programme, the audio file does not have to conform with any of the programme's broadcasting standards and will not be processed again during broadcast.

I know I have said this before, but it is so crucial that I'll point it out once again: You should have what you want to stage in front of your own ears. And you should know why you want it this way and not another way, why it serves the story. Then not much can go wrong. Because you will only ever use a fraction of all the technical possibilities in any one production. It should be the meaningful fraction. Sleep on elaborate productions. The final mixing, mastering and listen-through should be done with fresh ears, if possible.

No matter whether it's a podcast or radio production, it is advisable not to do everything all by yourself (at least when it comes to a certain level of complexity). Instead, it is worth getting a second opinion and set of ears. About the script and the production. Public broadcasters, for example, have a two-stage approval process: First, the script is approved by the editorial department. And then the actual production undergoes another round of approval by the commissioning editor. As a rule, there are then requests for smaller or larger changes. Here, too, it helps to have shared ideas beforehand—it avoids unpleasant surprises during the production approval process. I promise you: Music will always be a controversial topic. But it strengthens your argument if you can tell the editors the function and reasons for the music pieces you have chosen.

The last task is then to create the final broadcast documents, for the radio station, the archive, yourself, whoever. This includes the final manuscript (perhaps some minor changes or cuts were made during production) and the music report (whatever is necessary). And then you can download the piece to a USB stick, play it to your loved ones or yourself at home and be the first to notice any mistakes! That is simply par for the course.

8.7   CHECKLIST: STAGING

Making a story's voice heard, working in the studio or doing acoustic handicrafts at home—these are the activities that I personally enjoy the most. They are the moments when the story really comes to life, when what was previously only in your own head becomes sonic reality. In order to let your own creativity run wild, you are allowed to recruit some support. Like the following checklist.

Checklist staging

- Make sure you have good raw material. Your recordings should be as authentic and good as possible acoustically. The better the original sound, the more you can do with it in your production. And remember the obligatory ambiance of any recording situation

- every technician, sound engineer and you yourself will appreciate it later.

- Begin the staging at the latest while writing. Play with music, ambiance and sounds and test them out. It will change your writing and show whether the acoustic ideas match the recorded material.

- If circumstances permit: Don't do everything yourself. There are editors, directors and technicians. And they usually know what they are doing. If you're a reporter or a writer, and you have enough to do, that's fine. Involve the other trades early on. If you want to direct your own work, you should be able to do it.

- Stage a narrative attitude that fits your story. Dare to really tell it. Don't create an artificial distance to your story through the narrative attitude.

- Feel the music! It often carries the basic acoustic mood of a story. Give the music space so that it can breathe and unfold.

- Make your scenes really be heard. So that they come to life in the mind's ear and eye. Remember, scenes are the backbone of narration. You draw listeners into the story and keep them there. Use psycho-acoustic components, signature elements and Foley sound for this. it all helps to make the scenes sound particularly real.

- Know and use the opportunities offered by editing, mixing, mastering and effects. Very often it is like the old joke about the two actors who meet up. One says, "Ask me what's important in acting." The other one says, "What's import..."' The first interrupts: "Timing!"

- Stage consistently! Do not be afraid. If you have an idea, try it out until it sounds like you imagined it. Remember: everything you do should serve the story.

- Think sound design as a concept. How can you make leitmotifs that are important for your story tangible in sound? How does something like speed, movement, travel or discovery feel - and what emotions do these aspects evoke?

Personally, I love flowing staging: As a director, I often try to create an acoustically coherent sound image that is characterised by smooth transitions and acoustically binding scenes. As a listener, you can completely immerse yourself in this story. But it is precisely the craft of staging that repeatedly raises moral and ethical questions: What else is appropriate? Where is a line being crossed? There is a core issue at the heart of this: It is the subject of the next chapter.

Notes

1. There are online databases like this one: https://sound-effects.bbcrewind. co.uk/. Just make sure you have read the term of licence.
2. If you'd like to read something about voice recordings for radio plays cf. Grove and Wyatt (2013, 190 ff).
3. By the way, the name goes back to the inventor of these sound effects, the movie sound maker Jack Foley.

Bibliography

Abumrad, Jad. 2017. Avoiding Cheesy Sound Design. Accessed 14 April 2020. https://transom.org/2017/avoiding-cheesy-sound-design/.

Franklin, Jon. 1994. *Writing for Story*. New York: Plume.

Gervink, Manuel, and Robert Rabenalt (eds.). 2017. *Filmmusik und Narration. Über Musik im filmischen Erzählen*. Marburg: Tectum.

Grove, Claire, and Stephen Wyatt. 2013. *So You Want to Write Radio Drama?*. London: Nick Hern Books.

Henle, Hubert. 2001. *Das Tonstudio Handbuch*, 5th ed. Munich: GC Carstensen.

Pieper, Frank. 2004. *Das Effekte Praxisbuch*, 2nd ed. Munich: GC Carstensen.

Snyder, Blake. 2005. *Save the Cat: The Last Book on Screenwriting That You'll Ever Need*. Studio City: Michael Wiese Productions.

Strasberg, Lee. 1987. *A Dream of Passion: The Development of the Method*. Boston: Little, Brown.

S-Town. 2017. *S-Town*. Accessed 14 April 2020. https://stownpodcast.org/.

CHAPTER 9

Ethics and the Limits of Narrations: Is This Still Journalism?

9.1 News Factors Vs Story Factors

People are often enthusiastic both listeners, readers and viewers, as well as journalists. Thrilled when they listen to *Serial* (at least the first season) or watch the Netflix documentary series *Making a Murderer*. But if you want to understand and analyse what makes such productions stand out, so that you can transfer the craft techniques to your own products, you often encounter resistance. Yes of course, the stories behind *Serial* and *Making a Murderer* are special stories. And yes, behind these productions there are also corresponding resources that are hardly available, or not at all, in everyday working life, and maybe not even otherwise. But the way these stories are told, the techniques used to make them tangible, that's something you can learn about. And ask yourself which of these techniques can be applied to your own stories. Which techniques can help? And how? Then it quickly becomes clear that it is not only long documentaries that can benefit from this craft, but also current reporting and even hosting. However, many editorial offices don't even take the first step towards analysing the techniques. Resistance quickly flares up: Does every story have to be told the same way now? Do we have to imitate the Americans? And: With all this emotionalising and staging, this is no longer real journalism anyway! I personally was unable to resolve this contradiction for a long time. What's wrong with understanding how gripping stories are told? Why shouldn't I first try to understand how products that fascinate me actually work? That doesn't mean that I have to adopt everything uncritically. It remains my decision which narrative principles I want to try out in my own work. And sometimes, after trying things out, you can also discover whether something works for you or not.

© The Author(s), under exclusive license to Springer Nature Switzerland AG 2021
S. Preger, *Storytelling in Radio and Podcasts*,
https://doi.org/10.1007/978-3-030-73130-4_9

The resistance in many (at least German) editorial offices often seems to stem from a bizarre dichotomy: hearing and seeing as a normal audience (great story!) on the one hand, and working as a journalist (such stories are not journalism!) on the other. Where does that come from? What exactly creates the resistance? To answer these questions, a comparison between the classic news factors and what I call story factors helps:

News factors	Story factors
• Topicality	• The process
• Newness	• Scenes
• Temporal proximity	• Intention
• Physical proximity	• Change/Growth
• Social proximity	• Deeper insight
• Relevance	• Fundamentals
• Celebrities	• Latent topicality
• Discussion value	• Message
• Human interest	• Subject
• Conflicts	• Obstacles/Conflicts
• Emotions	• Emotions
• Surprises	• Surprises
Goal: Depict the topic	Goal: Deliver the experience

The list makes no claim to be complete nor the factors to be in the definitive order of importance. But even this rough overview illustrates three aspects fairly clearly:

- Firstly, some factors (such as conflicts, emotions and surprises) are the same. They are just as important for classic journalistic formats as for narrations and stories.
- Secondly, there are similar factors or overlaps. For example, the story factors 'deeper insight' and 'fundamentals' correspond to the news factor 'relevance.' If a story reveals a deeper insight into society, for example, then this story is also relevant in a journalistic sense. And the other way round: the news factor 'human interest' in the broadest sense also includes emotions.
- Thirdly, there are central factors that are very different. For journalistic products, topicality and newness will always play a major role in the decision for or against reporting. Both for the makers who decide to report on something and for the recipients. For narrations, topicality and news value play a much smaller role. The makers of narrations may pay more attention to these aspects than the recipients because they look at the topics that may be topical for months and might therefore warrant a longer narrative. For listeners, the subject of the narration may perhaps be one of the reasons to start listening to the story. But whether they keep listening (right through to the end) depends on completely different

factors. These include the process, scenes, intention and growth, factors which hardly play any role in journalistic products.

On a somewhat more systematic level, the clear differences can be seen in the answers to two questions: Why are reports made? And how is reporting done? News and story factors provide different answers to these questions. For, let's call it classical journalism, the answers are: There is a report because something new and important has just happened (Why?). The most important events or results are concisely summarised (How?). For narratives the answers are completely different. It is told because a deeper message about a fundamental human or social problem is to be conveyed (Why?). The main aim is to deliver an experience and make the process tangible (How?). News factors are there to judge issues. Story factors are there to judge stories. Just because the news factor categories are fulfilled does not mean there is automatically a story. The path from topic to story can be very long, complicated and sometimes impossible. If this is the case, then stick with a more classic form of presentation.

What this comparison calls to mind once again: Narrations are a form of representation in their own right. To judge them by the usual journalistic standards must inevitably lead to perplexity, perhaps even resistance and the feeling that this is not journalism. This impression is not entirely wrong either. Yet the narrations we are talking about here are documentaries, non-fictional narrations. So, they are part of the journalism system. They must also be measured against journalistic moral and ethical concepts otherwise they will not find a place in this system. Let us therefore consider the most frequent criticisms of narrations and narratives in detail.

9.2   Narrations Do not Reflect Reality!

There are two concerns at the source of this criticism:

- Concern one: Facts that do not fit the narrative are left out. Those who tell stories only use the facts and aspects that serve the story and/or message. Thus, a narration is a distorted image of reality.
- Concern two: The staging does not correspond to reality. Those who stage audio narratives often use non-real sounds and ambiance for the staging. This makes the narration a false reflection of reality.

On the concern about 'inappropriate' facts: a documentary narration must always deliver an appropriate representation of reality. If the story distorts this image, it is not a good story. So, the same standards apply for narrations as for all other journalistic formats and products. I would even go so far as to say that research for narrations must delve even deeper than for many other journalistic products. Because in narrations, it is not possible to simply fall back on different points of view, along the lines of "We have asked all groups in parliament for their opinion, here it comes." That doesn't work because of the structure of a narration. So as a reporter, I have to be even more certain that I have really understood a phenomenon or problem. All the necessary facts will always find a place in narrations because they are usually much longer than other formats. It is all about the best possible form of argumentation. I also need the space to design scenes. But (think of the ladder of abstraction), in many narrations there will be paragraphs and sections in which problems are debated and classified. In these passages there will be enough space to accommodate all the important facts and thus to work in a journalistically appropriate manner. This is precisely why the dramaturgy of a non-fictional narration is immensely complicated: it combines an exciting story with a journalistically sophisticated product. If reporters or editors fall short of their own standards, deliberately choose to invent scenes or leave out important facts, that's their decision. They are responsible for their actions, not the medium *podcast* nor the narrative technique *storytelling* (If you give too much credence, let's say, to the claims of a supposed former terrorist and then publish an award-winning podcast called *Caliphate* the problem, as the *New York Times* acknowledged, lies with journalistic standards.).

On the concern about non-real or fictional staging: that is indeed a very fine line. Does this ultimately mean I am not allowed to use sounds and ambiance from archives and databases because the story is then no longer a true reflection of reality? Isn't this applying much stricter standards to narration than to other forms of journalism? What about print reports or interviews, for example, with smoothed or even retrospectively (after authorisation) changed or introduced quotations and statements—something that happens in some countries, Germany included? Sentences have hardly ever been spoken the way we read them in journalistic products. The debate about the real image is as old as journalism itself.

My point is this: the first step is to admit to yourself that journalism always means distortion and subjectivity. But that does not mean arbitrariness. Rather, there must always be an attempt to come as close as possible to reality (Pörksen 2018). But what does that mean for an audio production? Personally, I find one thought helpful that at first glance may seem provocative or simply wrong in this context: Aaron Sorkin expresses it in his online masterclass. In one of the lessons he talks about what he calls 'the more important truth' or 'the fundamental truth.' What he means by this is that every scene in a story stands for a core statement that should convey that scene. Sorkin uses an example from the film *The Social Network*, a fictional movie that works with a real story. Sorkin wrote the screenplay. In an early version of the script, Mark Zuckerberg mixes himself a 'screwdriver' (a cocktail with orange juice and vodka) in one of the first scenes in the film. But shortly before the shooting Sorkin found out that Zuckerberg actually drank beer in this situation. So, what to do? For Sorkin the decisive factor is the message that the drink conveys and, for him, the 'screwdriver' says: I am drinking to get drunk (Zuckerberg has just returned from a date that didn't work out). Beer seems too profane a drink for Sorkin in this scene. The 'deeper truth' thus asks what the core of this situation or scene is.

So why does this idea help with non-fictional productions? After all, we can't just change reality the way we want to, then a narration really is no longer journalism. But it has led me to the following triad:

- Step 1: Explore reality. As far and as comprehensively as possible. This includes relevant sound and ambiance recordings.
- Step 2: Staging this reality. With the help of the original recordings as well as sounds and ambiance from the archive or database.
- Step 3: Check. Does the staged scene deliver an appropriate reflection of reality? Have I created a false impression? If the scene stands up to scrutiny, I can usually live with it. But there are always tough cases. That's why I try to be rather strict during the checking and, if in doubt, cut back a bit on the staging.

It helps me to think of a scene as condensed reality. This creates both a narration and a journalistic product. And I am not alone with this thought either. Support comes from Jon Franklin, who summarises the thought as follows: "But a story is the height of artificiality. Whether or not the story is true, you cannot recreate the character's world. You wouldn't if you could. It's too complicated, too confusing, too boring. Your tale represents an extract of reality, not reality itself" (Franklin 1994, 139). By the way, Aaron Sorkin's argument failed. In the film Mark Zuckerberg drinks beer, true to reality.

9.3   Narrations Rely on Emotions Only!

The main criticism behind this exclamation: Those who tell stories only pay attention to emotions. They are sometimes even artificially generated and exaggerated. The facts fall by the wayside.

This concern is not entirely unjustified either. It is possible that cause and effect are confused here. If a story shows the real challenge of a character who seriously wants to achieve something, and the story revolves around fundamental issues at the same time, then emotions are the logical consequence. After all, they are an integral part of human life. To negate them would not create an appropriate image of reality.

As a rule, we only perceive emotions as artificial or exaggerated if they are not derived from the narration. Then the story is usually flat because it is about trivialities and not real challenges. In such a case, it might not be worth telling this story in such detail, or at all. We also find emotions inappropriate or artificially exaggerated when someone tries to tell us how we as listeners should feel. But that is exactly what a narration should not do (keywords: depicting processes and not an omniscient, arrogant narrative attitude). Sometimes both even come together: a trivial or flat story that comes across as a huge drama. In the best case, it seems unintentionally funny, in the worst case it causes listeners to reject it completely. So, the criticism is often justified when trivialities are inflated. We would never do that in journalism, of course! Seriously: emotions are the result of a narration, not an end in themselves. Here, too, it is the author's task to deal with them responsibly and appropriately, and to deliver an appropriate reflection of reality. Sometimes, dealing with protagonists in a responsible way can also mean not publishing certain scenes and original sound bites.

9.4   Narrations Lack Journalistic Distance!

Counter question: What exactly is journalistic distance? If journalistic distance means the omniscient narrator who reports as distantly as possible? Then yes, that is what narration lacks. I at least hope so. There is an important problem underlying this criticism. If you want to get close to protagonists and characters, if you want to experience situations directly, you have to build trust and a real relationship. With this comes the danger of making the protagonist's goals and views your own or portraying the protagonists in a slightly better light than they deserve. This is indeed a great challenge for authors of narrations and can be a real problem. Two counter-strategies can help us to behave appropriately, both as journalists and human beings:

- Transparency in all directions. That means both with regard to characters and listeners. Make it clear to the people you work with what you want to do, what story you want to tell. To do this, you must first know that yourself. And if you're not ready, say so. That means building trust—which is the first thing we journalists have to do. It can also mean getting to know each other first, without recording equipment. Transparency with regard to characters does not, of course, mean playing with completely open cards, always and everywhere. There are good, journalistic reasons for not disclosing certain information at first: to get an appointment, for example, and to confront people with actions that are worthy of criticism. If the reporters had played with open cards from the beginning, they might not have been given an appointment at all.

  Transparency should also apply with regard to listeners. If there are conflicts of interest or similar things, let listeners know. It will increase your credibility, not least because you do not pretend to have the final answer to everything. The more complex a story is, the more likely it is that not everything is black and white, but much more differentiated and complicated. That's life. It is not good or bad, but often grey or colourful. In The Hitchhiker we deliberately decided to say that we had supported Heinrich both financially and with coffee and tobacco packages. What would have happened if we had kept this to ourselves and it had come out during or after release? Our credibility would have been called into question. And rightly so.

- Use the ladder of abstraction and debate the deeper ideas. This will enable you to keep creating distance in the piece. It is also where you can see how crucial story testing and development are. One of the essential elements for a story is the bigger or deeper idea (see Sect. 2.4), the fact that the story points beyond itself and gives a deeper insight into something. These aspects are more likely to be debated and explained in the sections of the story that are on the upper rungs of the ladder of abstraction. These passages create journalistic distance, also to the protagonist because here, amongst other things, it is explained why the story is worth telling and what the narration stands for.

It is therefore a pendulum moving between very close proximity and appropriate journalistic distance. This is also a great human challenge and emotionally exhausting for reporters. The meta-level has to be omnipresent and worked on continuously. If this is successful, then narrations also maintain an appropriate journalistic distance and human closeness. Hard on the subject, soft on the people.

9.5 NARRATIONS SERVE JOURNALISTIC GONZO EGOS!

The danger is indeed great that journalists only recount their own research and stage themselves as brilliant first-person narrators, with all the emotions. When reporters like Hunter S. Thompson embarked on gonzo journalism in the 1970s, subjective experience, the inner world and experience, was in the foreground: whether addressing the racetrack, drug use, or the search for the American dream. Thompson is also regarded as one of the forerunners or co-founders of New Journalism (Wolfe 1975). And it's true: long narrations, podcasts, but also shorter contributions, seem to have increasingly focused on the 'reporter ego.' There are, in my opinion, at least two aspects to consider:

- Reporters going somewhere and looking at something is not yet gonzo journalism. If it is, then the reporters really do have to expose themselves to a situation that hurts, challenges them or puts them in bizarre situations. This could be the roller coaster at a fairground just as well as high society at a racecourse. Of course, this also means that reporters have to give free rein to their perspective, experience, emotions and reveal them to the audience. Many reporters don't want to go that far, it's too personal for them. Which is totally okay, but it seems a bit like 'Wash me, but don't get me wet' (a German saying we use when somebody is a bit ambivalent). Which leads directly to my next point.
- There must be a good reason for saying 'I' in the narration. If there isn't, then don't do it. It's more likely to harm the story than to help it.

Gonzo journalism, moreover, should not be a justification for passing on research! *Serial* (by Sarah Koenig) as well as *S-Town* (by Brian Reed), *The Nobody Zone* (by Tim Hinman) or *The Other Latif* (by Latif Nasser) all use 'I' or 'we' stories, but are not gonzo journalism. They all know: The story is the star, not the journalists. They as narrators serve the story. And brilliantly so!

9.6   Narrations Force Out All Other Forms!

Sometimes this question sounds annoyed, sometimes rather anxious: 'Does everything have to be like this now?' 'This' often means narrations, narrative elements or serials. The answer is simple: no! News, articles, background, reportage, interviews, discussions, two ways, these and all other forms have their place. Especially in current reporting, these standards have established themselves for good reasons and these reasons have not suddenly disappeared. Certainly, there are narrative techniques and elements that can also be tried out and used in shorter forms (see Sect. 3.9). But if these techniques do not support the work, then they don't. In longer formats (background, feature, essay, etc.) I would personally prefer narrative techniques to be used more because they very often help to open listeners' minds to relevant arguments. Narrations can be a vehicle for important topics and debates. But a topic does not always deliver narrative elements. Then that's the way it is. Many topics can and must be reported on nevertheless. The (continued) development of narrative techniques must not lead to the exclusion of topics. At the same time, however, I would like to see more professionalism amongst editors with regard to narrations and storytelling so that they can recognise and exploit their potential.

9.7   Narrations Are Out of Date, Right?!

To close the chapter with a little cultural pessimism: We live in a postfactual age, which is characterised by fake news, felt truths and framing. A form such as narration with all its staging and emotions cannot provide appropriate answers to the pressing questions of our time. Especially in the debate about the postfactual age and fake news, facts must speak above all else. They should be the basis for opinions and provide orientation in our complex world. This argumentation is correct on the one hand. And on the other, it may be missing an important point. Feelings and perceptions (unfortunately) sometimes just don't have much to do with facts. The facts do not reach people. Especially if these facts come from people who are not very willing to be told anything. And let us not fool ourselves: We journalists often fall into that category. And that has something to do with us and our (narrative) attitude. At least we can change something about that.

My very personal conviction is that narrations and narrative techniques offer journalists the chance to regain more confidence amongst listeners, users, readers and viewers and to provide a suitable answer to the problems and questions of our time. For several reasons:

- Narrations depict the world more strongly in its complexity. They deliver experience as well as information and facts. Narrations thus provide much more orientation than an exclusively factual report.
- Narrations do not report from above. They embody an unknowing, in the best sense curious, and at the same time, life-wise narrative attitude. Listeners really take this seriously, in contrast to hollow talk of 'even playing fields' or merely reading irrelevant e-mails or social media messages from individual listeners on air.
- Narrations create understanding. They show that there can be no simple solutions to complex problems. Even journalists do not pretend to know all the answers.

Narrations are thus a means of counteracting fake news. People hear stories because they are looking for orientation and want to learn. Currently, there seems to be a greater focus on narrations by listeners and makers alike. This movement meets a long tradition of narration, in radio and podcasts. As creators in Germany, it sometimes feels like we are catching up on a bit of 'storytelling' professionalism or are continuing to develop together—which includes, for example, organising one's own work process for a narration appropriately, and quickly recognising and correcting the most common narrative errors. The next and final chapter deals with these aspects.

Bibliography

Franklin, Jon. 1994. *Writing for Story*. New York: Plume.
Pörksen, Bernhard. 2018. *Die große Gereiztheit. Wege aus der kollektiven Erregung*. Munich: Hanser.
Wolfe, Tom. 1975. *The New Journalism*. London: Picador.

CHAPTER 10

Work Routine for the Narrative Reporter

10.1 THE PERFECT PITCH

The first step is one of the most difficult. When you have once managed to work together with an editorial team in a trusting and successful manner, the next projects will be a little easier. At least selling the stories, that is. A good pitch is the first step on that path. It's actually old hat, but I'll say it again here: Make yourself familiar with the podcast channel, programme, publisher or label you want to work for. Check out the webpages, a lot of podcasts or programmes have guidelines on what they want to hear or read in a pitch. Adjust your pitch accordingly. Apart from this, a good pitch contains the following elements:

- Narrative sentence. It answers the question: What is the story?
- Plot ideas: Nobody will expect you to be able to present a completely elaborated plot. But you should be able to sketch the rough lines. Be guided by the elements of your story: characters, intentions, main conflicts, obstacles, plot points, possible ending. At the very least, you should have a rough idea of the starting point (triggering event) and the goal (where the story is heading). It always helps to be able to name the 'bigger idea'. It is the equivalent of journalistic relevance and answers the question: Why should we tell the story right now?
- Your perspective. Describe your motivation and angle: Why do *you* want to tell this particular story? How are you connected to the story and the people in it?
- Current status and planning: How far have you got? By when will you be able to complete the project? Is there possibly an event or date to

© The Author(s), under exclusive license to Springer Nature
Switzerland AG 2021
S. Preger, *Storytelling in Radio and Podcasts*,
https://doi.org/10.1007/978-3-030-73130-4_10

place the story, i.e. a relevant publishing date? Many editorial offices or publishers have long lead times. Six months to a year is not uncommon.

- Cost calculation. How time-consuming are the planned trips? What expenses, additional costs (possibly for music composition, etc.) might be incurred?
- Refer. If an editorial office, production company or label does not know you, attach references. Link to previous productions or send along a meaningful sound file.

Overall, the pitch should not be longer than a maximum of two pages, nobody reads more anyway. Don't give away too much either. You still want to have some strong elements on hand with which you can score. And don't oversell it. If you make promises you can't keep, it will be your loss in the end.

If you are familiar with the podcast, broadcast or label you can also adjust your pitch accordingly and thus increase your chances of selling a story. The final product should match the pitch as closely as possible and not deviate too far from it (if other developments become apparent, you should give an early signal). There is one question in particular that comes to mind: How far do I have to go with my research to pitch at all? The best way to answer this question is to take a look at the entire work process from the initial idea to the finished story. In recent years, I have often been asked at what point in the work process I decide on or implement something. That's why I'll play this through using the following example, a documentary for the WDR history programme *ZeitZeichen*. The programme has always meant a lot to me, not just because of the cooperation with the editorial staff and the varied material, but also the length. Fifteen minutes is almost ideal from a dramaturgical and narrative point of view. You have enough space to try out and implement ideas, but you don't have to invest months of time and effort as you do with very long formats. So, you can learn a lot, especially with these medium lengths. I think that's great. I myself divide the work process into seven phases.

10.2   Workflow for Narratives: The Seven Steps to a Finished Story

Step 1: Basic research

If you want to tell complex stories and concentrate on narrative composition, plot design and working with protagonists, you need to have the subject under control. Naivety and lack of expertise are unlikely to open doors later on. The more confident you are in handling a topic, the more likely people are to trust you. That means you must do your journalistic homework. Read up, get an overview of other publications on the topic under consideration and keep yourself up to date with the current state of developments and debates.

For me, this phase is a time of hunting and gathering. I start with the current findings on the subject and then work backwards. I quickly learn the difference between good and important sources on the one hand and less important sources on the other. I also recognise important players: These include the organisations and individuals involved (possible original sound sources, perhaps even protagonists). I already write them down at this stage. For an average *ZeitZeichen* I estimate a couple of days for this step, probably something like two and a half. Sometimes more, depending on how comprehensive the material or my previous knowledge of the respective topic is. For example, in order to get a reasonable grip on a life like Stephen Hawking's, at least three basic sources are important: autobiography (*My Brief History*), major popular publication (*A Brief History of Time*) and possibly one of the feature films about him (*The Theory of Everything*). The latter has, after all, strongly influenced the popular perception of Hawking. So, it helps me to work with listeners' potential expectations. In addition, there are excerpts from other books, some scientific papers and numerous lectures and original sounds from the archives of major broadcasting companies.

At the end of this step, I must have at least some mastery of the issue. In the case of the Hawking example this means at least the most important data on his life, milestones and his key scientific work. This research is the basis for developing the ideas for a story and for me to dare to make the first drafts of a narrative sentence. If I have no idea about the subject, I cannot form a narrative sentence because only when I am sure of my topic can I judge whether my intended narrative sentence is feasible and appropriate to reality. Of course, for every bigger documentary it helps if you do not start from scratch but are at least familiar with the context and basic information.

Step 2: Forming a narrative sentence

Books, essays and extracts from archives are now piled up on my desk. In the digital folder of the respective story, there are the audios from the archives. I've read through and listened to them once. If a topic turns out to be too confusing, I create a chronology of the most important events. This is an invaluable help, especially for documentaries. It also often helps me to find the bigger idea. When I look at the chronology, I become aware of the spirit of the different times and possible simultaneous events. It becomes clear to me what the time was like in which my story takes place and why it might be important for us today. This is always a great challenge for me when dealing with historical topics: to narrate them in a way that makes them relevant for us today. The deeper idea is often a good tool for finding an answer to that question.

All this helps me to find and form the narrative sentence, or at least a working version of it. This gives me the first ideas for the plot. I also realise what effort I have to put into the realisation. If unrealistic requirements arise,

I can still make adjustments. That's also the moment when I pitch or present the plot and my ideas to editors or colleagues. If we don't agree on something now, there are bound to be problems later! And it's really tedious to have to convince everyone else afterwards that your own ideas are actually much better and that the script has to stay as it is! So, this step is very focused. It brings order to the previous chaos. Sometimes it can be done within a few minutes because the story is clear in front of me. Sometimes it takes hours or days.

Step 3: Fieldwork

When editorial team and reporter agree, the actual fieldwork begins. This means above all: making appointments, travelling (if necessary and possible) and recording. Preliminary talks with potential protagonists and sound bites also make it possible to develop and refine the plot. As a general rule: the plot should be roughly ready before the recordings are made. Research and preliminary talks serve to get a realistic idea of the possible plot process. It often helps to allow some time to pass between the preliminary talk and the actual recording. Most people do not remember exactly what they have already told you. This way you can ask questions a second time without being afraid of getting strange answers ('I already told you that…').

For the actual interviews I prepare a story interview from the respective clusters (see Sect. 4.5) and make sure that my notes do not exceed one or two pages. I don't want to frighten anyone by bringing a lot of paperwork to the interview or meeting. In addition, I pay heed to these three tips for preparation, interviewing and follow-up:

- Tip One for the preparation comes from Ira Glass (*This American Life*): "And here's something counterintuitive. It's best to try to figure out the potential Big Ideas in any story before you go out interviewing people" (Glass 2017, 71).
- Tip Two for setting the recording or a special moment during the interview comes from Alix Spiegel (co-founder of Invisibilia): "So I have what I call 'five minutes of truth' in which I try to get a sense of whether the person needs anything or has any questions or is uncomfortable in any way, and I check to see if I've misunderstood something. (At the end of every interview, I try to get a sense of what I might not be getting. I just ask them, and that is usually a fruitful question.)" (Spiegel 2017, 52).
- And Tip Three for holding an interview comes from Davia Nelson and Nikki Silva (The Kitchen Sisters): "We don't turn off the microphone until we're out the door. As soon as the machine is off folks relax and invariably say the line that would work perfectly to start or end the piece. Or they reveal a secret or tell the best joke. When it's time to wrap up we lower our mics but don't turn off the machine. When they start talking again, which they always do, we just casually raise the mic and continue.

They're aware we're still recording; we never secretly tape or walk in recording before the person knows we've started" (The Kitchen Sisters 2017, 37). This tip I handle according to the situation. I do not want to treat people unfairly.

All three tips only produce good results if I manage to create a good atmosphere, take my interview partners seriously and bring about a situation that is as close as possible to a normal conversation. Combined with journalistic interview techniques, useful recordings often succeed.

When the actual recording work is complete, I sort and index my material. That means primarily listening and transcribing. I have got into the habit of neatly cataloguing all my recordings, that is, naming the files and transcribing nearly all the recordings. I usually transcribe the voice recordings completely. It reinforces the feeling of really having the story under control. Moreover, the tedious and boring transcription process gives me the best ideas for the production because I get a feeling for how the material and characters sound. Besides, transcribing is not nearly as tedious as it used to be. Depending on the production and the effort involved, I work with transcription software, for example, which automatically creates a first version of the transcript. The quality of these audio transcriptions has increased immensely over the last few years. Anyway, I always listen to the whole file again and correct any errors. In addition, I add my own personal notations. I mark quotes (quality and voice pitch, i.e. voice up, down or hanging) and note where in the story the quotes could come into play, for example as introduction, plot point or ending. Yes, this step is laborious, every time. But it gives me security. Afterwards I feel I know my material, not much can happen to me. Now the writing fun can begin. For an average *ZeitZeichen* episode I estimate about three days for this step.

Step 4: Making a storyboard or story sheet

Ideally, I now know how the story should run. But experience shows that I often overestimate myself a bit. I know what the rough narrative arc and plot elements should be, but I lack the exact details. Introductory scene including 'Save the Cat', triggering event, plot points and obstacles. That's why I fill in my story sheet or storyboard before I start writing. It usually includes the following elements, explained here with reference to the *ZeitZeichen* about the first intercontinental flight by solar plane:

- Occasion/Topic: First intercontinental flight in a solar plane (broadcast: 6 June 2017).
- Narrative sentence/Story: Bertrand Piccard wants to make the first flight around the world in a solar plane. He wants to show what renewable

energy can do. But there is no such technology as yet, nor can he get support or funding (e.g. from the aviation industry).

- Bigger Idea: Pioneering Spirit vs. Bureaucracy/Real Leadership/Renewable Energy.
- High Stakes/Risk: Piccard's self-image is in danger, after all, his father and grandfather achieved great things.
- Primal: ???
- Sound/Sonic atmosphere: Technical development, aviation, pioneers.

This sheet helps me because it shows me both possibilities and problems. First of all, it makes sure that I really form a narrative sentence from the actual occasion or topic and that I have my material in order. Furthermore, the question about 'High Stakes' shows that this is a personal risk, Piccard wants to prove that he is a worthy member of a great family. This also makes it clear that the information about Piccard's father and grandfather must appear early in the story otherwise the risk perceived by Bertrand Piccard will not be communicated. And the story sheet shows that I have a problem on the level of deeper insight ('Primal' only comes up with ???). It is not really a matter of life and death. So, the other levels have to develop enough power to carry the story. This review of the essential story principles is then supplemented by a plot draft which, in this case, looked like this (Fig. 10.1).

The plot design shows the essential elements of the story (see the plot of eleven elements in Sect. 3.7):

STORYBOARD

NARRATIVE SENTENCE / STORY: First intercontinental flight in a solar plane (broadcast date: 6 June 2017) Betrand Piccard wants to make the first flight around the world in a solar plane. He wants to show what renewable energy can do. But there is no such technology as yet, nor can he get support (for example from the aviation industry).

Bigger Idea: Pioneering Spirit vs Bureaucracy / Real Leadership / Renewable Energy

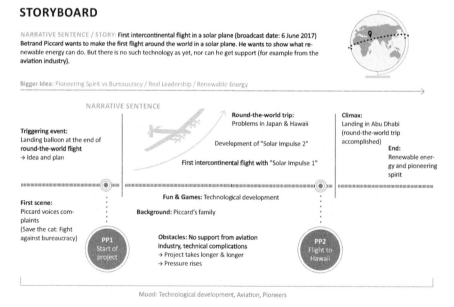

Fig. 10.1 Storyboard

- Promythion as a start.
- The introductory scene consists of Piccard giving a talk. Here Piccard is also introduced as a character. Save the Cat: Fight against bureaucracy.
- Triggering event: landing with the balloon at the end of the round-the-world flight (as a reconstructed scene, Piccard recounts it). This is also the basis for the narrative sentence or the story.
- First plot point: project start for 'Solar Impulse' in 2004.
- Increasing crises in four sections:
- First obstacle: technological developments/fundraising (acoustic implementation as 'Fun & Games Collage').
- Second obstacle: first intercontinental flight with 'Solar Impulse 1' (this is also the occasion or reason for the documentary).
- Third obstacle: development of 'Solar Impulse 2' for the round-the-world flight.
- Fourth obstacle: Biggest problems during the circumnavigation of the world (here problems in Japan and Hawaii). These reconstructed scenes also represent the deepest crisis. It looks like the project will fail.
- Second plot point: Successful departure from Japan to Hawaii.
- Highlight/special moment: Landing on the last leg of the journey in Abu Dhabi.
- New balance/conclusion: Piccard formulates what he has learned from the adventure and how he intends to build on this to develop environmentally friendly technologies.
- Closing with 'bigger idea': reference to the key themes 'Renewable energy', 'Leadership' and 'Pioneering Spirit'.

Depending on the material, the scenes are either reconstructed scenes which are told by Bertrand Piccard or a mixture of reconstructed and original scenes. Piccard recounts them in retrospect on the one hand, and on the other, can be heard every now and then in original recordings from the time. Thus, the scenes deliver a strong experience.

I don't start writing until the story sheet or board is finished. This is the only way I can be sure that the story is really working. Also, it's much easier to interrupt the writing process because I only have to take a look at the storyboard to know where I am again, at least roughly. It simply forces me to really think the story through. Once I've taped all the material, I make the storyboard and finalise the plot. That can take between one and three hours. Then the writing can begin.

Step 5: Writing manuscript, correction and approval included

The most important rule for me is to write in peace with a clear head. Okay, those are actually two rules. I usually start in the morning with a new script or with the development of the storyboard and then move on to the script.

This I know about myself: I can work well on scripts in the morning and midmorning. For me it's also important to clear my desk of all other subjects and not look at my e-mails. I write. Of course, everyone has to develop their own working rhythm. But it helps me to take my biorhythm into account and to focus fully on the story.

What is also important for me personally is to start the staging and sound design now at the very latest. I pick out music, let it run alongside, cut sound bites cleanly and so on. This is the only way I can, for example, write special sentences in the story that fit the music and create a coherent sound. Writing a *ZeitZeichen* manuscript usually takes me between one and two days. One day, if it really runs smoothly and goes fast. If it is more laborious, it can take two full days. Of course, I don't write for eight or ten hours at a stretch. That includes breaks from time to time. Which is why I say this: where I am in the story is important when it comes to taking breaks. I try to take them when I already know what I'm going to write next, when I know relatively precisely how to continue. I don't usually take a break when I'm stuck. Unless there is really no other alternative. Otherwise, the inhibition threshold for re-entry is too high for me.

Investing a disproportionate amount of time into writing the manuscript often means that there are problems with the story that I didn't manage to control while working on the storyboard. Now I have to solve bigger plot problems during the writing process. In the case of *ZeitZeichen* this also includes finding compromises between an exciting story on the one hand and the appropriate portrayal of the event or biography on the other. With a format like this, there is an implicit promise that listeners will receive the most important information about the event or person, and this always resonates with them. So, it can't be absent, it is simply part of the programme. For this reason, I often use the form of the scenic-reflective narrative for *ZeitZeichen* (see Sect. 3.8). It is not always possible to incorporate the actual event (which, in this case, after all, determines the date of publication) into the story as gently and fluently as with the documentary on 'Solar Impulse.' I probably deviate from the storyboard by 10–15% (estimate!) when I write because I have new (hopefully better) ideas, add or delete small details or transitions that don't work as I had imagined them when I created the storyboard. But that also means that for 85–90% I have clear ideas in my head beforehand. That helps a lot.

Even if the writing goes smoothly, I leave the finished script overnight and rework it with fresh eyes and ears the next day. I also use the correction process to check the most important facts again, especially names and dates. It may be that even the very last gaps in the research have to be filled. Most of the time this is about odd facts or wordings. The revision is also good for checking your own position on the story. Do I build up enough journalistic distance again after a close relationship to a protagonist? The documentary about 'Solar Impulse,' for example, thrives on Piccard's story. This is another reason why it is appropriate from a journalistic point of view to take critical stock at the end.

Just do yourself a favour: Don't kill your darlings. If you have strong scenes that are important to the story and carry them, don't cut them in favour of more information.

My own 50:50 rule, which I mentioned earlier, helps me to make listeners feel as though they are following a story and not just a series of information blocks. Fifty per cent scenes and real story (I'm already weaving in information there, too) and fifty per cent background information and debates. These must be necessary for the story. If the ratio tilts too much in the info direction, the scenes are chopped off, they don't seem real, just like short examples. The more I can narrate scenically, the better.

When all this has been done, the script is sent to the editor or colleagues for approval or correction. The more these people knew about the story beforehand, the fewer unpleasant surprises there are on both sides now. A long and trusting collaboration helps, of course. As a rule, two or three proofreading rounds are sufficient. The longer and more complex a production, the more rounds there may, of course, be (if there are more than three meetings, then there probably wasn't enough advance coordination and common understanding of the story). While the script is in the editorial office, you can already start the next step.

Step 6: Production

Now at least the preparations for the actual production can begin, even if there is no final approval yet. The type of preparation depends on whether you produce alone or with a technician, whether you direct or not. So, I cut all the original sound clips and search for the final sounds and ambiance. As soon as the script has been finally approved and is available in a production version, the production can begin. For a *ZeitZeichen* documentary you can estimate one day for production. This depends on many factors, of course: How good is your own preparation? How complex is the production? For me, staging the production work is one of the most glorious moments of the whole process. The story is now really coming alive. Whenever possible, I try to spread the production over two days in order to do the final mix and mastering with fresh ears. The finished audio file goes to the editors, followed by approval and possible reworking until the final bounce. Only the paperwork is still missing then. Time to wrap up.

Step 7: Paperwork

Personally, I even find this step quite contemplative at times. I produce the final version of the manuscript (in the production a few things usually change) and whatever else an editorial office, a publishing house or a label needs. Done! Reward now!

WORKFLOW FOR NARRATION

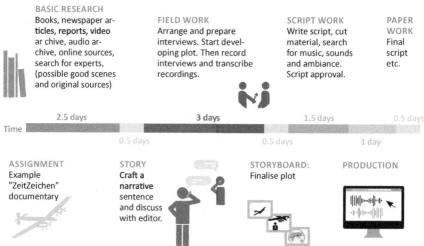

BASIC RESEARCH
Books, newspaper articles, reports, video archive, audio archive, online sources, search for experts, (possible good scenes and original sources)

FIELD WORK
Arrange and prepare interviews. Start developing plot. Then record interviews and transcribe recordings.

SCRIPT WORK
Write script, cut material, search for music, sounds and ambiance. Script approval.

PAPER WORK
Final script etc.

Time   2.5 days   3 days   1.5 days   0.5 days

0.5 days   0.5 days   1 day

ASSIGNMENT
Example "ZeitZeichen" documentary

STORY
Craft a narrative sentence and discuss with editor.

STORYBOARD:
Finalise plot

PRODUCTION

Fig. 10.2 Workflow for Narration

If you add up all the time spent on an average *ZeitZeichen*, for example, in my case it looks something like this (Fig. 10.2).

So, 9.5 days, just under two working weeks. Of course, that's only a very rough estimate, played out on a clear 15-minute documentary. The pitch is omitted here because the date determines the occasion and the topic (which is not yet a story!). If I am working on a story where I already know people and background very well, the basic research is reduced. Sometimes it can take much longer at other steps. Basic research and fieldwork for *The Hitchhiker*, for example, took longer (much longer!) and so did everything else.

However, as an average value for the given length, this is quite a good order of magnitude. The two weeks of work are spread over several months (the editorial staff plans long term). Personally, this means I will condense at the end. The basic research can sometimes be done over a longer time: I read and listen and get an impression. At the latest when I start working in the field and do the actual recordings, I try to concentrate on the product. Because then I know my material and work faster. But as I said: Everyone has to develop their own working style. I just think we talk about these things too rarely. And the questions have been put to me very often. That's why I have made my modus operandi transparent. On this path there are numerous places where problems and/or mistakes can creep in. To recognise them and to have a solution strategy ready helps immensely, irrespective of your role in the production, whether you are working in a team or as a lone fighter. That's why I would like to conclude this book with my fix list for the biggest story problems we encountered in Chapter 1.

10.3 Fixes for the Ten Most Common Story Problems

In my work as a writer, director, editor and story consultant, I encounter similar problems time and again. I tried to summarise them meaningfully at the beginning of this book and, as far as possible, will now try to provide some solutions:

- The hell of the second act. Solution: Force yourself to form a narrative sentence and a storyboard. The work and time you invest here will always pay dividends as you write, creating a much better product. And if you discover that you don't have a real story, then write a classic report. Nothing wrong with that. But then not lasting 30 minutes, please. If you do this, you already solve the next problem!
- The two-story or parallel strand problem. Solution: Decide on one story. No, two stories at once are not possible. If you have more than one strand (which is, of course, conceivable), then these strands must be connected to each other, but in the sense of the story, not thematically. The political and economic dimensions of a topic do not make a story connection. *Game of Thrones* also has many strands, but it's always about who sits on the throne in the end. Another example: In March 2018, *This American Life* released 'Five Women.' A different kind of #MeToo story.' In it, five women talk about their experiences. What at first glance looks like five stories in one is not because the women not only all talk about their experiences with one and the same man, but their experiences and stories have points of contact with each other, as well. So here we have different perspectives on a narrative. An impressive story, in many ways.
- No triggering event. Solution: Make a plot draft and take the following advice to heart: Stories are told forwards. One scene follows the other, this is the only way to create a narrative flow. If you follow this advice, especially at the beginning, you will not be able to avoid a triggering event.
- Results are anticipated: the exposition problem. Solution: Remember what Jon Franklin writes: "You could, of course, set aside a dozen paragraphs or so at the top of your story and give a mini-lecture on the subject at hand. You could... but you won't, not if you want to sell your story" (Franklin 1994, 151). Try to deliver an experience and make the facts tangible. Ask yourself when your information will have the most impact on the story (keyword: list of revelations). Try to think in scenes.
- No true-to-scene recordings. Solution: Just record true to scene! To do so, it helps to know in advance which recording situations are possible and what you want to narrate there. This is a question of research and planning. If, however, recordings for one scene have been taken at several locations for whatever reason, use the better half. Tell the rest of the story yourself.

- There are no scenes/no action at all. Solution: The honest answer? Then you can't tell the story! At least not like that. Sounds hard, but it's true. At this point, many journalists make the decision to give it a go anyway. Just as long and detailed as planned, just with more information paragraphs. If you do it that way, it will definitely sound like it. To put it rather less harshly: Then it'll just be a normal report. Be honest and ask yourself how much time people will really want to spend listening to that. It's usually less than we would like.
- Weak and boring tape and original sounds. Solution: Prepare the story interview beforehand and then lead people during the interview into the experience and create dialogues. Understand your characters as acting persons. Often journalists don't even try this, jumping to the conclusion that a character wouldn't have done that anyway. Remember: It is your story that will be boring afterwards.
- Multiple breaks in the narrative: the lost perspective. Solution: Follow your characters. They carry the plot and therefore carry the story. Once you have established a protagonist, he or she will show you the way. And if you need to explain things in between to keep the story moving forward, you are welcome to do so. Even with the help of experts. You only need a dramaturgical reason to integrate information and interviews into the story. Or in other words: The information comes then and there in the story, if and where it serves the story. If the story runs without a specific explanatory passage, then be courageous: think about cutting it!
- The omniscient narrator. Solution: Rethink your own role and establish a narrator who serves the story.
- The narrative problem: stories not so well told. Solution: Be demanding, ambitious and professionalise yourself. Just as news or hosting obey certain craft rules, so must stories. It is just a different craft. Learn it! If you master all the rules and principles, you can deviate from it again.

Very often the solution to story problems lies in a structured approach. You must know what you want and keep control of the process. Then chance won't rule your story, you will. Structure creates the frame of reference in which creativity can really thrive. It can never become arbitrary.

If I may make two wishes to conclude, they are the following:

- First, let's talk more: about stories, our profession, our ways of working, our ideas and our concerns. Then we can learn from each other, get inspiration and refine our storytelling skills. From this follows my other wish.
- Second, let's try out something more. Those who do, make mistakes. That's a good thing. Because we can learn from mistakes. Just as we can learn from great productions.

There is a long feature tradition in Europe and a very agile podcast scene, which can also draw on a lot of experience. Perhaps something completely new can emerge from the interaction between these two elements, paired perhaps with more Anglo-American storytelling craft. That would be a great story, at least for me.

BIBLIOGRAPHY

Franklin, Jon. 1994. *Writing for Story*. New York: Plume.

Glass, Ira. 2017. Harnessing Luck as an Industrial Product. In *Reality Radio*, ed. John Biewen and Alexa Dilworth, 2nd ed., 64–76. Durham: University of North Carolina Press.

Preger, Sven. 2017. 'Erster Interkontinentalflug mit Solarflugzeug gelingt'. Accessed 20 December 2020. https://www1.wdr.de/radio/wdr5/sendungen/zeitzeichen/solar-flugzeug-100.html.

Spiegel, Alix. 2017. Variations in Tape Use and the Position of the Narrator. In *Reality Radio*, ed. John Biewen and Alexa Dilworth, 2nd ed., 42–53. Durham: University of North Carolina Press.

The Kitchen Sisters. 2017. Talking to Strangers. In *Reality Radio*, ed. John Biewen and Alexa Dilworth, 2nd ed., 34–41. Durham: University of North Carolina Press.

This American Life. 2018. Five Women. Accessed 20 December 2020. https://www.thisamericanlife.org/640/five-women.

INDEX

A

Act structure, 14, 49, 50, 57, 58, 66, 67

Analepsis/flashback, 138

Anticipation, 2, 81, 116, 117, 125, 127, 136, 167, 208, 212

B

Beliefs, 3, 60, 108, 124, 179, 180, 192

C

Campbell, Joseph, 57–60, 62, 63, 70, 93, 105

Cliché plus X, 137

Collage, 70–72, 84, 122, 123, 125, 131–133, 177, 191, 211, 212, 235

Condensed reality, 97, 131, 166, 223

Conflict, 4, 15–17, 28, 31, 43, 49, 50, 52–55, 57, 66, 71, 72, 78, 80, 84–86, 93–97, 102, 113, 120, 162–164, 166, 169, 197, 212, 220, 224, 229

D

Directing, 105, 189, 191, 202, 205, 214

E

Editing, 166, 196, 200–202, 205, 216

Emotions, 2, 4–6, 13, 24, 47, 97, 101, 107, 127, 133–137, 144, 148, 185, 196, 197, 216, 220, 223, 225, 226

Expectation management, 127, 144

F

Fake news, 226, 227

False reportage, 151

Feature, 6, 9–12, 16, 52, 82, 102, 115, 117, 125, 162, 163, 167, 173, 176, 182, 183, 188, 189, 192, 202, 207, 212, 226, 231, 241

The Final Sentence, 73, 139, 144

First-Person Narrator, 16, 179, 183–185, 192, 225

Foley sound, 196, 210, 216

G

German narrator, 175, 181, 191

Gonzo journalism, 225, 226

H

Hero's journey, 14, 58, 62–64, 66–68, 124

Hierarchy of needs, 95, 136

J

Journalistic distance, 168, 224, 225, 236

© The Editor(s) (if applicable) and The Author(s), under exclusive
license to Springer Nature Switzerland AG 2021
S. Preger, *Storytelling in Radio and Podcasts*,
https://doi.org/10.1007/978-3-030-73130-4

L

Ladder of abstraction, 47–49, 69, 74,
    105, 122, 129, 167, 171, 172, 181,
    182, 192, 222, 225
List of revelations, 69, 72, 117, 128,
    129, 144, 154, 239
Live feeling, 121, 189, 190
Live impression, 189–191

M

Maximum capacity, 97, 113, 150
Meta-structures for audio narratives, 74,
    77, 78, 108

N

Narrative attitude, 2, 11, 20, 21, 30, 85,
    112, 176–182, 184, 186, 190, 192,
    193, 204, 205, 214, 216, 223, 227
Narrative podcasts, 4, 7, 18
Narrative sentence, 31–36, 38–40, 44,
    46, 50, 66, 68, 71, 72, 75, 86,
    94, 97, 107, 108, 111, 119, 129,
    138, 150, 171, 188, 200, 229, 231,
    233–235, 239
Narrator's mindset, 179
New Journalism, 13, 98, 225
News factors, 2, 220, 221

O

One-liner, 29, 30
On the nose dialogue, 163, 164

P

Pitch, 29, 30, 34, 159, 204, 229, 230,
    232, 233, 238
Plot point paradigm, 14, 65–67, 69, 72,
    74, 75, 83, 85–87, 108, 124, 129,
    154, 229, 233, 235
Podcast, 2, 4, 6, 7, 9, 10, 12, 13, 16–18,
    30, 40, 45, 74, 82–84, 91, 98, 106,
    118, 121, 125, 138, 152, 179–181,
    190, 214, 215, 225, 227, 229, 230,
    241
Prolepsis, 124, 131, 138, 208
Promythion, 123–125, 235

Protagonist, 7, 14, 31–33, 35, 38, 39,
    54, 73–76, 79, 80, 83, 85, 91–93,
    95–97, 102, 108, 111–113, 116,
    117, 119, 134, 140, 141, 150, 156,
    157, 163, 171, 180, 183, 184, 192,
    214, 224, 225, 230–232, 236, 240
Psychoacoustics, 197, 211

R

Real and reconstructed scenes, 50, 86
Rhythm & Tempo, 12, 103, 125,
    129–131, 144, 154, 189, 191, 197,
    199, 205, 206, 210, 212, 236

S

Scene sentence, 150
Serial, 3, 6–10, 18, 25, 26, 28, 29, 34,
    35, 37–40, 47, 48, 75, 81–85, 96,
    100, 101, 111, 115, 118, 125, 134,
    136, 140, 142, 143, 168, 182–185,
    187, 196, 206, 208, 214, 219, 226
Serials, 81, 82, 85, 226
Signature elements, 196, 197, 209, 216
Sound design, 84, 112, 196–198, 201,
    202, 206, 216, 236
Staging, 6, 8, 11, 21, 95, 191, 193,
    195–199, 202–204, 206, 209, 210,
    216, 219, 221–223, 226, 236, 237
Staging characters, 93
Staging narrative attitude, 177
Staging techniques, 219
Status detail, 98, 99, 113
Storyboard, 67, 83, 85–87, 97, 234,
    235, 239
Story check, 38–40
Story cosmos, 21, 122
Story engines, 35, 36, 39
Story factors, 219–221
Story feedback, 7, 117, 203
Story fixes, 239
Story interview, 106, 107, 109–111,
    113, 166, 198, 232, 240
Story principles, 24, 27–29, 33, 38, 108,
    234
Story problems, 19, 238, 240
Story sounds, 16, 20, 176, 177, 189
Storytelling, 2, 4, 6, 7, 9, 10, 12–15,
    18, 19, 24, 43, 62, 81, 82, 106,

113, 115, 119, 120, 123, 133, 137, 143, 153, 189, 192, 202, 226, 227, 240, 241
Subtext, 3, 20, 77, 124, 164, 165, 173, 184, 186
Suspense killer, 118, 144

T
Tasks for the narrator, 177
3D relationship, 100, 113
Transparency, 151, 177, 183, 184, 190, 224

True-to-scene, 20, 110, 158–160, 173, 212, 239

U
Use of music, 208, 209

W
Workflow, 34, 86, 200, 230, 238
Writing for narratives, 186, 188, 189

Made in the USA
Coppell, TX
08 December 2022

88283225R00144